BIGG TIME

WRITER
Ty Templeton

PENCILLER
Ty Templeton

INKER
Ty Templeton

LETTERER
Ty Templeton

COLORIST
Ty Templeton

SEPARATOR
Ty Templeton

DC COMICS

Jenette Kahn PRESIDENT & EDITOR-IN-CHIEF
Paul Levitz EXECUTIVE VICE PRESIDENT & PUBLISHER
Karen Berger VP-EXECUTIVE EDITOR
Heidi MacDonald & Joan Hilty EDITORS
Zachary Rau ASSISTANT EDITOR
Amie Brockway-Metcalf ART DIRECTOR
Georg Brewer VP-DESIGN & RETAIL PRODUCT DEVELOPMENT
Richard Bruning VP-CREATIVE DIRECTOR
Patrick Caldon SENIOR VP-FINANCE & OPERATIONS
Terri Cunningham VP-MANAGING EDITOR
Dan DiDio VP-EDITORIAL
Joel Ehrlich SENIOR VP-ADVERTISING & PROMOTIONS
Alison Gill VP-MANUFACTURING
Lillian Laserson VP & GENERAL COUNSEL
Jim Lee EDITORIAL DIRECTOR-WILDSTORM
David McKillips VP-ADVERTISING
John Nee VP-BUSINESS DEVELOPMENT
Cheryl Rubin VP-LICENSING & MERCHANDISING
Bob Wayne VP-SALES & MARKETING

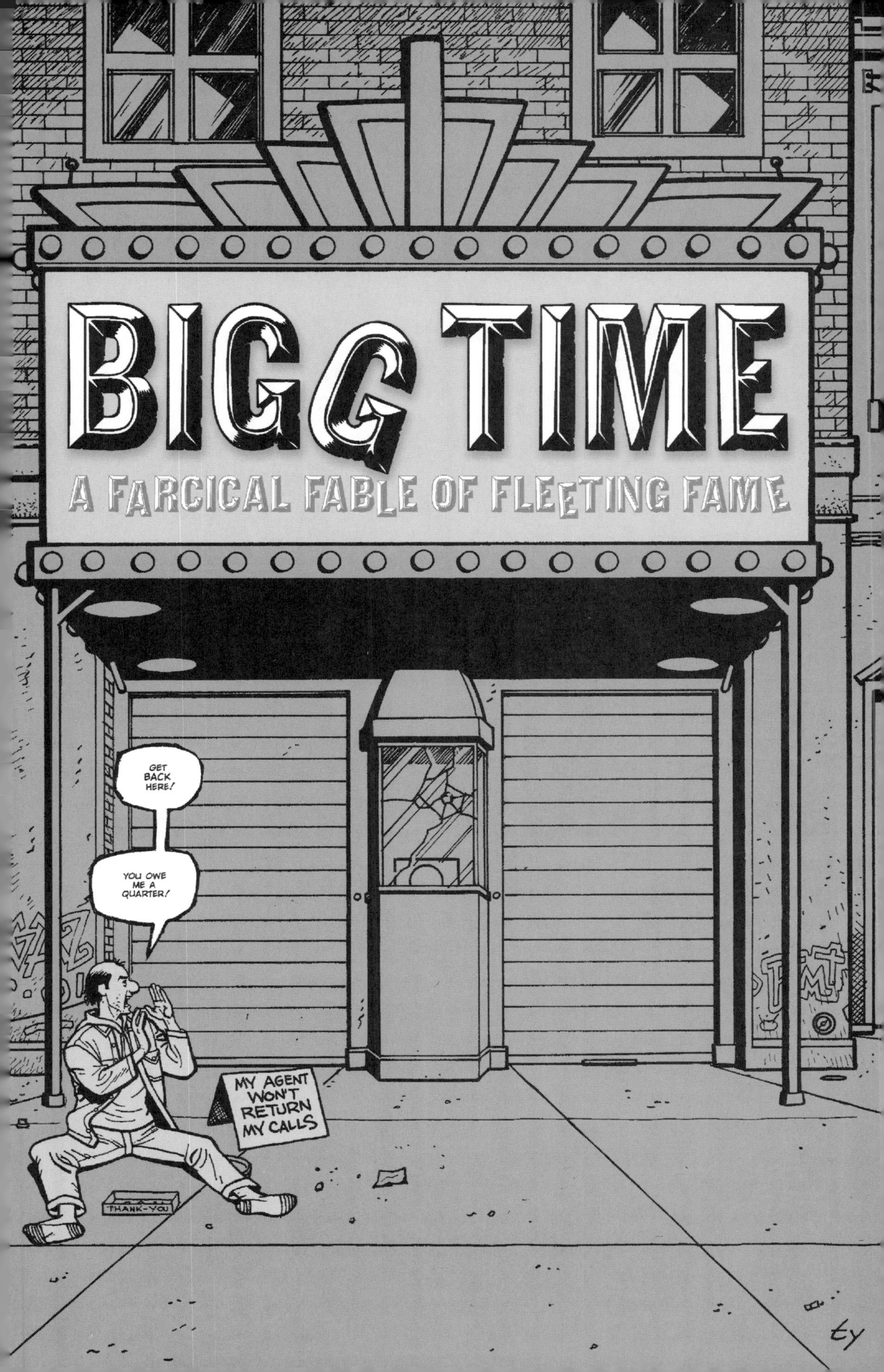
BIGG TIME
A FARCICAL FABLE OF FLEETING FAME
GET BACK HERE!
YOU OWE ME A QUARTER!
MY AGENT WON'T RETURN MY CALLS
THANK-YOU

BIGG TIME. Published by DC Comics, 1700 Broadway, New York, NY 10019. Copyright © 2002 Ty Templeton. All Rights Reserved.
All characters featured in this issue, the distinctive likenesses thereof, and all related indicia are trademarks of Ty Templeton.
VERTIGO is a trademark of DC Comics. The stories, characters and incidents mentioned in this magazine are entirely fictional.
DC Comics does not read or accept unsolicited submissions of ideas, stories or artwork.
Printed in Canada. DC Comics. A division of Warner Bros.-An AOL Time Warner Company.
ISBN 1-56389-905-1. First Printing. Cover art by Ty Templeton. Cover color by Lee Loughridge. Logo by Todd Klein.

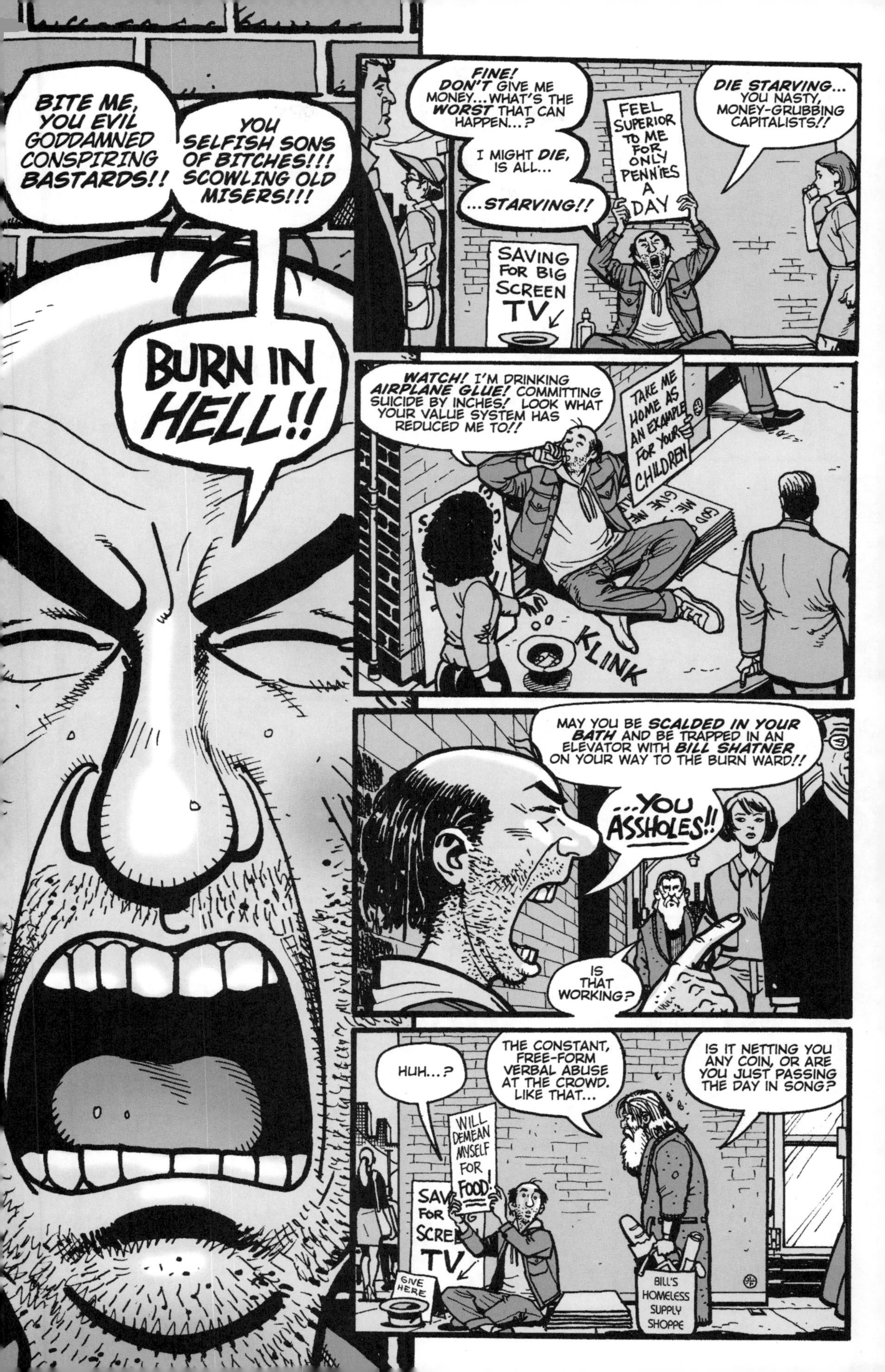
BITE ME, YOU EVIL GODDAMNED CONSPIRING BASTARDS!!
YOU SELFISH SONS OF BITCHES!!! SCOWLING OLD MISERS!!!
BURN IN HELL!!
FINE! DON'T GIVE ME MONEY... WHAT'S THE WORST THAT CAN HAPPEN...?
I MIGHT DIE, IS ALL...
...STARVING!!
FEEL SUPERIOR TO ME FOR ONLY PENNIES A DAY
SAVING FOR BIG SCREEN TV
DIE STARVING... YOU NASTY, MONEY-GRUBBING CAPITALISTS!!
WATCH! I'M DRINKING AIRPLANE GLUE! COMMITTING SUICIDE BY INCHES! LOOK WHAT YOUR VALUE SYSTEM HAS REDUCED ME TO!!
TAKE ME HOME AS AN EXAMPLE FOR YOUR CHILDREN
KLINK
MAY YOU BE SCALDED IN YOUR BATH AND BE TRAPPED IN AN ELEVATOR WITH BILL SHATNER ON YOUR WAY TO THE BURN WARD!!
...YOU ASSHOLES!!
IS THAT WORKING?
HUH...?
THE CONSTANT, FREE-FORM VERBAL ABUSE AT THE CROWD. LIKE THAT...
IS IT NETTING YOU ANY COIN, OR ARE YOU JUST PASSING THE DAY IN SONG?
WILL DEMEAN MYSELF FOR FOOD!
GIVE HERE
BILL'S HOMELESS SUPPLY SHOPPE

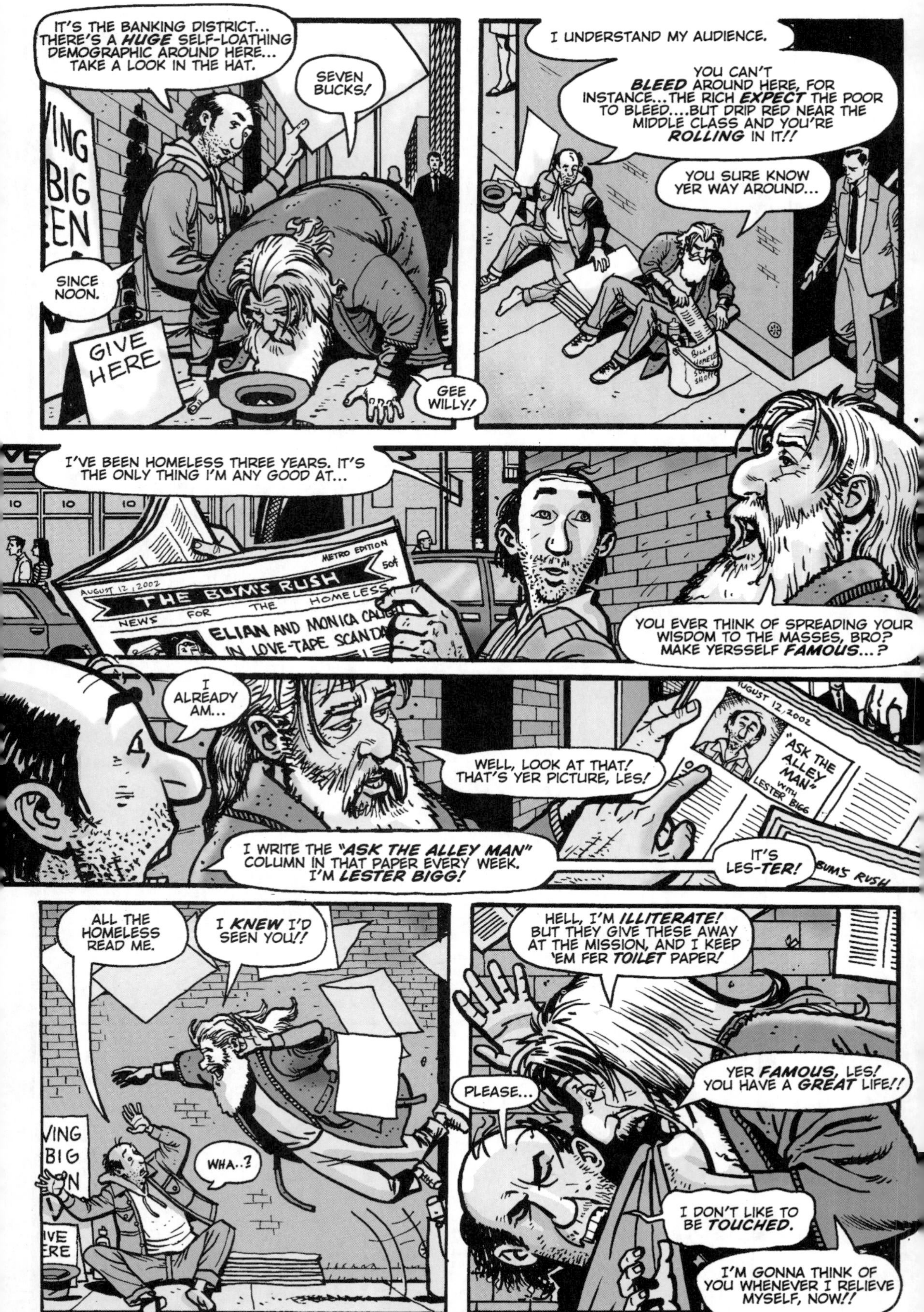

IT'S THE BANKING DISTRICT... THERE'S A HUGE SELF-LOATHING DEMOGRAPHIC AROUND HERE... TAKE A LOOK IN THE HAT.
SEVEN BUCKS!
SINCE NOON.
GIVE HERE
GEE WILLY!
I UNDERSTAND MY AUDIENCE.
YOU CAN'T BLEED AROUND HERE, FOR INSTANCE...THE RICH EXPECT THE POOR TO BLEED....BUT DRIP RED NEAR THE MIDDLE CLASS AND YOU'RE ROLLING IN IT!!
YOU SURE KNOW YER WAY AROUND...
I'VE BEEN HOMELESS THREE YEARS. IT'S THE ONLY THING I'M ANY GOOD AT...
AUGUST 12, 2002
METRO EDITION
50¢
THE BUM'S RUSH
NEWS FOR THE HOMELESS
ELIAN AND MONICA CAUGHT IN LOVE-TAPE SCANDAL
YOU EVER THINK OF SPREADING YOUR WISDOM TO THE MASSES, BRO? MAKE YERSSELF FAMOUS...?
I ALREADY AM...
WELL, LOOK AT THAT! THAT'S YER PICTURE, LES!
AUGUST 12, 2002
"ASK THE ALLEY MAN" WITH LESTER BIGG
I WRITE THE "ASK THE ALLEY MAN" COLUMN IN THAT PAPER EVERY WEEK. I'M LESTER BIGG!
IT'S LES-TER!
BUM'S RUSH
ALL THE HOMELESS READ ME.
I KNEW I'D SEEN YOU!!
WHA..?
HELL, I'M ILLITERATE! BUT THEY GIVE THESE AWAY AT THE MISSION, AND I KEEP 'EM FER TOILET PAPER!
PLEASE...
YER FAMOUS, LES! YOU HAVE A GREAT LIFE!!
I DON'T LIKE TO BE TOUCHED.
I'M GONNA THINK OF YOU WHENEVER I RELIEVE MYSELF, NOW!!

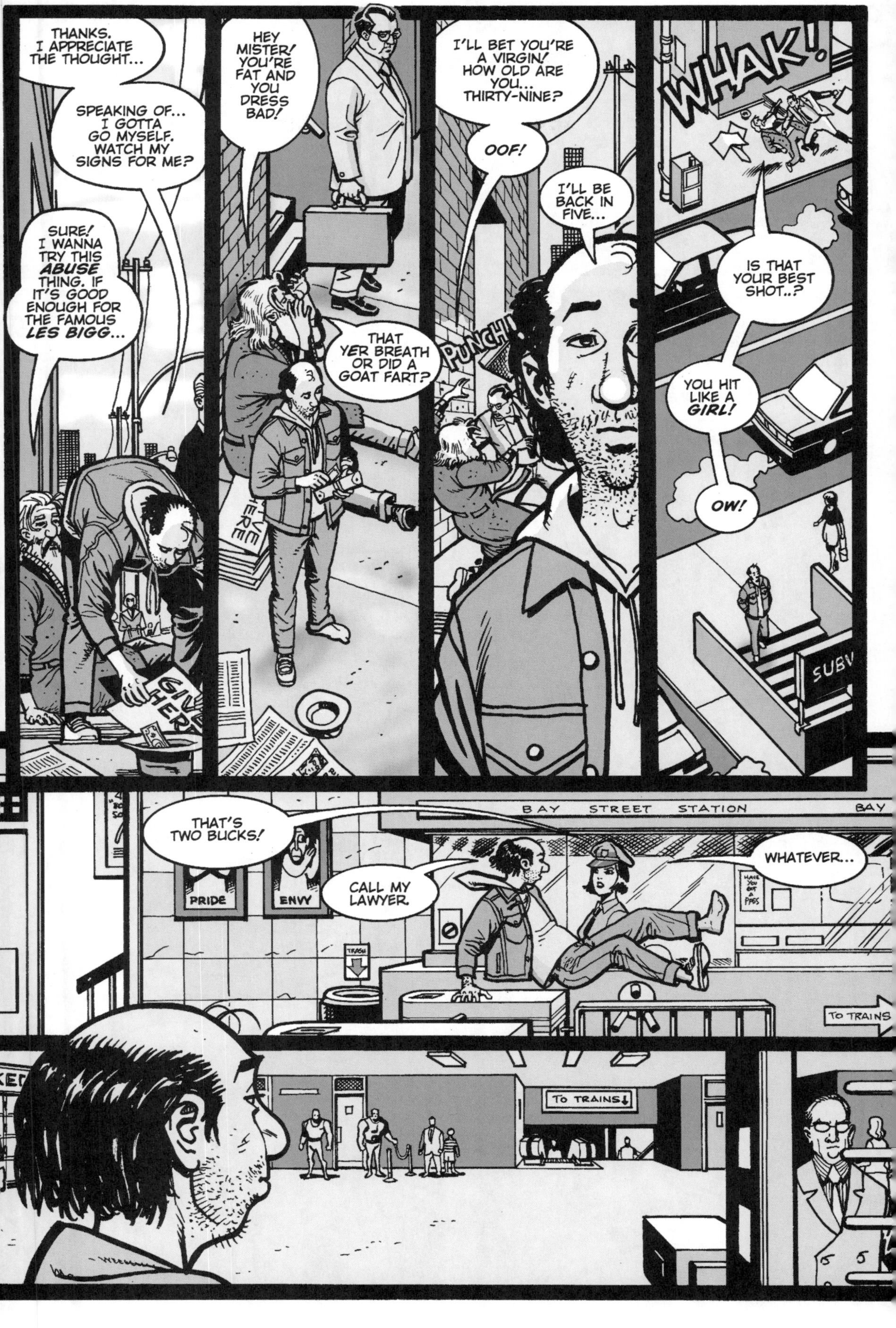
THANKS. I APPRECIATE THE THOUGHT...
SPEAKING OF... I GOTTA GO MYSELF. WATCH MY SIGNS FOR ME?
SURE! I WANNA TRY THIS ABUSE THING. IF IT'S GOOD ENOUGH FOR THE FAMOUS LES BIGG...
HEY MISTER! YOU'RE FAT AND YOU DRESS BAD!
THAT YER BREATH OR DID A GOAT FART?
I'LL BET YOU'RE A VIRGIN! HOW OLD ARE YOU... THIRTY-NINE?
OOF!
PUNCH!
I'LL BE BACK IN FIVE...
WHAK!
IS THAT YOUR BEST SHOT..?
YOU HIT LIKE A GIRL!
OW!
BAY STREET STATION
PRIDE
ENVY
THAT'S TWO BUCKS!
CALL MY LAWYER.
WHATEVER...
TRASH
TO TRAINS
TO TRAINS

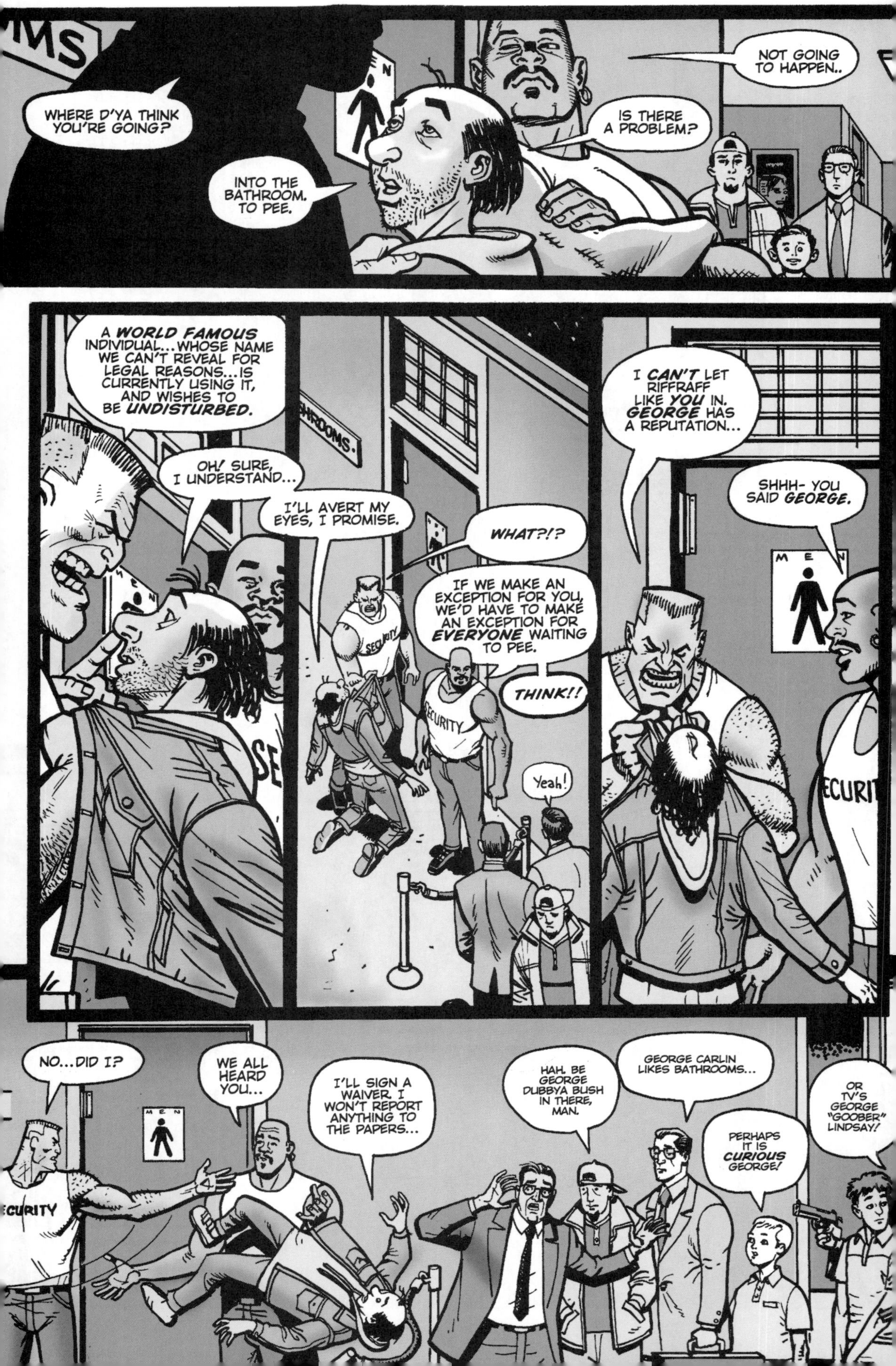

WHERE D'YA THINK YOU'RE GOING?
INTO THE BATHROOM. TO PEE.
IS THERE A PROBLEM?
NOT GOING TO HAPPEN..
A **WORLD FAMOUS** INDIVIDUAL...WHOSE NAME WE CAN'T REVEAL FOR LEGAL REASONS...IS CURRENTLY USING IT, AND WISHES TO BE **UNDISTURBED.**
OH! SURE, I UNDERSTAND...
I'LL AVERT MY EYES, I PROMISE.
WHAT?!?
IF WE MAKE AN EXCEPTION FOR YOU, WE'D HAVE TO MAKE AN EXCEPTION FOR **EVERYONE** WAITING TO PEE.
THINK!!
Yeah!
I **CAN'T** LET RIFFRAFF LIKE **YOU** IN. **GEORGE** HAS A REPUTATION...
SHHH- YOU SAID **GEORGE.**
MEN
SECURITY
NO...DID I?
WE ALL HEARD YOU...
I'LL SIGN A WAIVER. I WON'T REPORT ANYTHING TO THE PAPERS...
HAH. BE GEORGE DUBBYA BUSH IN THERE, MAN.
GEORGE CARLIN LIKES BATHROOMS...
PERHAPS IT IS **CURIOUS** GEORGE!
OR TV'S GEORGE "GOOBER" LINDSAY!

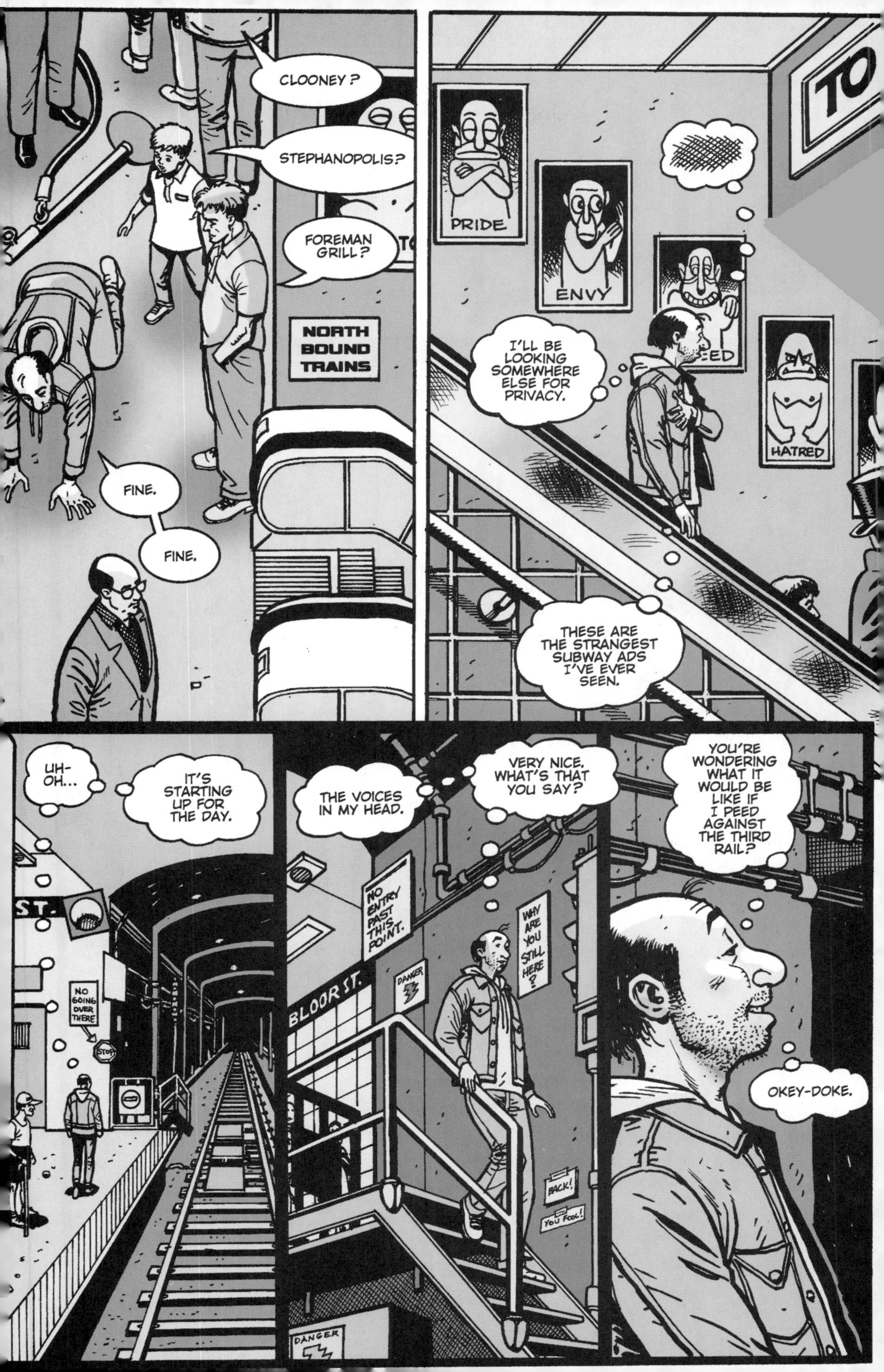
CLOONEY?
STEPHANOPOLIS?
FOREMAN GRILL?
NORTH BOUND TRAINS
FINE.
FINE.
PRIDE
ENVY
HATRED
I'LL BE LOOKING SOMEWHERE ELSE FOR PRIVACY.
THESE ARE THE STRANGEST SUBWAY ADS I'VE EVER SEEN.
UH-OH...
IT'S STARTING UP FOR THE DAY.
NO GOING OVER THERE
STOP
THE VOICES IN MY HEAD.
VERY NICE. WHAT'S THAT YOU SAY?
NO ENTRY PAST THIS POINT.
WHY ARE YOU STILL HERE?
BLOOR ST.
DANGER
BACK!
YOU FOOL!
DANGER
YOU'RE WONDERING WHAT IT WOULD BE LIKE IF I PEED AGAINST THE THIRD RAIL?
OKEY-DOKE.

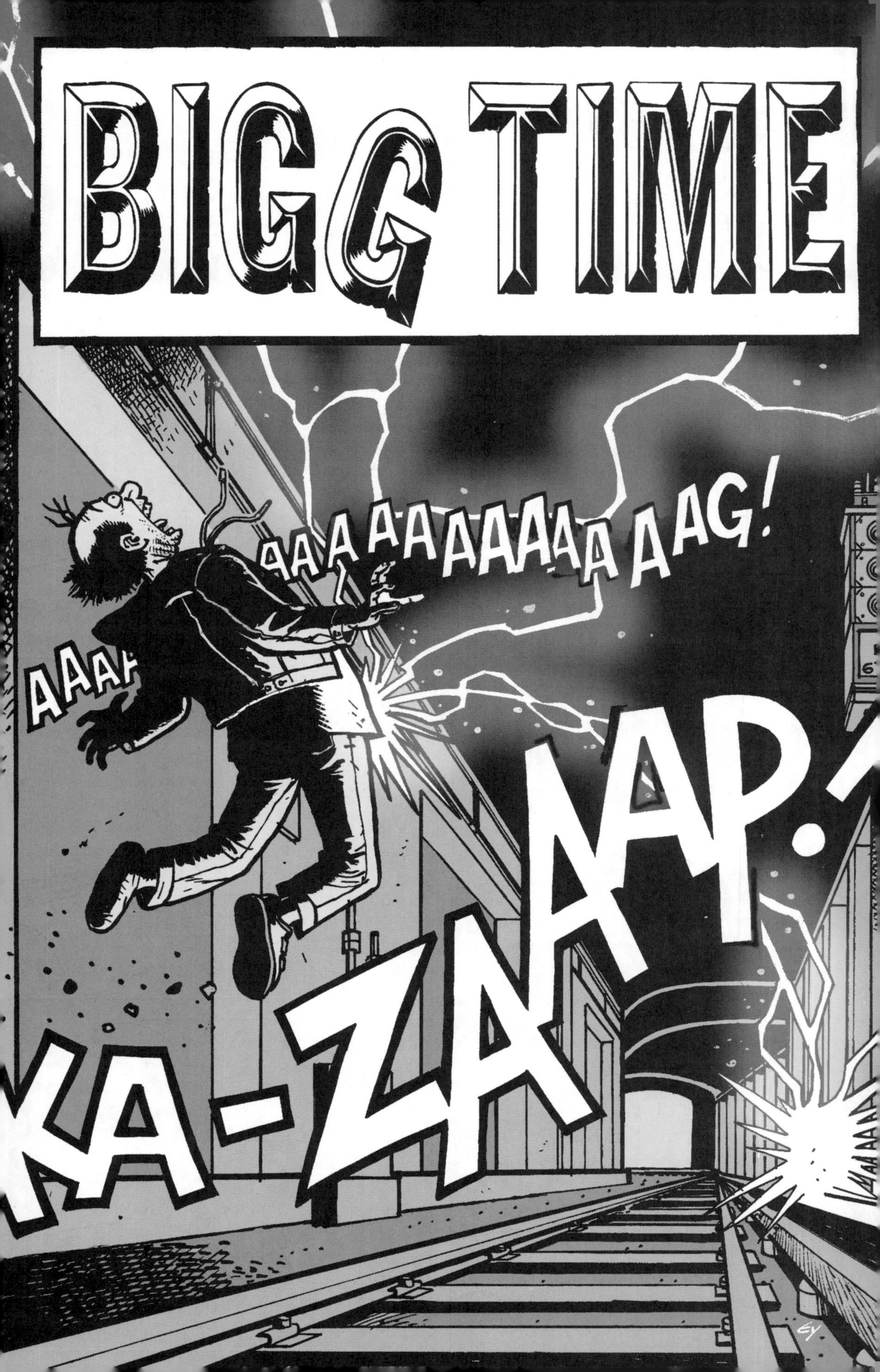
BIGG TIME
AAAAAAAAAAAAG!
AAAA
KA-ZAAAP!

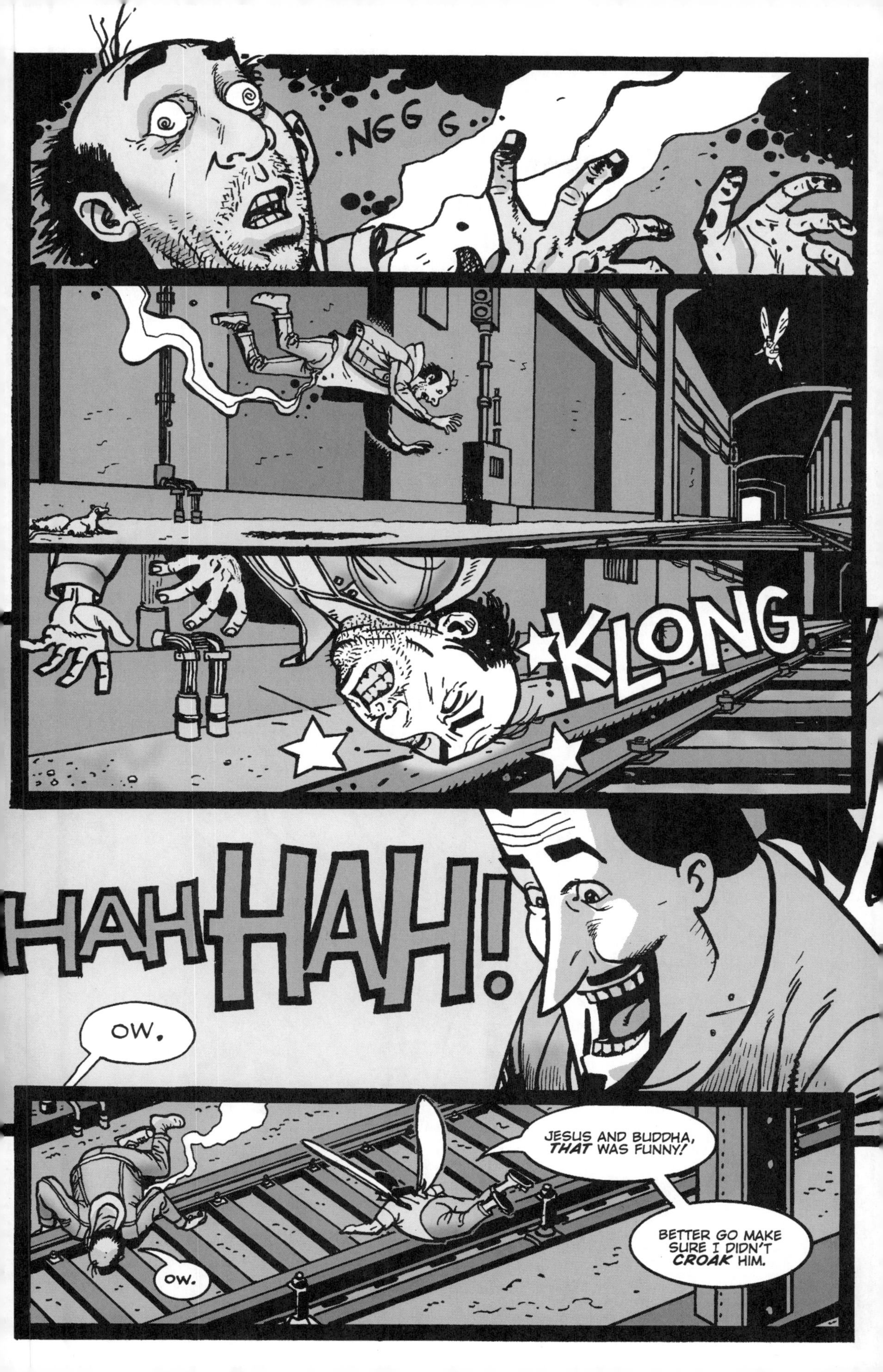
NGGG
KLONG
HAHHAH!
OW.
JESUS AND BUDDHA, THAT WAS FUNNY!
BETTER GO MAKE SURE I DIDN'T CROAK HIM.
OW.

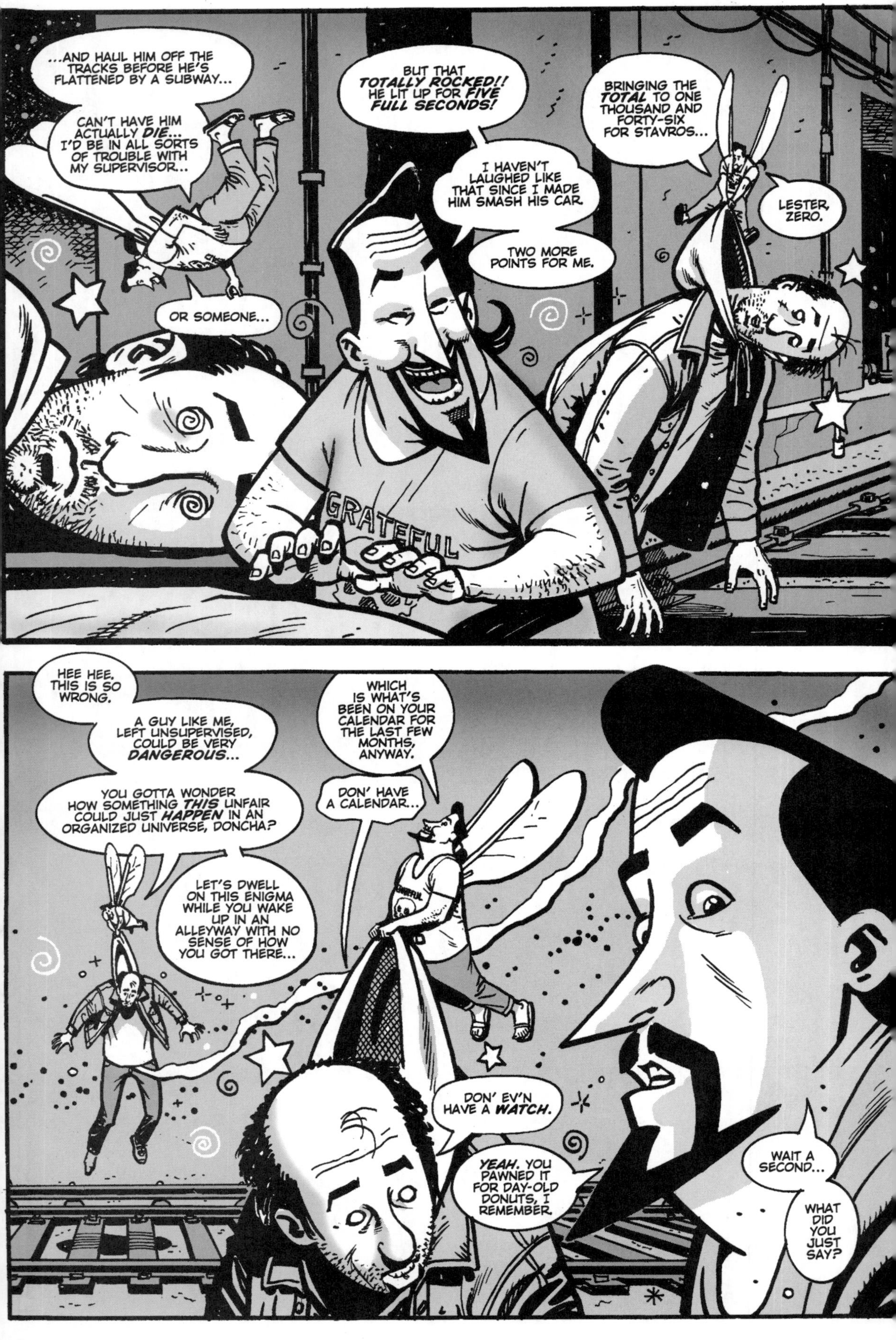
...AND HAUL HIM OFF THE TRACKS BEFORE HE'S FLATTENED BY A SUBWAY...
CAN'T HAVE HIM ACTUALLY DIE... I'D BE IN ALL SORTS OF TROUBLE WITH MY SUPERVISOR...
OR SOMEONE...
BUT THAT TOTALLY ROCKED!! HE LIT UP FOR FIVE FULL SECONDS!
I HAVEN'T LAUGHED LIKE THAT SINCE I MADE HIM SMASH HIS CAR.
TWO MORE POINTS FOR ME.
BRINGING THE TOTAL TO ONE THOUSAND AND FORTY-SIX FOR STAVROS...
LESTER, ZERO.
GRATEFUL
HEE HEE. THIS IS SO WRONG.
A GUY LIKE ME, LEFT UNSUPERVISED, COULD BE VERY DANGEROUS...
YOU GOTTA WONDER HOW SOMETHING THIS UNFAIR COULD JUST HAPPEN IN AN ORGANIZED UNIVERSE, DONCHA?
LET'S DWELL ON THIS ENIGMA WHILE YOU WAKE UP IN AN ALLEYWAY WITH NO SENSE OF HOW YOU GOT THERE...
WHICH IS WHAT'S BEEN ON YOUR CALENDAR FOR THE LAST FEW MONTHS, ANYWAY.
DON' HAVE A CALENDAR...
DON' EV'N HAVE A WATCH.
YEAH. YOU PAWNED IT FOR DAY-OLD DONUTS, I REMEMBER.
WAIT A SECOND...
WHAT DID YOU JUST SAY?

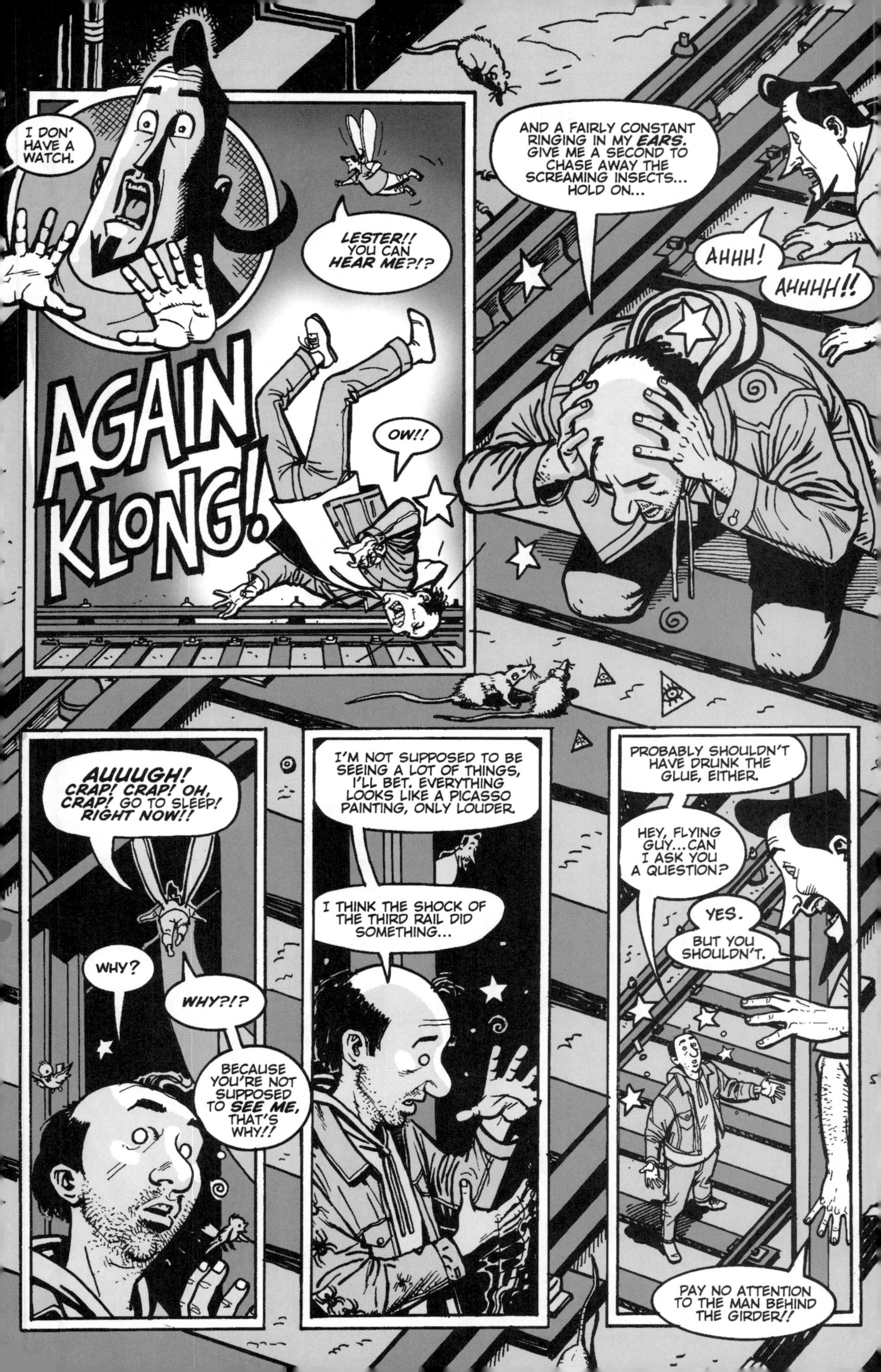
I DON' HAVE A WATCH.
LESTER!! YOU CAN HEAR ME?!?
AGAIN KLONG!
OW!!
AND A FAIRLY CONSTANT RINGING IN MY EARS. GIVE ME A SECOND TO CHASE AWAY THE SCREAMING INSECTS... HOLD ON...
AHHH!
AHHHH!!
AUUUGH! CRAP! CRAP! OH, CRAP! GO TO SLEEP! RIGHT NOW!!
WHY?
WHY?!?
BECAUSE YOU'RE NOT SUPPOSED TO SEE ME, THAT'S WHY!!
I'M NOT SUPPOSED TO BE SEEING A LOT OF THINGS, I'LL BET. EVERYTHING LOOKS LIKE A PICASSO PAINTING, ONLY LOUDER.
I THINK THE SHOCK OF THE THIRD RAIL DID SOMETHING...
PROBABLY SHOULDN'T HAVE DRUNK THE GLUE, EITHER.
HEY, FLYING GUY...CAN I ASK YOU A QUESTION?
YES.
BUT YOU SHOULDN'T.
PAY NO ATTENTION TO THE MAN BEHIND THE GIRDER!!

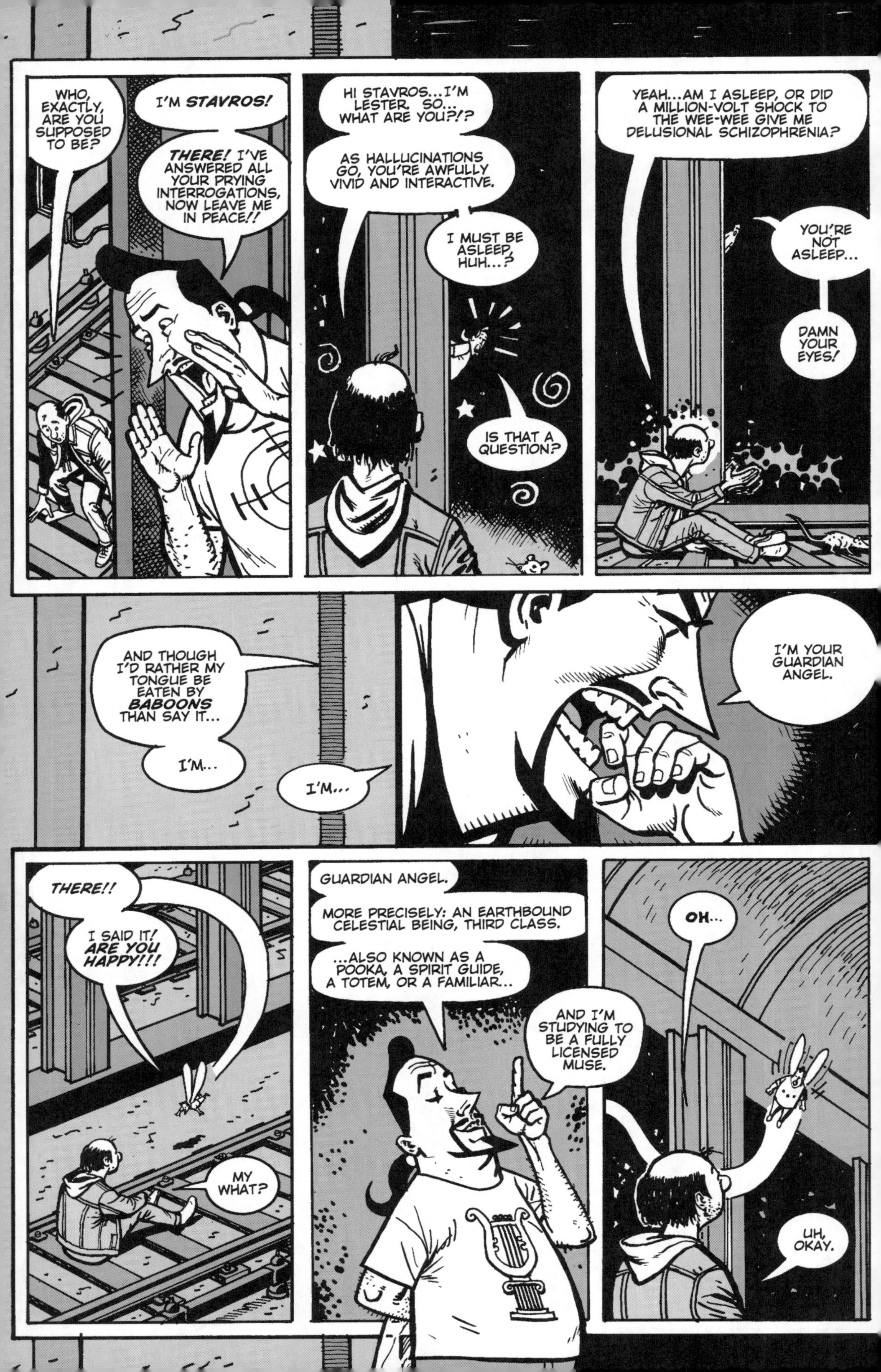
WHO, EXACTLY, ARE YOU SUPPOSED TO BE?
I'M STAVROS!
THERE! I'VE ANSWERED ALL YOUR PRYING INTERROGATIONS, NOW LEAVE ME IN PEACE!!
HI STAVROS...I'M LESTER. SO... WHAT ARE YOU?!?
AS HALLUCINATIONS GO, YOU'RE AWFULLY VIVID AND INTERACTIVE.
I MUST BE ASLEEP, HUH...?
IS THAT A QUESTION?
YEAH...AM I ASLEEP, OR DID A MILLION-VOLT SHOCK TO THE WEE-WEE GIVE ME DELUSIONAL SCHIZOPHRENIA?
YOU'RE NOT ASLEEP...
DAMN YOUR EYES!
AND THOUGH I'D RATHER MY TONGUE BE EATEN BY BABOONS THAN SAY IT...
I'M...
I'M...
I'M YOUR GUARDIAN ANGEL.
THERE!!
I SAID IT! ARE YOU HAPPY!!!
MY WHAT?
GUARDIAN ANGEL.
MORE PRECISELY: AN EARTHBOUND CELESTIAL BEING, THIRD CLASS.
...ALSO KNOWN AS A POOKA, A SPIRIT GUIDE, A TOTEM, OR A FAMILIAR...
AND I'M STUDYING TO BE A FULLY LICENSED MUSE.
OH...
UH, OKAY.

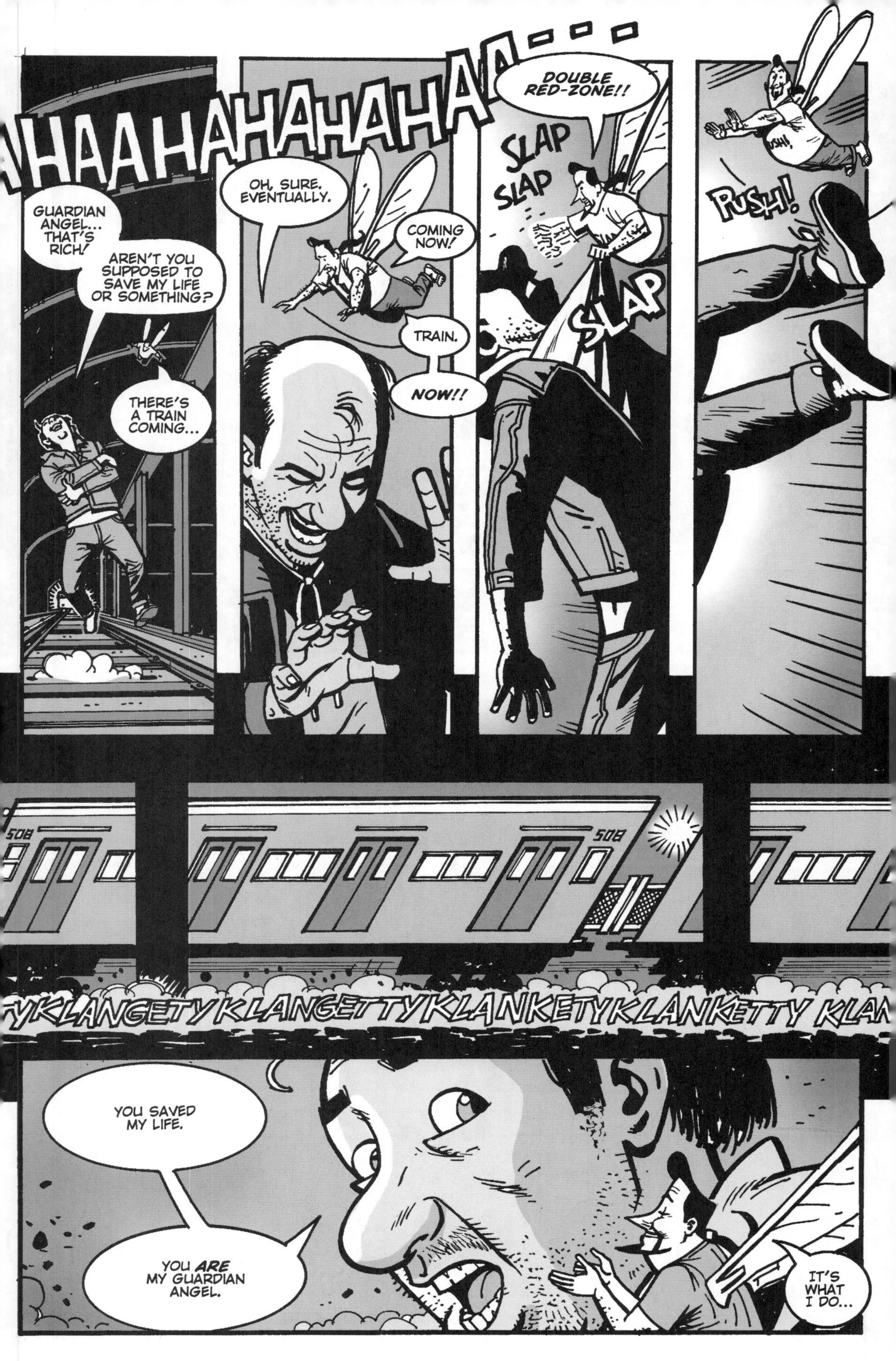
HAAHAHAHAHAHAA---
GUARDIAN ANGEL... THAT'S RICH!
AREN'T YOU SUPPOSED TO SAVE MY LIFE OR SOMETHING?
THERE'S A TRAIN COMING...
OH, SURE. EVENTUALLY.
COMING NOW!
TRAIN.
NOW!!
DOUBLE RED-ZONE!!
SLAP
SLAP
SLAP
PUSH!
PUSH!
KLANGETYKLANGETTYKLANKETYKLANKETTY KLAN
YOU SAVED MY LIFE.
YOU ARE MY GUARDIAN ANGEL.
IT'S WHAT I DO...

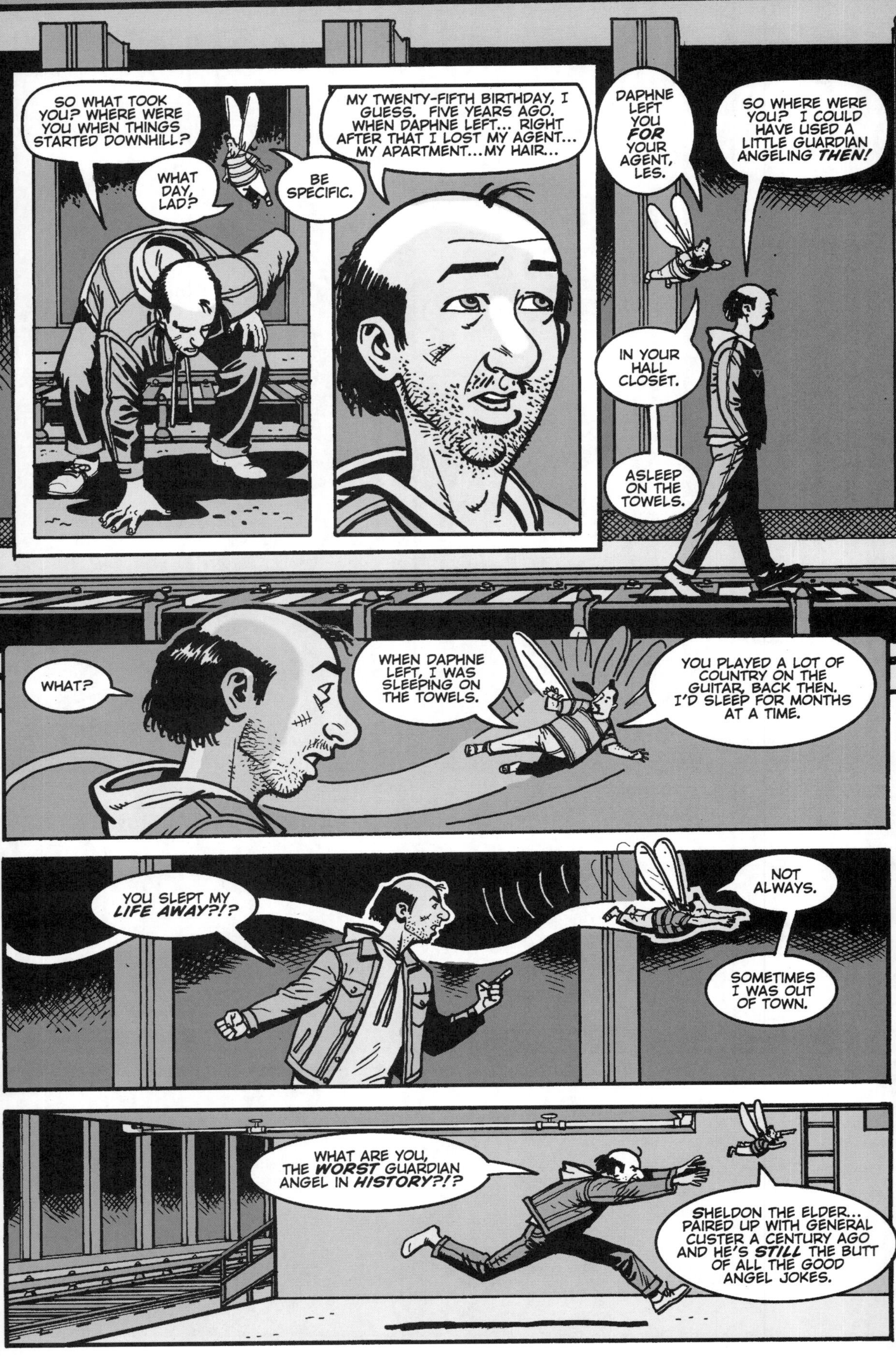
SO WHAT TOOK YOU? WHERE WERE YOU WHEN THINGS STARTED DOWNHILL?
WHAT DAY, LAD?
BE SPECIFIC.
MY TWENTY-FIFTH BIRTHDAY, I GUESS. FIVE YEARS AGO. WHEN DAPHNE LEFT... RIGHT AFTER THAT I LOST MY AGENT... MY APARTMENT... MY HAIR...
DAPHNE LEFT YOU **FOR** YOUR AGENT, LES.
SO WHERE WERE YOU? I COULD HAVE USED A LITTLE GUARDIAN ANGELING ***THEN!***
IN YOUR HALL CLOSET.
ASLEEP ON THE TOWELS.
WHAT?
WHEN DAPHNE LEFT, I WAS SLEEPING ON THE TOWELS.
YOU PLAYED A LOT OF COUNTRY ON THE GUITAR, BACK THEN. I'D SLEEP FOR MONTHS AT A TIME.
YOU SLEPT MY ***LIFE AWAY?!?***
NOT ALWAYS.
SOMETIMES I WAS OUT OF TOWN.
WHAT ARE YOU, THE ***WORST*** GUARDIAN ANGEL IN ***HISTORY?!?***
SHELDON THE ELDER... PAIRED UP WITH GENERAL CUSTER A CENTURY AGO AND HE'S ***STILL*** THE BUTT OF ALL THE GOOD ANGEL JOKES.

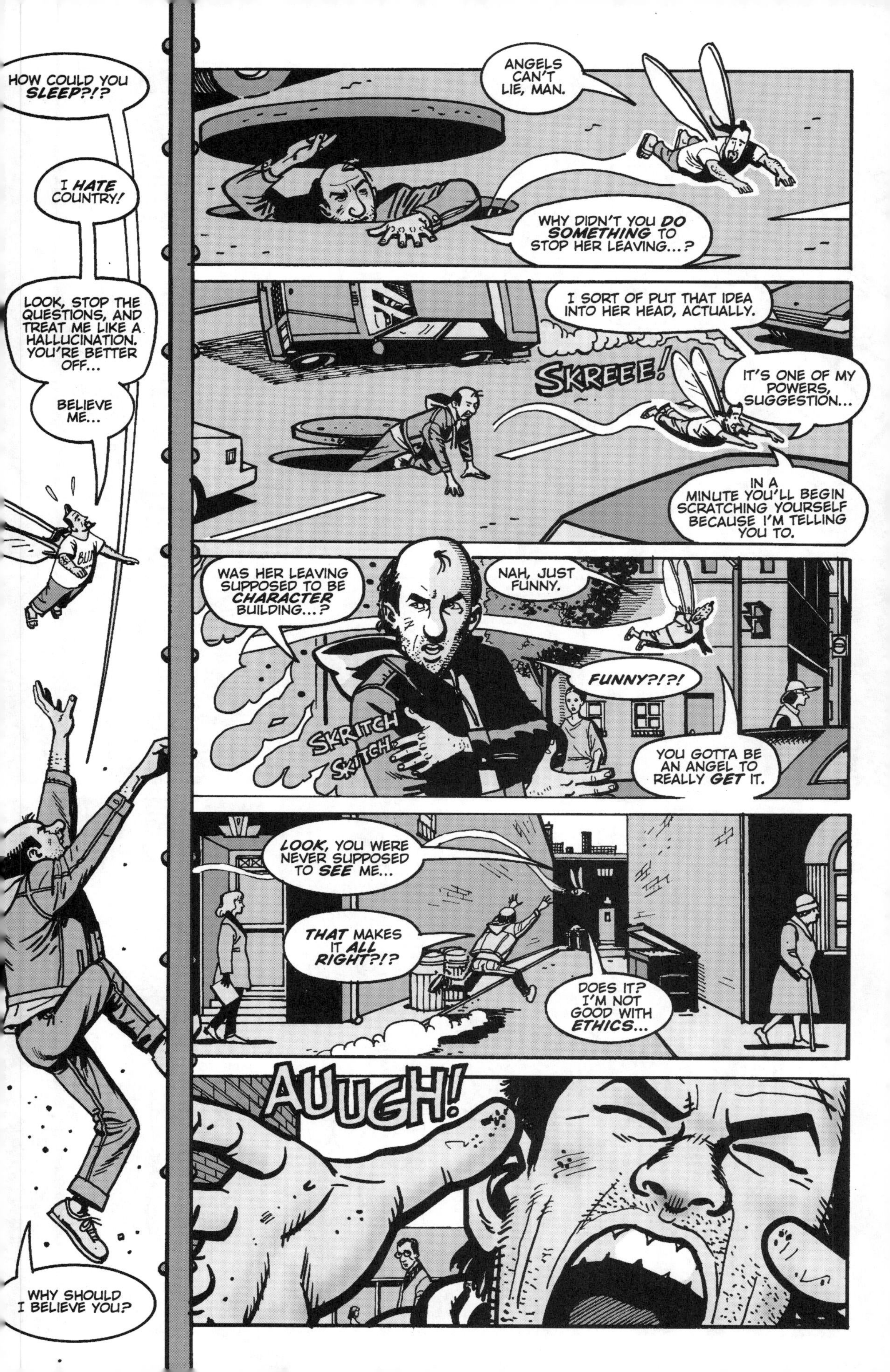

ANGELS CAN'T LIE, MAN.
WHY DIDN'T YOU DO SOMETHING TO STOP HER LEAVING...?
HOW COULD YOU SLEEP?!?
I HATE COUNTRY!
I SORT OF PUT THAT IDEA INTO HER HEAD, ACTUALLY.
SKREEE!
IT'S ONE OF MY POWERS, SUGGESTION...
IN A MINUTE YOU'LL BEGIN SCRATCHING YOURSELF BECAUSE I'M TELLING YOU TO.
LOOK, STOP THE QUESTIONS, AND TREAT ME LIKE A HALLUCINATION. YOU'RE BETTER OFF...
BELIEVE ME...
WAS HER LEAVING SUPPOSED TO BE CHARACTER BUILDING...?
NAH, JUST FUNNY.
FUNNY?!?!
SKRITCH SKITCH
YOU GOTTA BE AN ANGEL TO REALLY GET IT.
LOOK, YOU WERE NEVER SUPPOSED TO SEE ME...
THAT MAKES IT ALL RIGHT?!?
DOES IT? I'M NOT GOOD WITH ETHICS...
AUUCH!
WHY SHOULD I BELIEVE YOU?

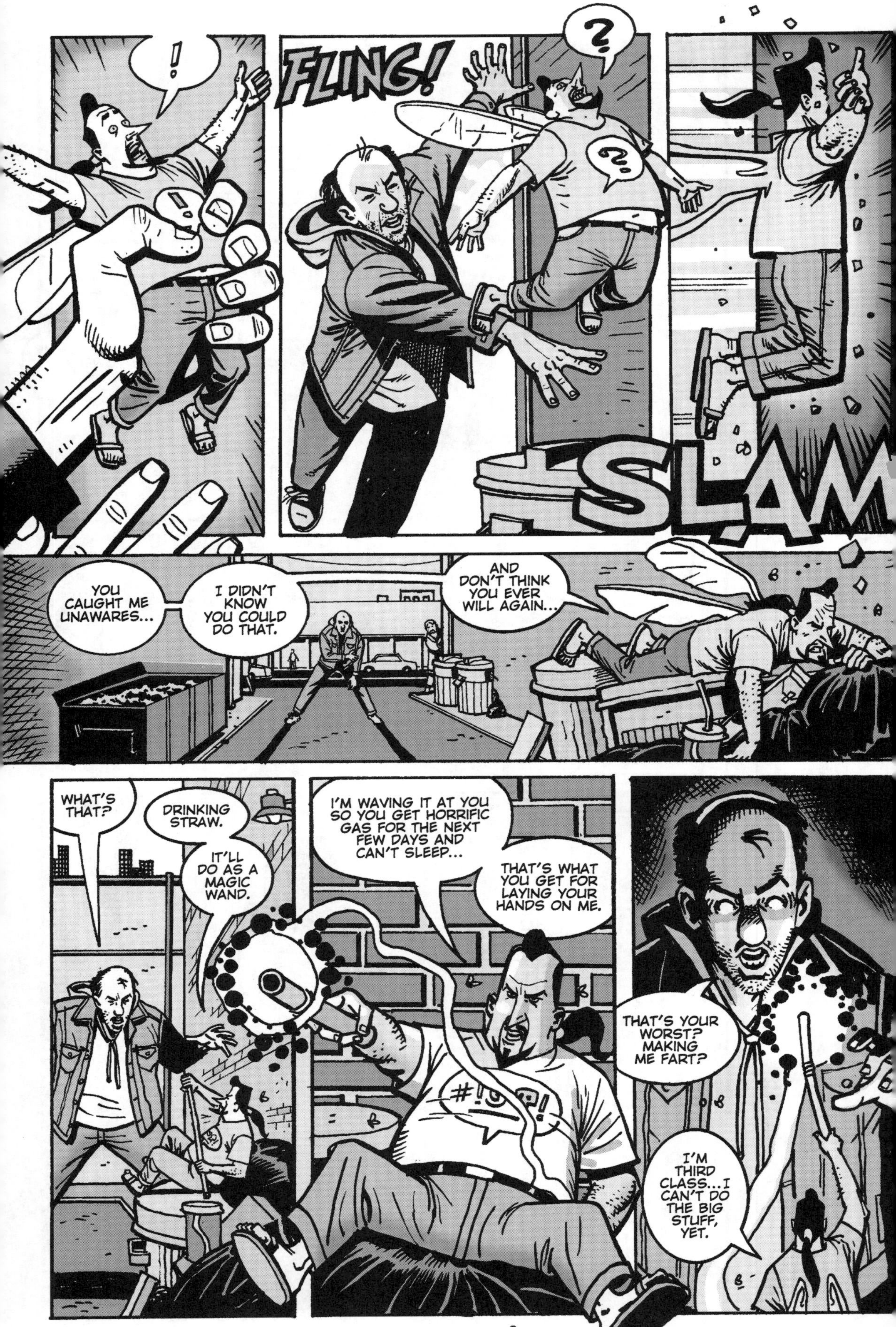

!
!
FLING!
?
?
SLAM
YOU CAUGHT ME UNAWARES...
I DIDN'T KNOW YOU COULD DO THAT.
AND DON'T THINK YOU EVER WILL AGAIN...
WHAT'S THAT?
DRINKING STRAW.
IT'LL DO AS A MAGIC WAND.
I'M WAVING IT AT YOU SO YOU GET HORRIFIC GAS FOR THE NEXT FEW DAYS AND CAN'T SLEEP...
THAT'S WHAT YOU GET FOR LAYING YOUR HANDS ON ME.
#!$@!
THAT'S YOUR WORST? MAKING ME FART?
I'M THIRD CLASS...I CAN'T DO THE BIG STUFF, YET.

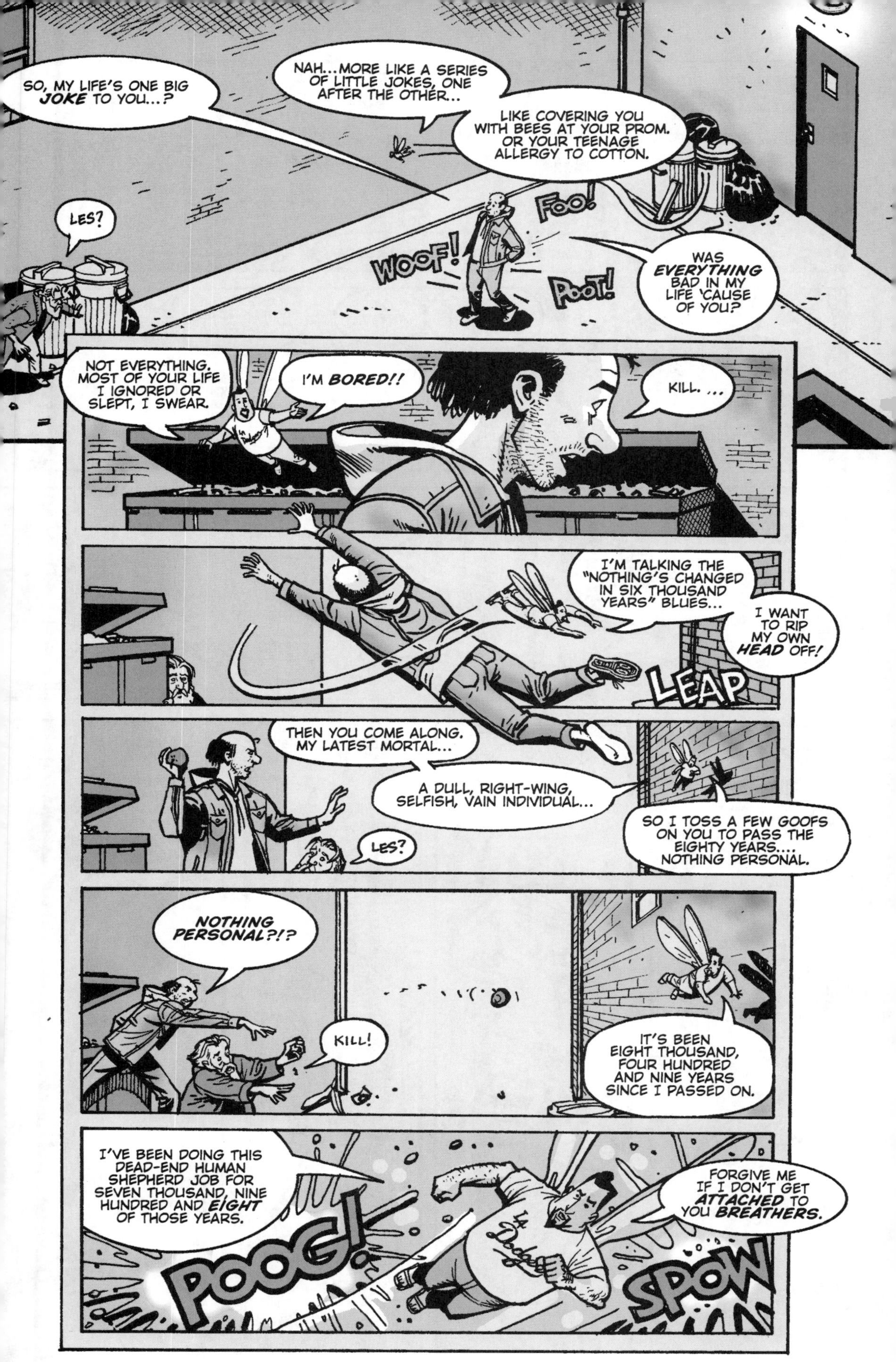
SO, MY LIFE'S ONE BIG *JOKE* TO YOU...?
NAH...MORE LIKE A SERIES OF LITTLE JOKES, ONE AFTER THE OTHER...
LIKE COVERING YOU WITH BEES AT YOUR PROM. OR YOUR TEENAGE ALLERGY TO COTTON.
LES?
FOO!
WOOF!
POOT!
WAS *EVERYTHING* BAD IN MY LIFE 'CAUSE OF YOU?
NOT EVERYTHING. MOST OF YOUR LIFE I IGNORED OR SLEPT, I SWEAR.
I'M *BORED!!*
KILL. ...
I'M TALKING THE "NOTHING'S CHANGED IN SIX THOUSAND YEARS" BLUES...
I WANT TO RIP MY OWN *HEAD* OFF!
LEAP
THEN YOU COME ALONG. MY LATEST MORTAL...
A DULL, RIGHT-WING, SELFISH, VAIN INDIVIDUAL...
LES?
SO I TOSS A FEW GOOFS ON YOU TO PASS THE EIGHTY YEARS.... NOTHING PERSONAL.
NOTHING PERSONAL?!?
KILL!
IT'S BEEN EIGHT THOUSAND, FOUR HUNDRED AND NINE YEARS SINCE I PASSED ON.
I'VE BEEN DOING THIS DEAD-END HUMAN SHEPHERD JOB FOR SEVEN THOUSAND, NINE HUNDRED AND *EIGHT* OF THOSE YEARS.
FORGIVE ME IF I DON'T GET *ATTACHED* TO YOU *BREATHERS.*
POOG!
SPOW

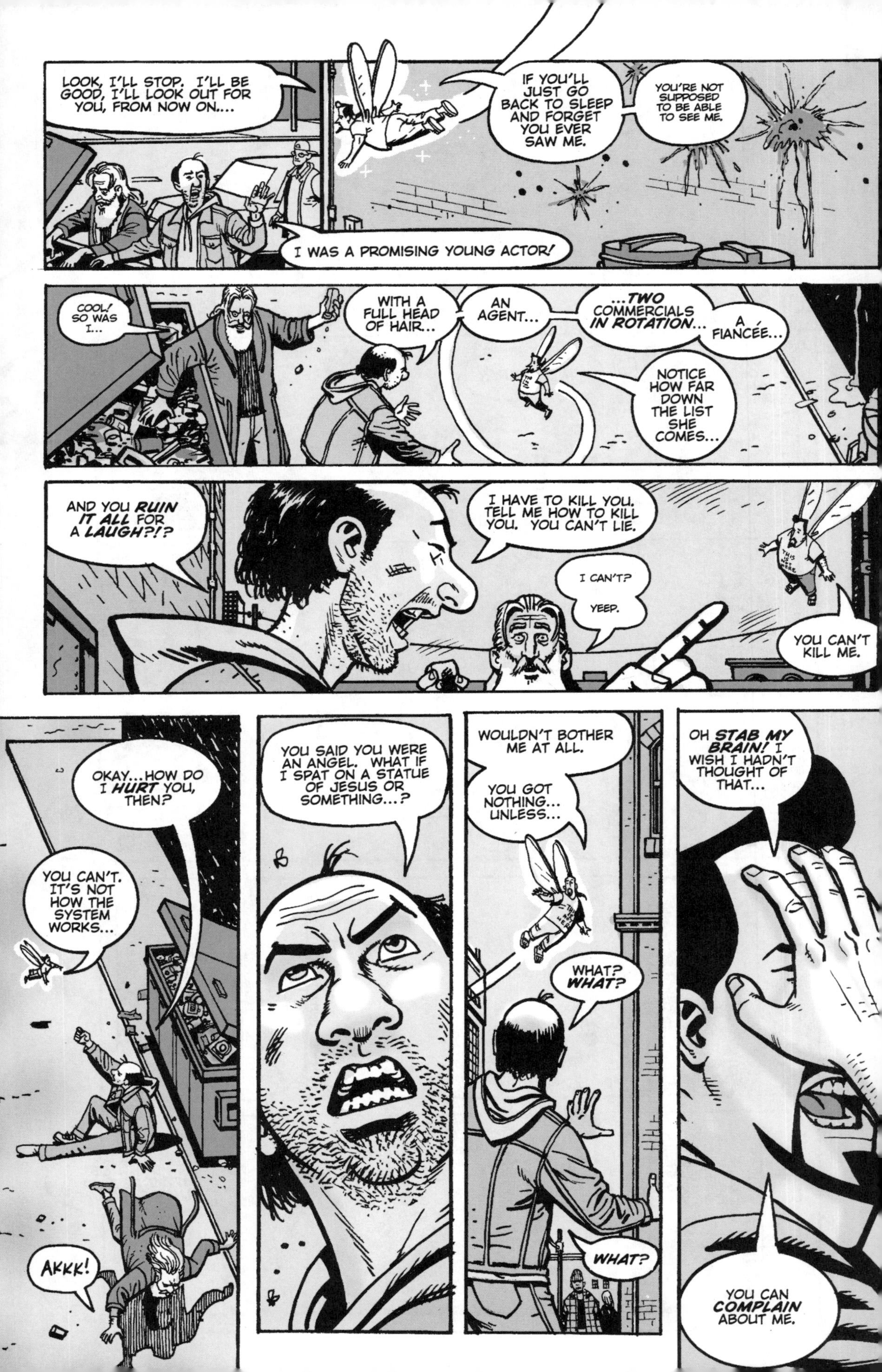
LOOK, I'LL STOP. I'LL BE GOOD, I'LL LOOK OUT FOR YOU, FROM NOW ON....
IF YOU'LL JUST GO BACK TO SLEEP AND FORGET YOU EVER SAW ME.
YOU'RE NOT SUPPOSED TO BE ABLE TO SEE ME.
I WAS A PROMISING YOUNG ACTOR!
COOL! SO WAS I...
WITH A FULL HEAD OF HAIR...
AN AGENT...
...TWO COMMERCIALS IN ROTATION...
A FIANCÉE...
NOTICE HOW FAR DOWN THE LIST SHE COMES...
AND YOU RUIN IT ALL FOR A LAUGH?!?
I HAVE TO KILL YOU. TELL ME HOW TO KILL YOU. YOU CAN'T LIE.
I CAN'T?
YEEP.
YOU CAN'T KILL ME.
OKAY...HOW DO I HURT YOU, THEN?
YOU CAN'T. IT'S NOT HOW THE SYSTEM WORKS...
AKKK!
YOU SAID YOU WERE AN ANGEL. WHAT IF I SPAT ON A STATUE OF JESUS OR SOMETHING...?
WOULDN'T BOTHER ME AT ALL.
YOU GOT NOTHING... UNLESS...
WHAT? WHAT?
WHAT?
OH STAB MY BRAIN! I WISH I HADN'T THOUGHT OF THAT...
YOU CAN COMPLAIN ABOUT ME.

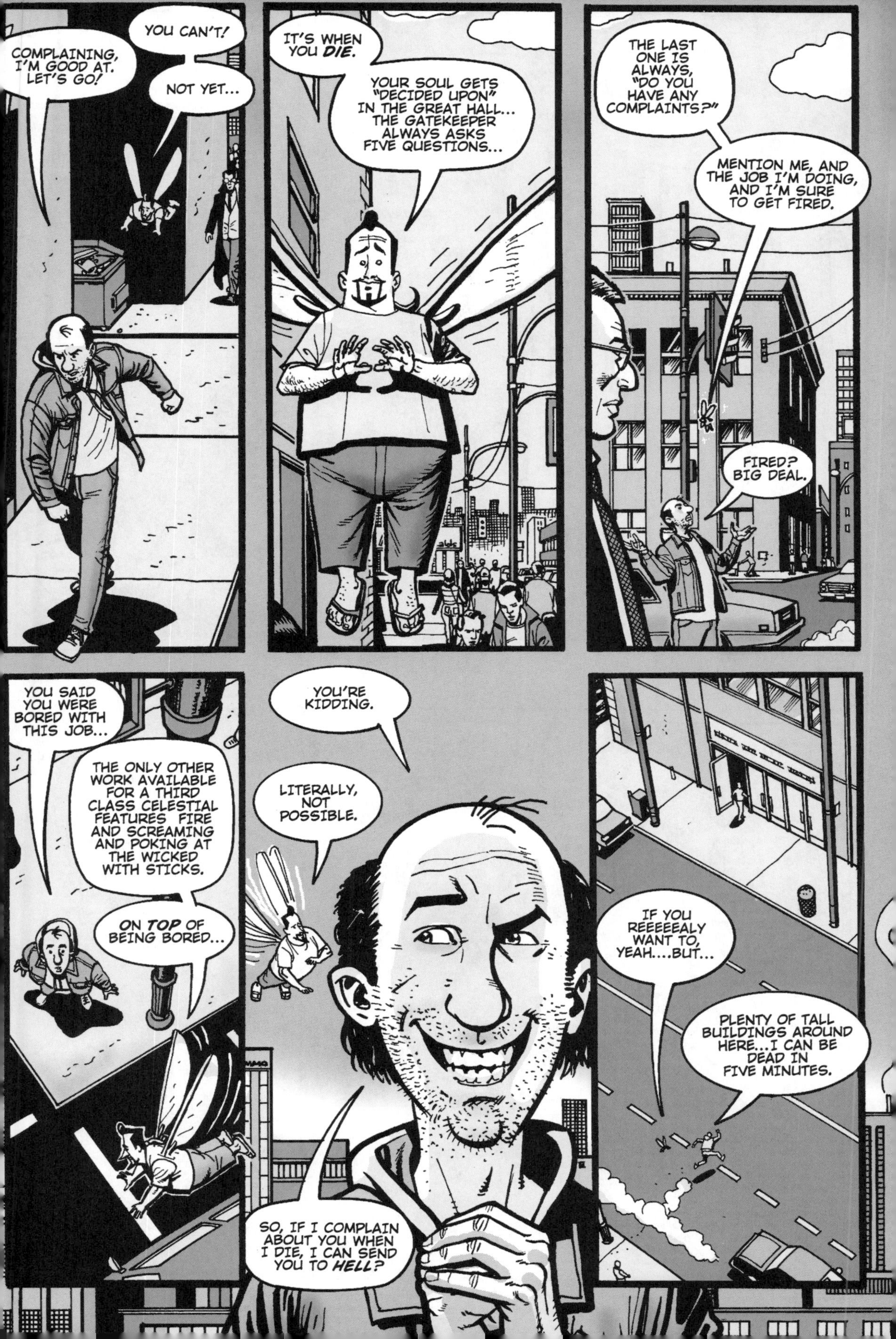
COMPLAINING, I'M GOOD AT. LET'S GO!
YOU CAN'T!
NOT YET...
IT'S WHEN YOU DIE.
YOUR SOUL GETS "DECIDED UPON" IN THE GREAT HALL... THE GATEKEEPER ALWAYS ASKS FIVE QUESTIONS...
THE LAST ONE IS ALWAYS, "DO YOU HAVE ANY COMPLAINTS?"
MENTION ME, AND THE JOB I'M DOING, AND I'M SURE TO GET FIRED.
FIRED? BIG DEAL.
YOU SAID YOU WERE BORED WITH THIS JOB...
THE ONLY OTHER WORK AVAILABLE FOR A THIRD CLASS CELESTIAL FEATURES FIRE AND SCREAMING AND POKING AT THE WICKED WITH STICKS.
ON TOP OF BEING BORED...
YOU'RE KIDDING.
LITERALLY, NOT POSSIBLE.
SO, IF I COMPLAIN ABOUT YOU WHEN I DIE, I CAN SEND YOU TO HELL?
IF YOU REEEEEALY WANT TO, YEAH....BUT...
PLENTY OF TALL BUILDINGS AROUND HERE...I CAN BE DEAD IN FIVE MINUTES.

YOU'RE NOT SERIOUS...

YOU'RE COMPELLING EVIDENCE FOR AN AFTERLIFE...

IT'S GOT TO BE BETTER THAN WHAT I'VE GOT GOING HERE...

VERY TALL BUILDING

WAIT! WE COULD MAKE A *DEAL*... WHAT'S YOUR FONDEST WISH?

TO SCREW YOU OVER. I'M WORKING ON THAT RIGHT NOW.

ELEVATOR TO VERY TALL BUILDING ROOF

C'MON...I'M A MAGICAL CREATURE. I CAN DO *ANYTHING*.

I'VE SEEN YOUR MAGIC.

A LIFETIME OF FARTING ISN'T MY FONDEST WISH.

VTB VERY TALL BUILDINGS INC.

EXCUSE ME?

NO, NO! I KNOW PEOPLE IN THE ANGELLING GAME...I CAN GET THINGS *DONE*!

ATTILA THE HUN WAS ONE OF MINE, YOU KNOW...

OKAY...SO WHAT KIND OF "ANYTHING" ARE WE TALKING ABOUT?

WELL....ANYTHING WITHIN *REASON*...

I KNEW IT.

SEE YOU IN HELL.

NO!

NO!

GIVE ME A MONTH!

IN A MONTH, I'LL *GUARANTEE* YOUR FONDEST WISH. PROMISE.

THAT'S NOT BAD... A MONTH, EH? I GUARANTEE IT!

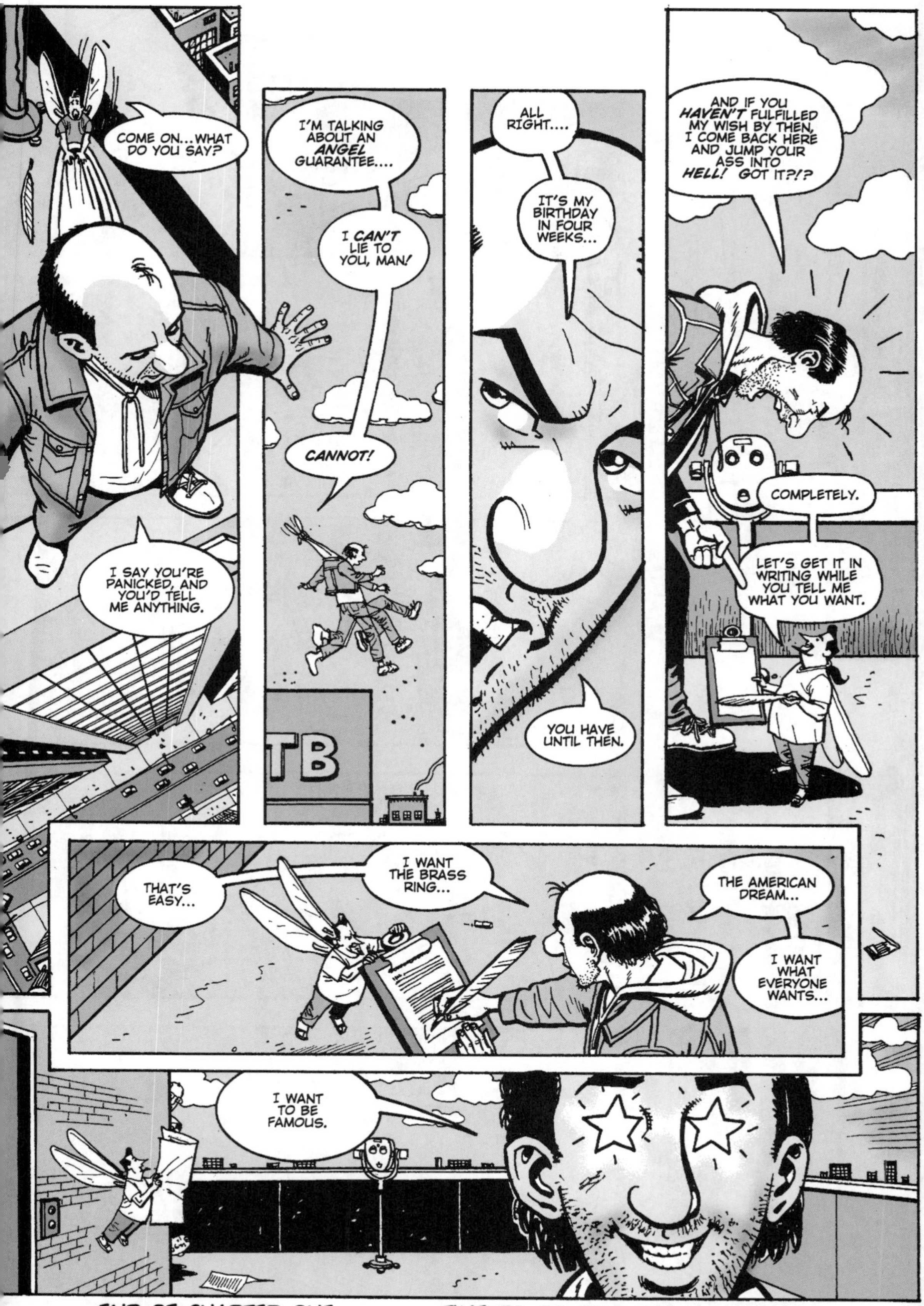
COME ON...WHAT DO YOU SAY?
I SAY YOU'RE PANICKED, AND YOU'D TELL ME ANYTHING.
I'M TALKING ABOUT AN ANGEL GUARANTEE....
I CAN'T LIE TO YOU, MAN!
CANNOT!
TB
ALL RIGHT....
IT'S MY BIRTHDAY IN FOUR WEEKS...
YOU HAVE UNTIL THEN.
AND IF YOU HAVEN'T FULFILLED MY WISH BY THEN, I COME BACK HERE AND JUMP YOUR ASS INTO HELL! GOT IT?!?
COMPLETELY.
LET'S GET IT IN WRITING WHILE YOU TELL ME WHAT YOU WANT.
I WANT THE BRASS RING...
THAT'S EASY...
THE AMERICAN DREAM...
I WANT WHAT EVERYONE WANTS...
I WANT TO BE FAMOUS.
END OF CHAPTER ONE
TIME TO GO AND GET A SANDWICH.

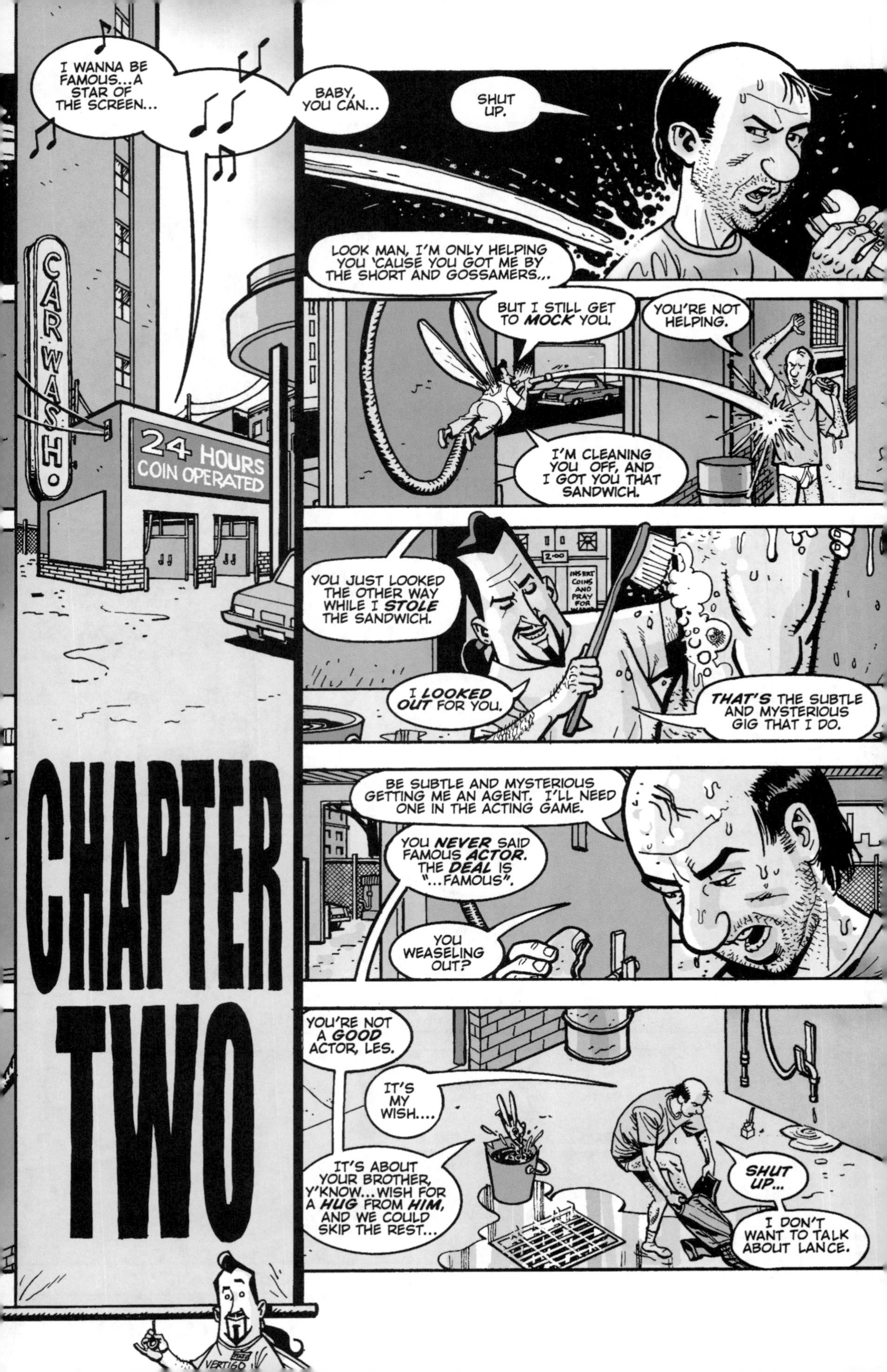
I WANNA BE FAMOUS...A STAR OF THE SCREEN...
BABY, YOU CAN...
SHUT UP.
CAR WASH
24 HOURS
COIN OPERATED
LOOK MAN, I'M ONLY HELPING YOU 'CAUSE YOU GOT ME BY THE SHORT AND GOSSAMERS...
BUT I STILL GET TO ***MOCK*** YOU.
YOU'RE NOT HELPING.
I'M CLEANING YOU OFF, AND I GOT YOU THAT SANDWICH.
YOU JUST LOOKED THE OTHER WAY WHILE I ***STOLE*** THE SANDWICH.
INSERT COINS AND PRAY FOR
I ***LOOKED OUT*** FOR YOU.
THAT'S THE SUBTLE AND MYSTERIOUS GIG THAT I DO.
CHAPTER TWO
BE SUBTLE AND MYSTERIOUS GETTING ME AN AGENT. I'LL NEED ONE IN THE ACTING GAME.
YOU ***NEVER*** SAID FAMOUS ***ACTOR***. THE ***DEAL*** IS "...FAMOUS".
YOU WEASELING OUT?
YOU'RE NOT A ***GOOD*** ACTOR, LES.
IT'S MY WISH....
IT'S ABOUT YOUR BROTHER, Y'KNOW...WISH FOR A ***HUG*** FROM ***HIM***, AND WE COULD SKIP THE REST...
SHUT UP...
I DON'T WANT TO TALK ABOUT LANCE.
VERTIGO

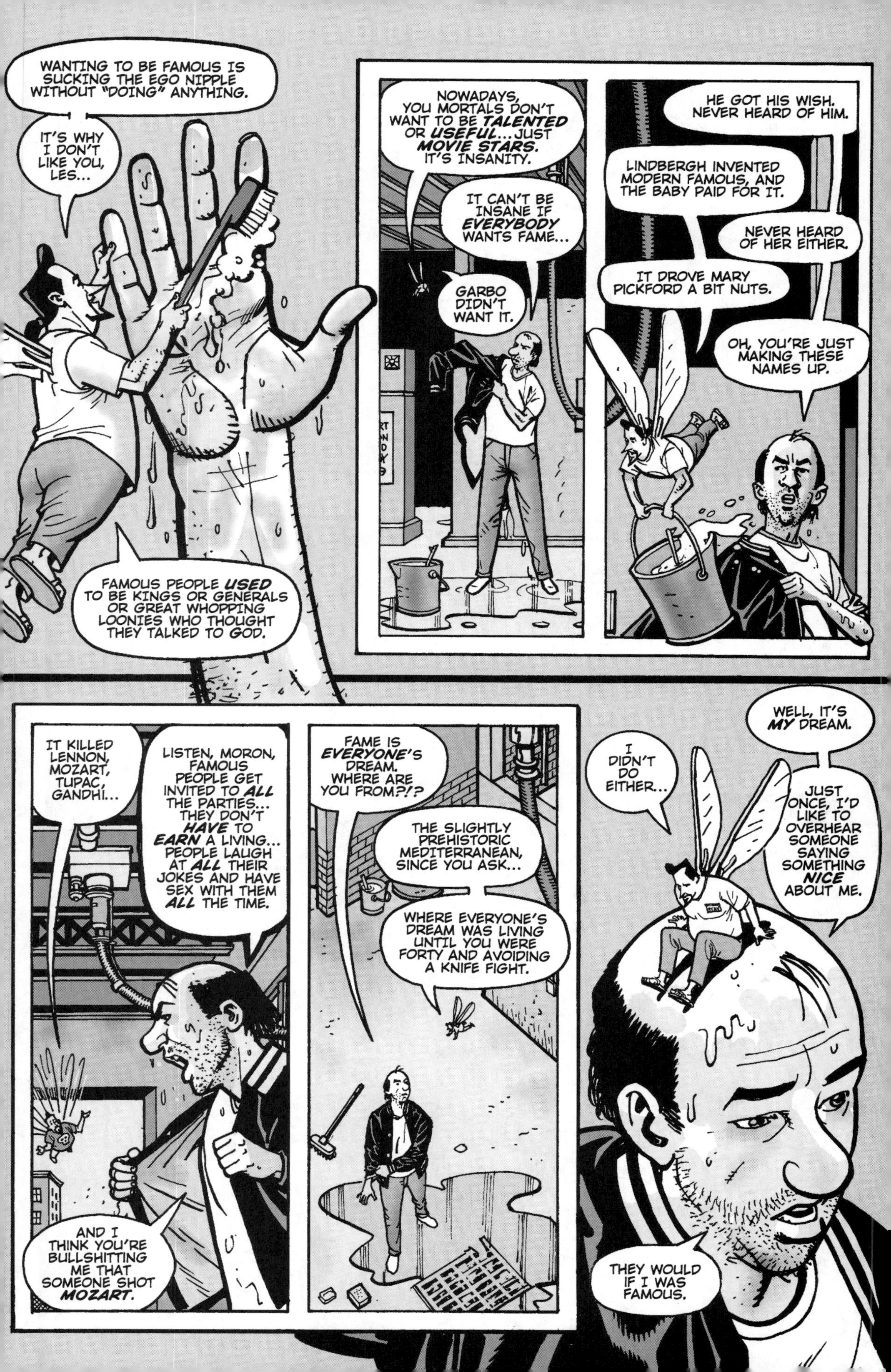
WANTING TO BE FAMOUS IS SUCKING THE EGO NIPPLE WITHOUT "DOING" ANYTHING.
IT'S WHY I DON'T LIKE YOU, LES...
FAMOUS PEOPLE USED TO BE KINGS OR GENERALS OR GREAT WHOPPING LOONIES WHO THOUGHT THEY TALKED TO GOD.
NOWADAYS, YOU MORTALS DON'T WANT TO BE TALENTED OR USEFUL...JUST MOVIE STARS. IT'S INSANITY.
IT CAN'T BE INSANE IF EVERYBODY WANTS FAME...
GARBO DIDN'T WANT IT.
LINDBERGH INVENTED MODERN FAMOUS, AND THE BABY PAID FOR IT.
HE GOT HIS WISH. NEVER HEARD OF HIM.
IT DROVE MARY PICKFORD A BIT NUTS.
NEVER HEARD OF HER EITHER.
OH, YOU'RE JUST MAKING THESE NAMES UP.
IT KILLED LENNON, MOZART, TUPAC, GANDHI...
LISTEN, MORON, FAMOUS PEOPLE GET INVITED TO ALL THE PARTIES... THEY DON'T HAVE TO EARN A LIVING... PEOPLE LAUGH AT ALL THEIR JOKES AND HAVE SEX WITH THEM ALL THE TIME.
AND I THINK YOU'RE BULLSHITTING ME THAT SOMEONE SHOT MOZART.
FAME IS EVERYONE'S DREAM. WHERE ARE YOU FROM?!?
THE SLIGHTLY PREHISTORIC MEDITERRANEAN, SINCE YOU ASK...
WHERE EVERYONE'S DREAM WAS LIVING UNTIL YOU WERE FORTY AND AVOIDING A KNIFE FIGHT.
WELL, IT'S MY DREAM.
I DIDN'T DO EITHER...
JUST ONCE, I'D LIKE TO OVERHEAR SOMEONE SAYING SOMETHING NICE ABOUT ME.
THEY WOULD IF I WAS FAMOUS.

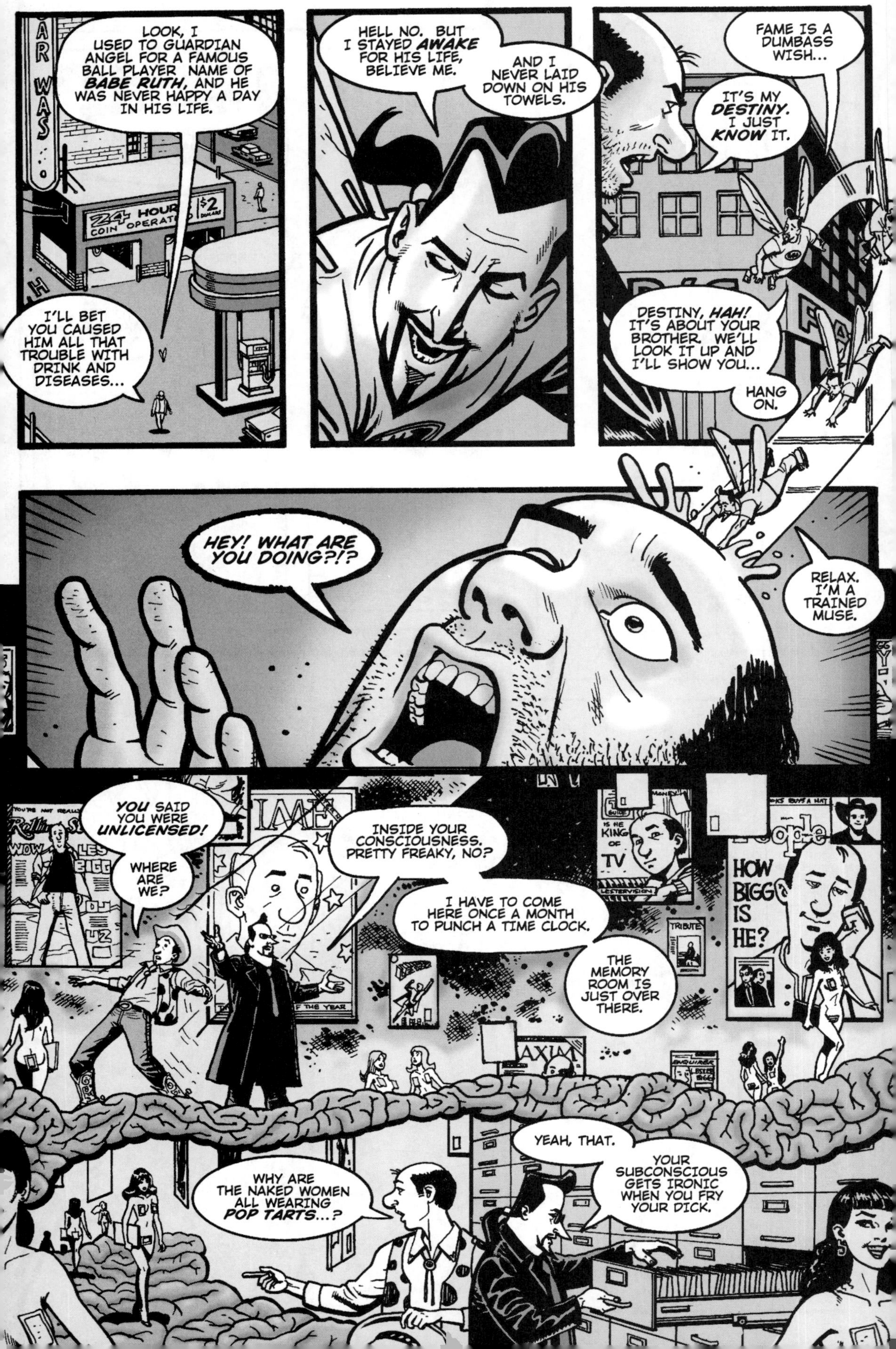
LOOK, I USED TO GUARDIAN ANGEL FOR A FAMOUS BALL PLAYER NAME OF *BABE RUTH*, AND HE WAS NEVER HAPPY A DAY IN HIS LIFE.
24 HOURS COIN OPERATED
$2
I'LL BET YOU CAUSED HIM ALL THAT TROUBLE WITH DRINK AND DISEASES...
HELL NO. BUT I STAYED ***AWAKE*** FOR HIS LIFE, BELIEVE ME.
AND I NEVER LAID DOWN ON HIS TOWELS.
FAME IS A DUMBASS WISH...
IT'S MY ***DESTINY.*** I JUST ***KNOW*** IT.
DESTINY, ***HAH!*** IT'S ABOUT YOUR BROTHER. WE'LL LOOK IT UP AND I'LL SHOW YOU...
HANG ON.
HEY! WHAT ARE YOU DOING?!?
RELAX. I'M A TRAINED MUSE.
YOU SAID YOU WERE ***UNLICENSED!***
WHERE ARE WE?
INSIDE YOUR CONSCIOUSNESS. PRETTY FREAKY, NO?
I HAVE TO COME HERE ONCE A MONTH TO PUNCH A TIME CLOCK.
THE MEMORY ROOM IS JUST OVER THERE.
HOW BIGG IS HE?
WHY ARE THE NAKED WOMEN ALL WEARING ***POP TARTS...?***
YEAH, THAT.
YOUR SUBCONSCIOUS GETS IRONIC WHEN YOU FRY YOUR DICK.

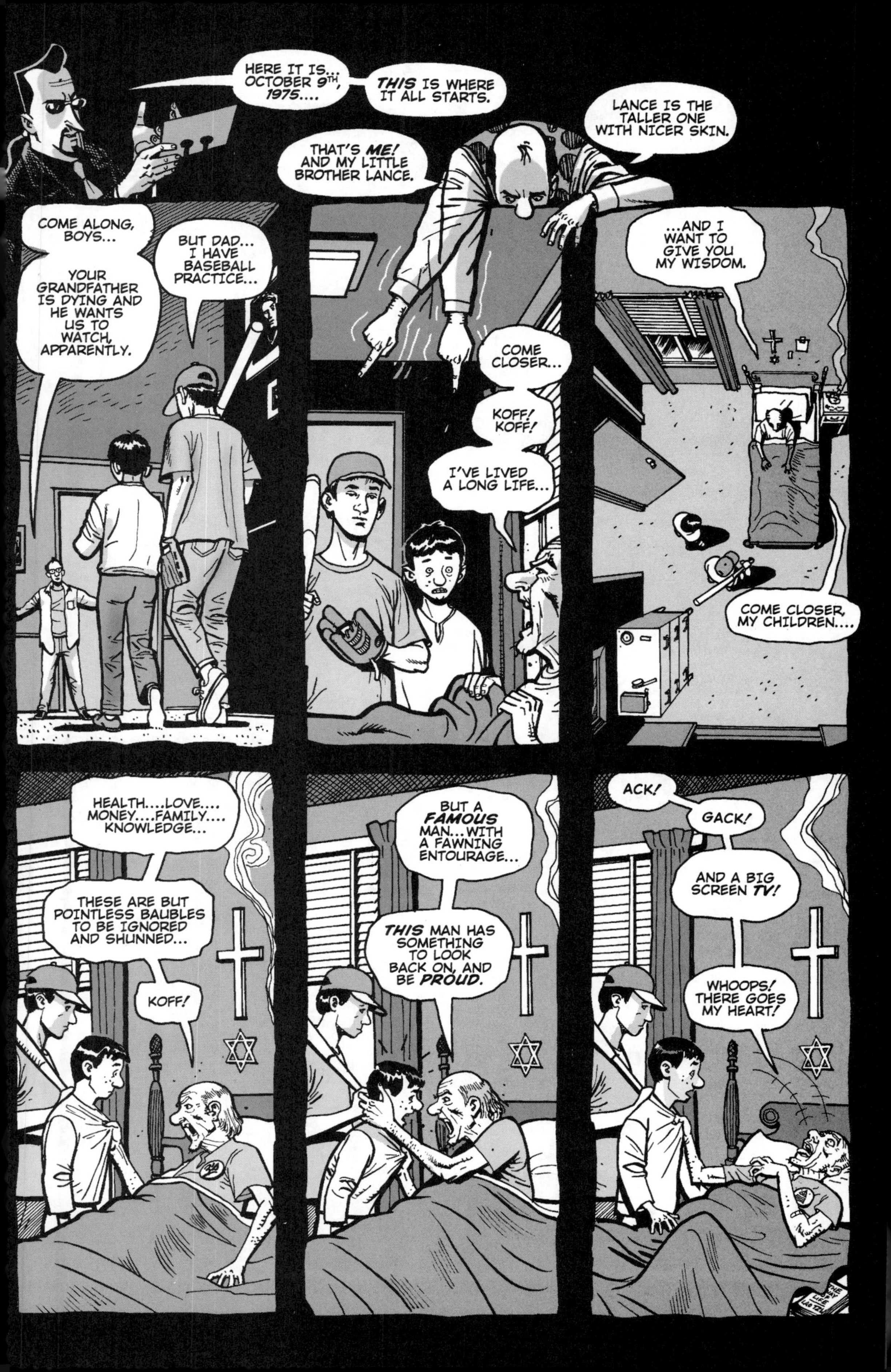
HERE IT IS... OCTOBER 9TH, 1975....
THIS IS WHERE IT ALL STARTS.
THAT'S ME! AND MY LITTLE BROTHER LANCE.
LANCE IS THE TALLER ONE WITH NICER SKIN.
COME ALONG, BOYS...
YOUR GRANDFATHER IS DYING AND HE WANTS US TO WATCH, APPARENTLY.
BUT DAD... I HAVE BASEBALL PRACTICE...
COME CLOSER...
KOFF! KOFF!
I'VE LIVED A LONG LIFE...
...AND I WANT TO GIVE YOU MY WISDOM.
COME CLOSER, MY CHILDREN....
HEALTH....LOVE.... MONEY....FAMILY.... KNOWLEDGE...
THESE ARE BUT POINTLESS BAUBLES TO BE IGNORED AND SHUNNED...
KOFF!
BUT A FAMOUS MAN...WITH A FAWNING ENTOURAGE...
THIS MAN HAS SOMETHING TO LOOK BACK ON, AND BE PROUD.
ACK!
GACK!
AND A BIG SCREEN TV!
WHOOPS! THERE GOES MY HEART!

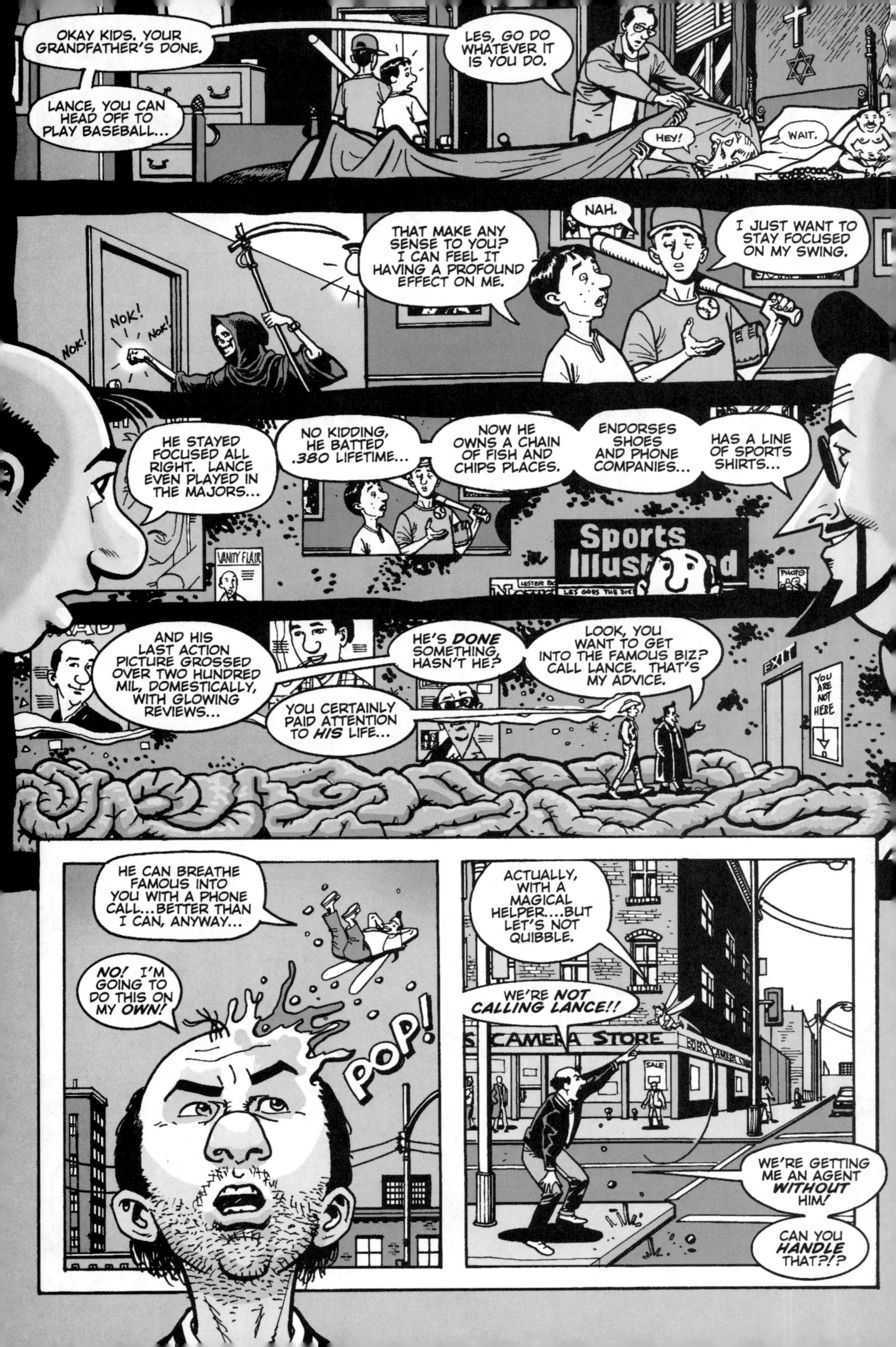
OKAY KIDS. YOUR GRANDFATHER'S DONE.
LANCE, YOU CAN HEAD OFF TO PLAY BASEBALL...
LES, GO DO WHATEVER IT IS YOU DO.
HEY!
WAIT.
NOK! NOK! NOK!
THAT MAKE ANY SENSE TO YOU? I CAN FEEL IT HAVING A PROFOUND EFFECT ON ME.
NAH.
I JUST WANT TO STAY FOCUSED ON MY SWING.
HE STAYED FOCUSED ALL RIGHT. LANCE EVEN PLAYED IN THE MAJORS...
NO KIDDING, HE BATTED .380 LIFETIME...
NOW HE OWNS A CHAIN OF FISH AND CHIPS PLACES.
ENDORSES SHOES AND PHONE COMPANIES...
HAS A LINE OF SPORTS SHIRTS...
VANITY FLAIR
Sports
AND HIS LAST ACTION PICTURE GROSSED OVER TWO HUNDRED MIL, DOMESTICALLY, WITH GLOWING REVIEWS...
HE'S *DONE* SOMETHING, HASN'T HE?
YOU CERTAINLY PAID ATTENTION TO *HIS* LIFE...
LOOK, YOU WANT TO GET INTO THE FAMOUS BIZ? CALL LANCE. THAT'S MY ADVICE.
EXIT
YOU ARE NOT HERE
HE CAN BREATHE FAMOUS INTO YOU WITH A PHONE CALL...BETTER THAN I CAN, ANYWAY...
NO! I'M GOING TO DO THIS ON MY *OWN!*
POP!
ACTUALLY, WITH A MAGICAL HELPER...BUT LET'S NOT QUIBBLE.
WE'RE *NOT CALLING LANCE!!*
CAMERA STORE
SALE
WE'RE GETTING ME AN AGENT *WITHOUT* HIM!
CAN YOU *HANDLE* THAT?!?

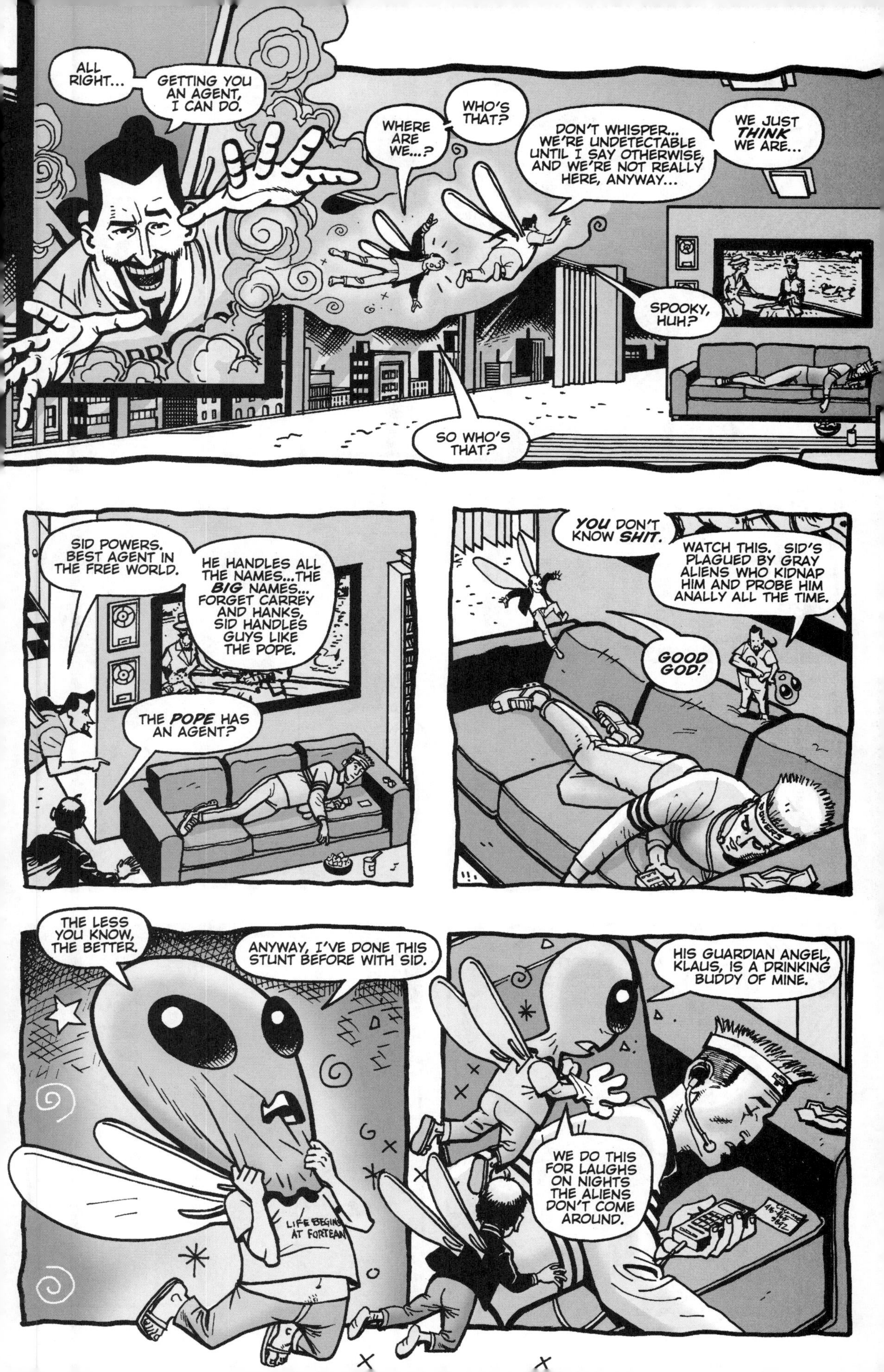
ALL RIGHT...
GETTING YOU AN AGENT, I CAN DO.
WHERE ARE WE...?
WHO'S THAT?
DON'T WHISPER... WE'RE UNDETECTABLE UNTIL I SAY OTHERWISE, AND WE'RE NOT REALLY HERE, ANYWAY...
WE JUST THINK WE ARE...
SPOOKY, HUH?
SO WHO'S THAT?
SID POWERS. BEST AGENT IN THE FREE WORLD.
HE HANDLES ALL THE NAMES...THE BIG NAMES... FORGET CARREY AND HANKS, SID HANDLES GUYS LIKE THE POPE.
THE POPE HAS AN AGENT?
YOU DON'T KNOW SHIT.
WATCH THIS. SID'S PLAGUED BY GRAY ALIENS WHO KIDNAP HIM AND PROBE HIM ANALLY ALL THE TIME.
GOOD GOD!
THE LESS YOU KNOW, THE BETTER.
ANYWAY, I'VE DONE THIS STUNT BEFORE WITH SID.
HIS GUARDIAN ANGEL, KLAUS, IS A DRINKING BUDDY OF MINE.
WE DO THIS FOR LAUGHS ON NIGHTS THE ALIENS DON'T COME AROUND.
LIFE BEGINS AT FORTEAN

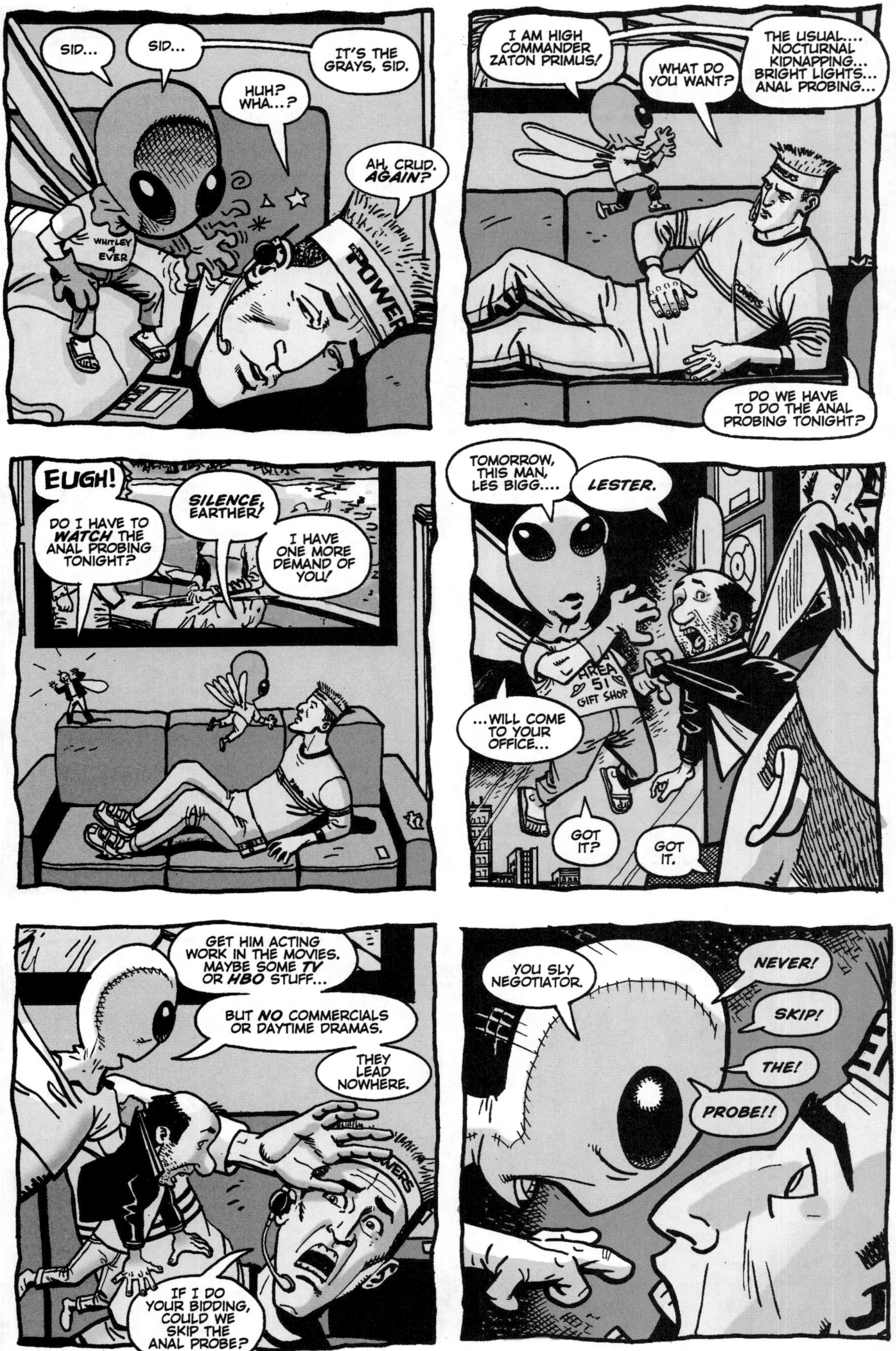
SID...
SID...
IT'S THE GRAYS, SID.
HUH? WHA...?
WHITLEY 4 EVER
AH, CRUD. AGAIN?
POWER
I AM HIGH COMMANDER ZATON PRIMUS!
WHAT DO YOU WANT?
THE USUAL.... NOCTURNAL KIDNAPPING... BRIGHT LIGHTS... ANAL PROBING...
DO WE HAVE TO DO THE ANAL PROBING TONIGHT?
EUGH!
DO I HAVE TO WATCH THE ANAL PROBING TONIGHT?
SILENCE, EARTHER!
I HAVE ONE MORE DEMAND OF YOU!
TOMORROW, THIS MAN, LES BIGG....
LESTER.
AREA 51 GIFT SHOP
...WILL COME TO YOUR OFFICE...
GOT IT?
GOT IT.
GET HIM ACTING WORK IN THE MOVIES. MAYBE SOME TV OR HBO STUFF...
BUT NO COMMERCIALS OR DAYTIME DRAMAS.
THEY LEAD NOWHERE.
IF I DO YOUR BIDDING, COULD WE SKIP THE ANAL PROBE?
YOU SLY NEGOTIATOR.
NEVER!
SKIP!
THE!
PROBE!!

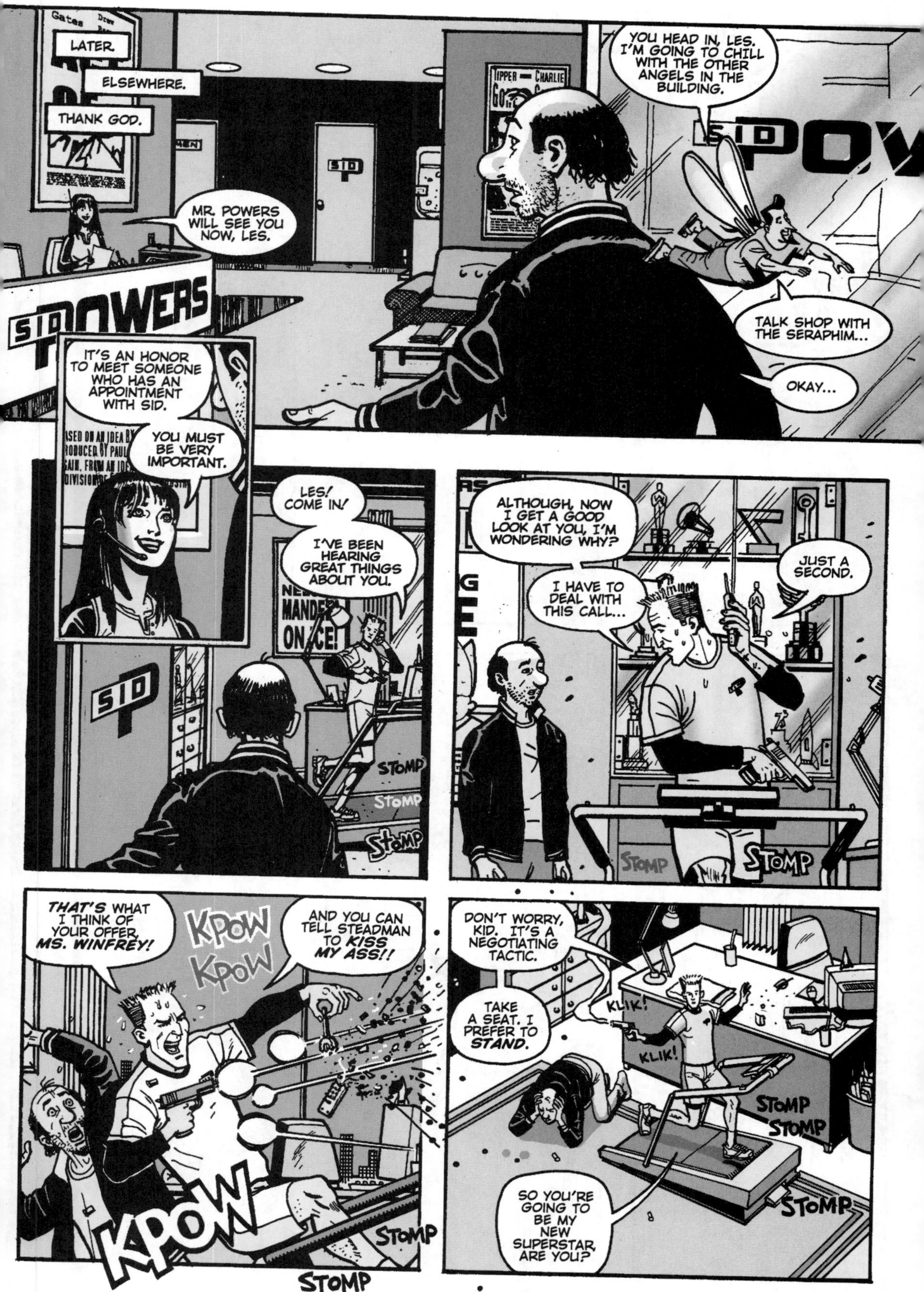
LATER.
ELSEWHERE.
THANK GOD.
MR. POWERS WILL SEE YOU NOW, LES.
YOU HEAD IN, LES. I'M GOING TO CHILL WITH THE OTHER ANGELS IN THE BUILDING.
TALK SHOP WITH THE SERAPHIM...
OKAY...
IT'S AN HONOR TO MEET SOMEONE WHO HAS AN APPOINTMENT WITH SID.
YOU MUST BE VERY IMPORTANT.
LES! COME IN!
I'VE BEEN HEARING GREAT THINGS ABOUT YOU.
STOMP
STOMP
STOMP
ALTHOUGH, NOW I GET A GOOD LOOK AT YOU, I'M WONDERING WHY?
I HAVE TO DEAL WITH THIS CALL...
JUST A SECOND.
STOMP
STOMP
THAT'S WHAT I THINK OF YOUR OFFER, MS. WINFREY!
KPOW
KPOW
AND YOU CAN TELL STEADMAN TO KISS MY ASS!!
KPOW
STOMP
STOMP
DON'T WORRY, KID. IT'S A NEGOTIATING TACTIC.
TAKE A SEAT. I PREFER TO STAND.
KLIK!
KLIK!
STOMP
STOMP
STOMP
SO YOU'RE GOING TO BE MY NEW SUPERSTAR, ARE YOU?

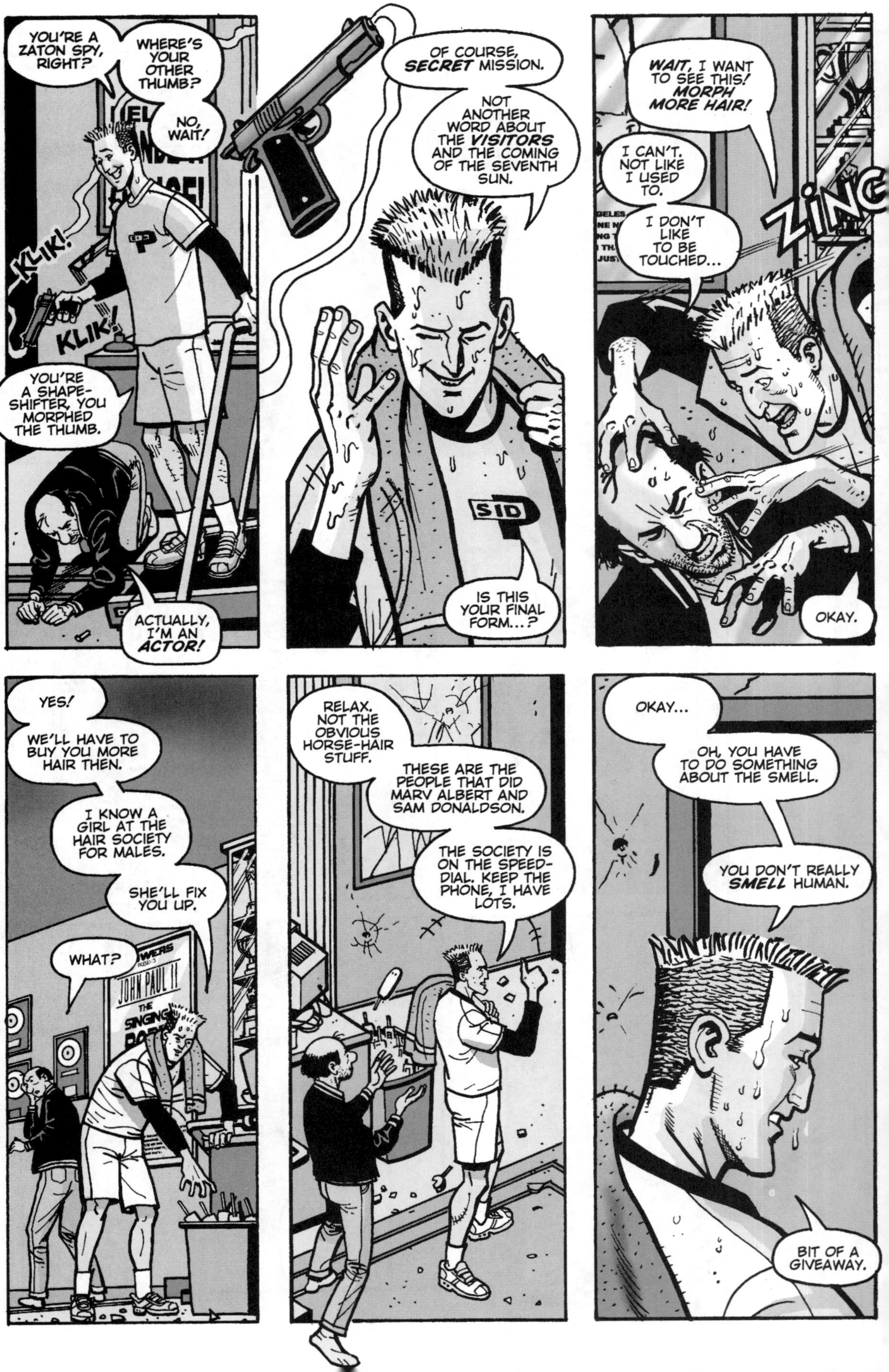
YOU'RE A ZATON SPY, RIGHT?
WHERE'S YOUR OTHER THUMB?
NO, WAIT!
KLIK!
KLIK!
YOU'RE A SHAPE-SHIFTER, YOU MORPHED THE THUMB.
ACTUALLY, I'M AN ACTOR!
OF COURSE, SECRET MISSION.
NOT ANOTHER WORD ABOUT THE VISITORS AND THE COMING OF THE SEVENTH SUN.
SID
IS THIS YOUR FINAL FORM...?
WAIT, I WANT TO SEE THIS! MORPH MORE HAIR!
I CAN'T. NOT LIKE I USED TO.
I DON'T LIKE TO BE TOUCHED...
ZING
OKAY.
YES!
WE'LL HAVE TO BUY YOU MORE HAIR THEN.
I KNOW A GIRL AT THE HAIR SOCIETY FOR MALES.
SHE'LL FIX YOU UP.
WHAT?
JOHN PAUL II
RELAX. NOT THE OBVIOUS HORSE-HAIR STUFF.
THESE ARE THE PEOPLE THAT DID MARV ALBERT AND SAM DONALDSON.
THE SOCIETY IS ON THE SPEED-DIAL. KEEP THE PHONE, I HAVE LOTS.
OKAY...
OH, YOU HAVE TO DO SOMETHING ABOUT THE SMELL.
YOU DON'T REALLY SMELL HUMAN.
BIT OF A GIVEAWAY.

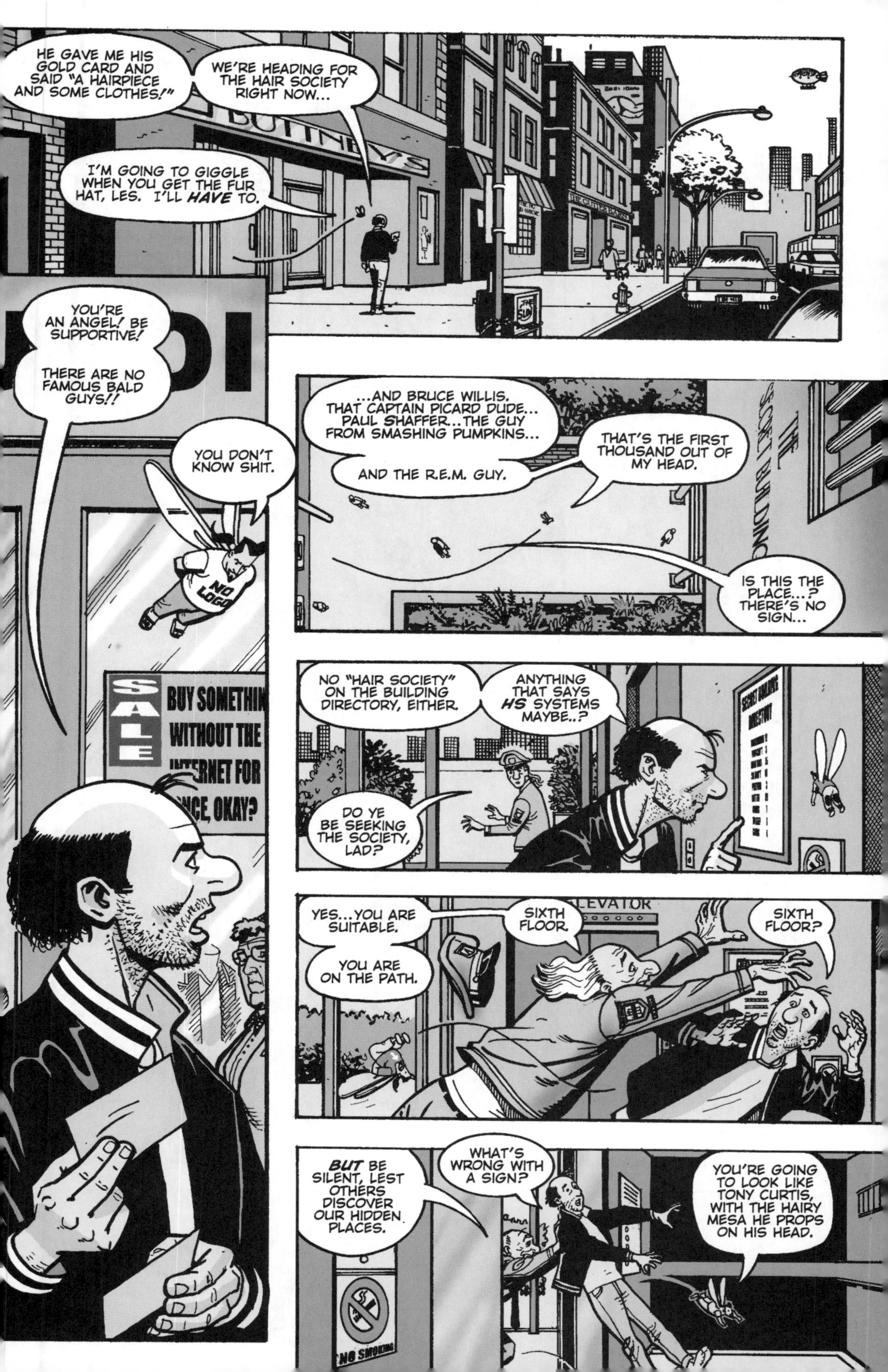
HE GAVE ME HIS GOLD CARD AND SAID "A HAIRPIECE AND SOME CLOTHES!"
WE'RE HEADING FOR THE HAIR SOCIETY RIGHT NOW...
I'M GOING TO GIGGLE WHEN YOU GET THE FUR HAT, LES. I'LL *HAVE* TO.
THE SUN
YOU'RE AN ANGEL! BE SUPPORTIVE!
THERE ARE NO FAMOUS BALD GUYS!!
YOU DON'T KNOW SHIT.
NO LOGO
BUY SOMETHIN WITHOUT THE INTERNET FOR NCE, OKAY?
...AND BRUCE WILLIS. THAT CAPTAIN PICARD DUDE... PAUL SHAFFER...THE GUY FROM SMASHING PUMPKINS...
AND THE R.E.M. GUY.
THAT'S THE FIRST THOUSAND OUT OF MY HEAD.
IS THIS THE PLACE...? THERE'S NO SIGN...
NO "HAIR SOCIETY" ON THE BUILDING DIRECTORY, EITHER.
ANYTHING THAT SAYS *HS* SYSTEMS MAYBE..?
DO YE BE SEEKING THE SOCIETY, LAD?
YES...YOU ARE SUITABLE.
YOU ARE ON THE PATH.
SIXTH FLOOR.
SIXTH FLOOR?
ELEVATOR
BUT BE SILENT, LEST OTHERS DISCOVER OUR HIDDEN PLACES.
WHAT'S WRONG WITH A SIGN?
YOU'RE GOING TO LOOK LIKE TONY CURTIS, WITH THE HAIRY MESA HE PROPS ON HIS HEAD.
NO SMOKING

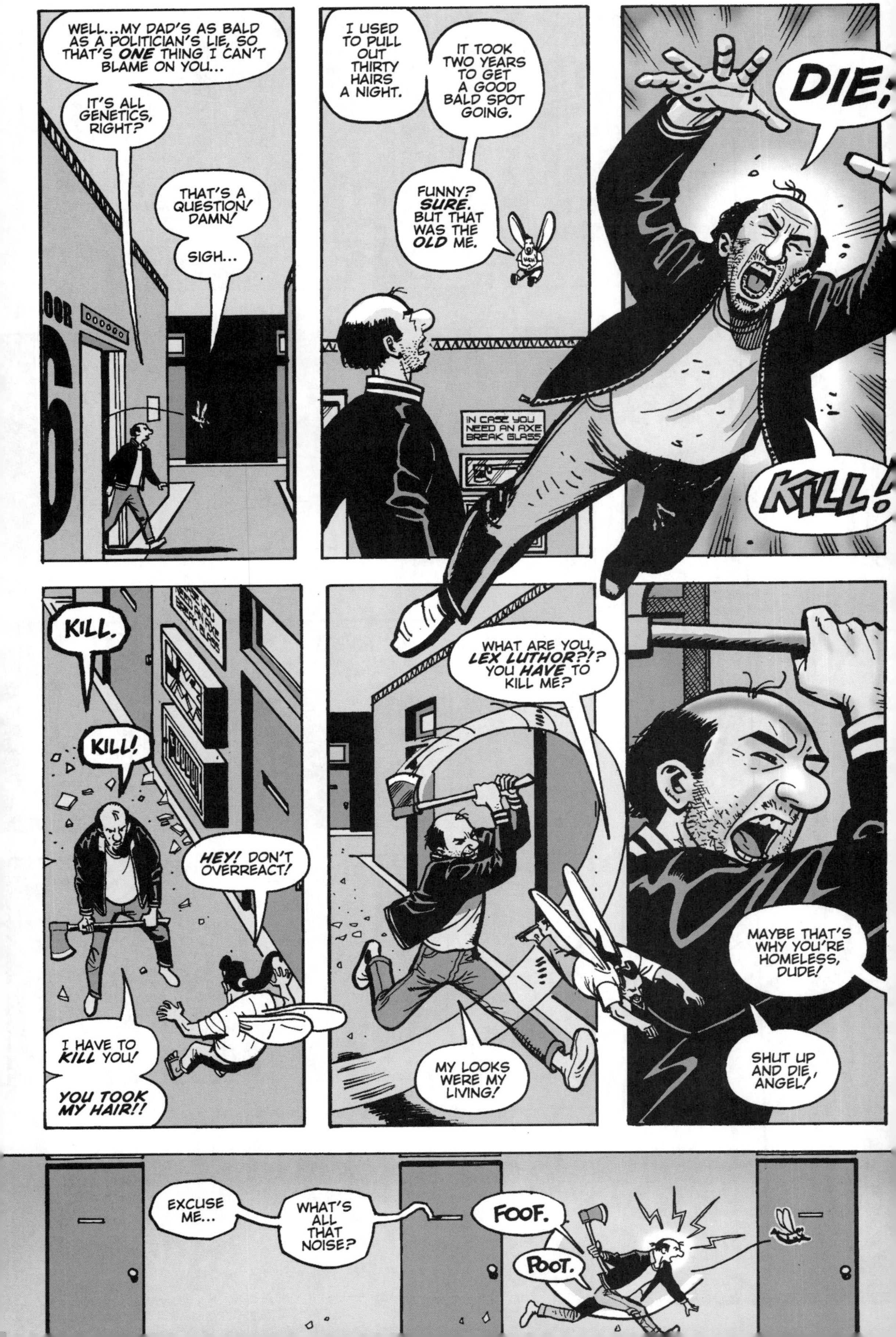
WELL...MY DAD'S AS BALD AS A POLITICIAN'S LIE, SO THAT'S ONE THING I CAN'T BLAME ON YOU...
IT'S ALL GENETICS, RIGHT?
THAT'S A QUESTION! DAMN!
SIGH...
I USED TO PULL OUT THIRTY HAIRS A NIGHT.
IT TOOK TWO YEARS TO GET A GOOD BALD SPOT GOING.
FUNNY? SURE. BUT THAT WAS THE OLD ME.
IN CASE YOU NEED AN AXE BREAK GLASS
DIE,
KILL!
KILL.
KILL!
HEY! DON'T OVERREACT!
I HAVE TO KILL YOU!
YOU TOOK MY HAIR!!
WHAT ARE YOU, LEX LUTHOR?!? YOU HAVE TO KILL ME?
MY LOOKS WERE MY LIVING!
MAYBE THAT'S WHY YOU'RE HOMELESS, DUDE!
SHUT UP AND DIE, ANGEL!
EXCUSE ME...
WHAT'S ALL THAT NOISE?
FOOF.
POOT.

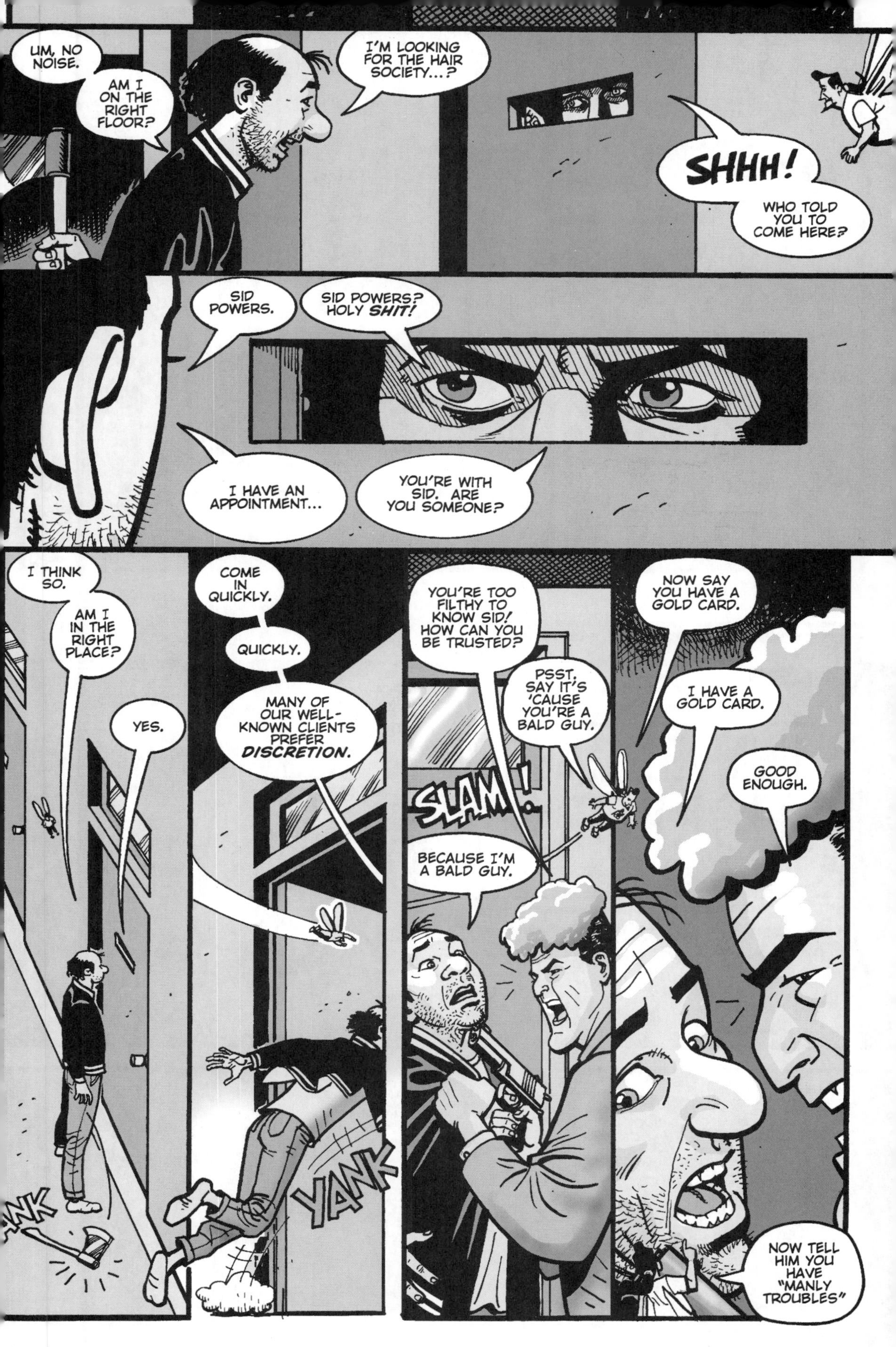
UM, NO NOISE.
AM I ON THE RIGHT FLOOR?
I'M LOOKING FOR THE HAIR SOCIETY...?
SHHH!
WHO TOLD YOU TO COME HERE?
SID POWERS.
SID POWERS? HOLY SHIT!
I HAVE AN APPOINTMENT...
YOU'RE WITH SID. ARE YOU SOMEONE?
I THINK SO.
AM I IN THE RIGHT PLACE?
YES.
YANK
COME IN QUICKLY.
QUICKLY.
MANY OF OUR WELL-KNOWN CLIENTS PREFER DISCRETION.
YANK
YOU'RE TOO FILTHY TO KNOW SID! HOW CAN YOU BE TRUSTED?
PSST, SAY IT'S 'CAUSE YOU'RE A BALD GUY.
SLAM!
BECAUSE I'M A BALD GUY.
NOW SAY YOU HAVE A GOLD CARD.
I HAVE A GOLD CARD.
GOOD ENOUGH.
NOW TELL HIM YOU HAVE "MANLY TROUBLES"

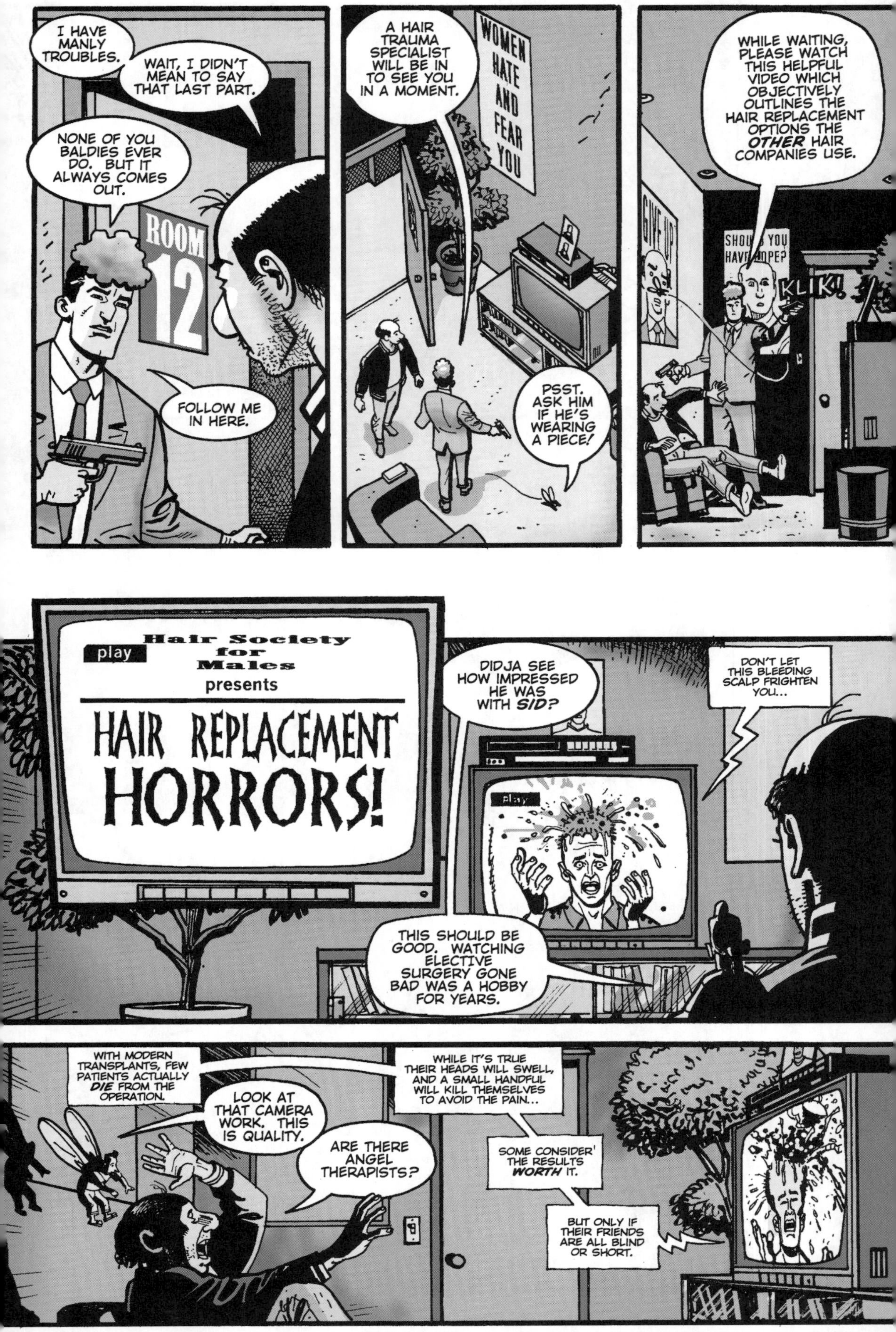

I HAVE MANLY TROUBLES.
WAIT, I DIDN'T MEAN TO SAY THAT LAST PART.
NONE OF YOU BALDIES EVER DO. BUT IT ALWAYS COMES OUT.
ROOM 12
FOLLOW ME IN HERE.
A HAIR TRAUMA SPECIALIST WILL BE IN TO SEE YOU IN A MOMENT.
WOMEN HATE AND FEAR YOU
PSST. ASK HIM IF HE'S WEARING A PIECE!
WHILE WAITING, PLEASE WATCH THIS HELPFUL VIDEO WHICH OBJECTIVELY OUTLINES THE HAIR REPLACEMENT OPTIONS THE OTHER HAIR COMPANIES USE.
GIVE UP
KLIK!
play
Hair Society for Males
presents
HAIR REPLACEMENT HORRORS!
DIDJA SEE HOW IMPRESSED HE WAS WITH SID?
DON'T LET THIS BLEEDING SCALP FRIGHTEN YOU...
play
THIS SHOULD BE GOOD. WATCHING ELECTIVE SURGERY GONE BAD WAS A HOBBY FOR YEARS.
WITH MODERN TRANSPLANTS, FEW PATIENTS ACTUALLY DIE FROM THE OPERATION.
LOOK AT THAT CAMERA WORK. THIS IS QUALITY.
WHILE IT'S TRUE THEIR HEADS WILL SWELL, AND A SMALL HANDFUL WILL KILL THEMSELVES TO AVOID THE PAIN...
ARE THERE ANGEL THERAPISTS?
SOME CONSIDER THE RESULTS WORTH IT.
BUT ONLY IF THEIR FRIENDS ARE ALL BLIND OR SHORT.

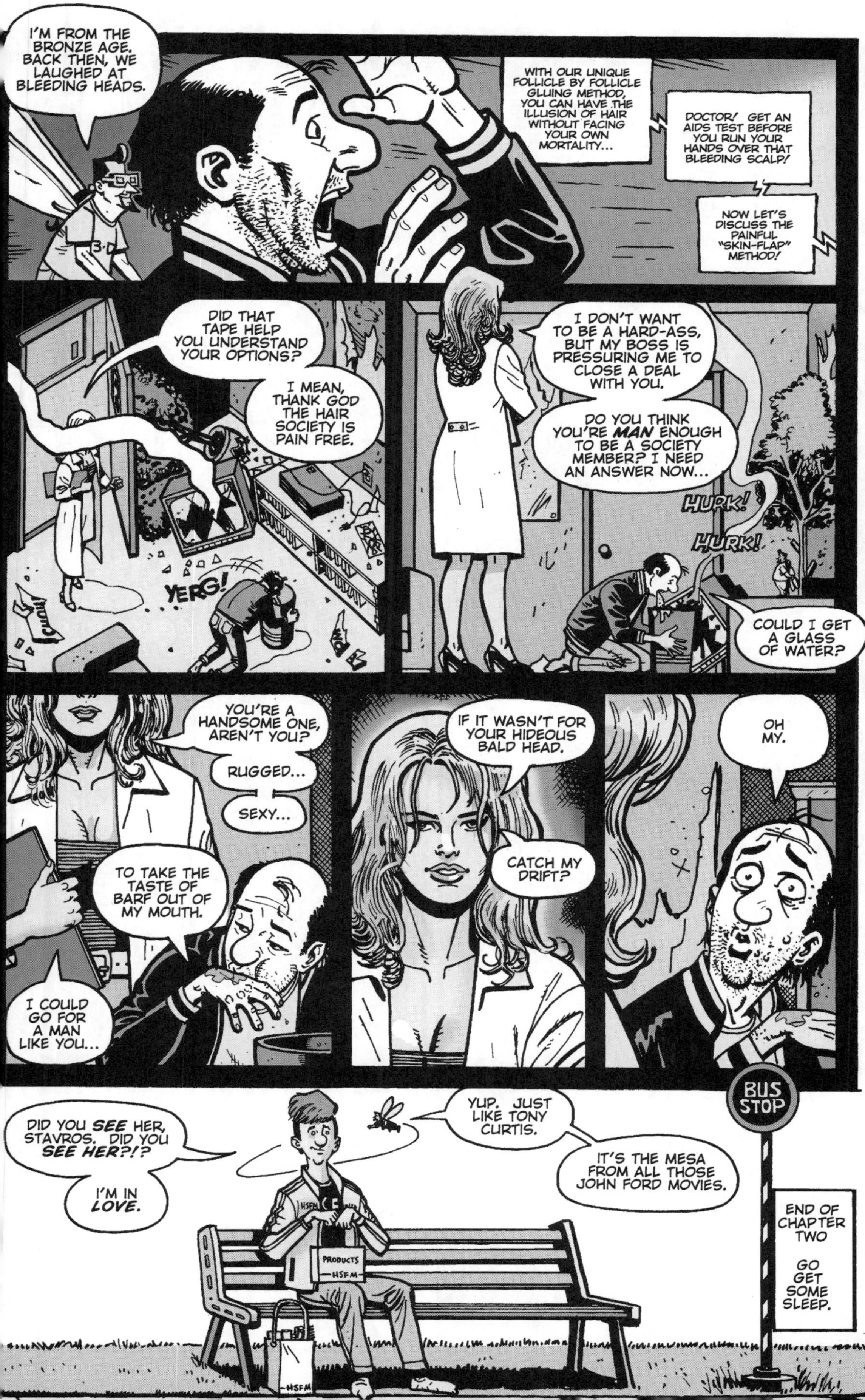
I'M FROM THE BRONZE AGE. BACK THEN, WE LAUGHED AT BLEEDING HEADS.
WITH OUR UNIQUE FOLLICLE BY FOLLICLE GLUING METHOD, YOU CAN HAVE THE ILLUSION OF HAIR WITHOUT FACING YOUR OWN MORTALITY...
DOCTOR! GET AN AIDS TEST BEFORE YOU RUN YOUR HANDS OVER THAT BLEEDING SCALP!
NOW LET'S DISCUSS THE PAINFUL "SKIN-FLAP" METHOD!
DID THAT TAPE HELP YOU UNDERSTAND YOUR OPTIONS?
I MEAN, THANK GOD THE HAIR SOCIETY IS PAIN FREE.
YERG!
I DON'T WANT TO BE A HARD-ASS, BUT MY BOSS IS PRESSURING ME TO CLOSE A DEAL WITH YOU.
DO YOU THINK YOU'RE MAN ENOUGH TO BE A SOCIETY MEMBER? I NEED AN ANSWER NOW...
HURK!
HURK!
COULD I GET A GLASS OF WATER?
YOU'RE A HANDSOME ONE, AREN'T YOU?
RUGGED...
SEXY...
TO TAKE THE TASTE OF BARF OUT OF MY MOUTH.
I COULD GO FOR A MAN LIKE YOU...
IF IT WASN'T FOR YOUR HIDEOUS BALD HEAD.
CATCH MY DRIFT?
OH MY.
BUS STOP
DID YOU SEE HER, STAVROS. DID YOU SEE HER?!?
I'M IN LOVE.
YUP. JUST LIKE TONY CURTIS.
IT'S THE MESA FROM ALL THOSE JOHN FORD MOVIES.
PRODUCTS
HSFM
END OF CHAPTER TWO
GO GET SOME SLEEP.

chapter three

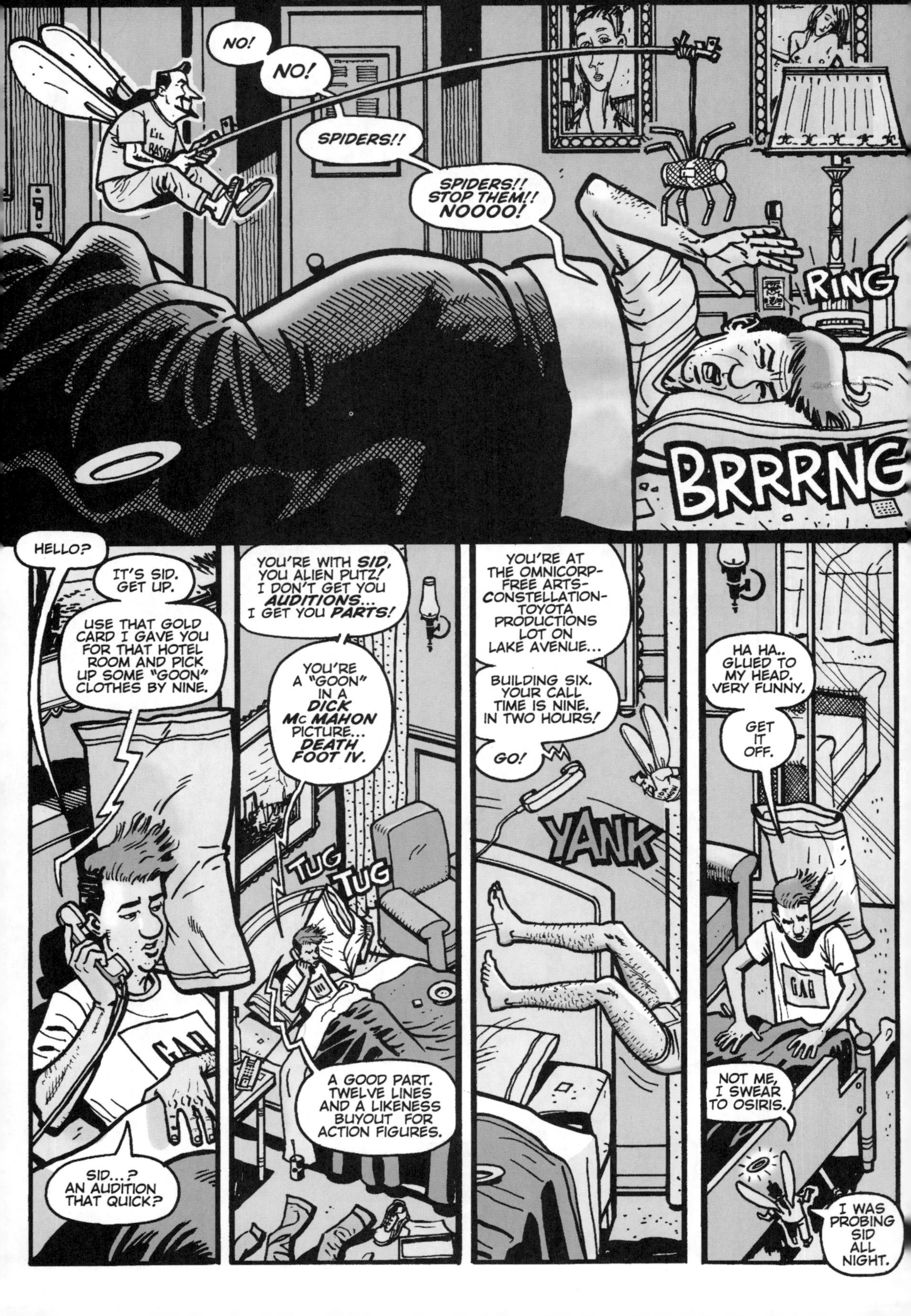
NO!
NO!
SPIDERS!!
SPIDERS!! STOP THEM!! NOOOO!
RING
BRRRNG
HELLO?
IT'S SID. GET UP.
USE THAT GOLD CARD I GAVE YOU FOR THAT HOTEL ROOM AND PICK UP SOME "GOON" CLOTHES BY NINE.
SID...? AN AUDITION THAT QUICK?
YOU'RE WITH SID, YOU ALIEN PUTZ! I DON'T GET YOU AUDITIONS... I GET YOU PARTS!
YOU'RE A "GOON" IN A DICK McMAHON PICTURE... DEATH FOOT IV.
TUG TUG
A GOOD PART. TWELVE LINES AND A LIKENESS BUYOUT FOR ACTION FIGURES.
YOU'RE AT THE OMNICORP-FREE ARTS-CONSTELLATION-TOYOTA PRODUCTIONS LOT ON LAKE AVENUE...
BUILDING SIX. YOUR CALL TIME IS NINE. IN TWO HOURS!
GO!
YANK
HA HA.. GLUED TO MY HEAD. VERY FUNNY.
GET IT OFF.
NOT ME, I SWEAR TO OSIRIS.
I WAS PROBING SID ALL NIGHT.

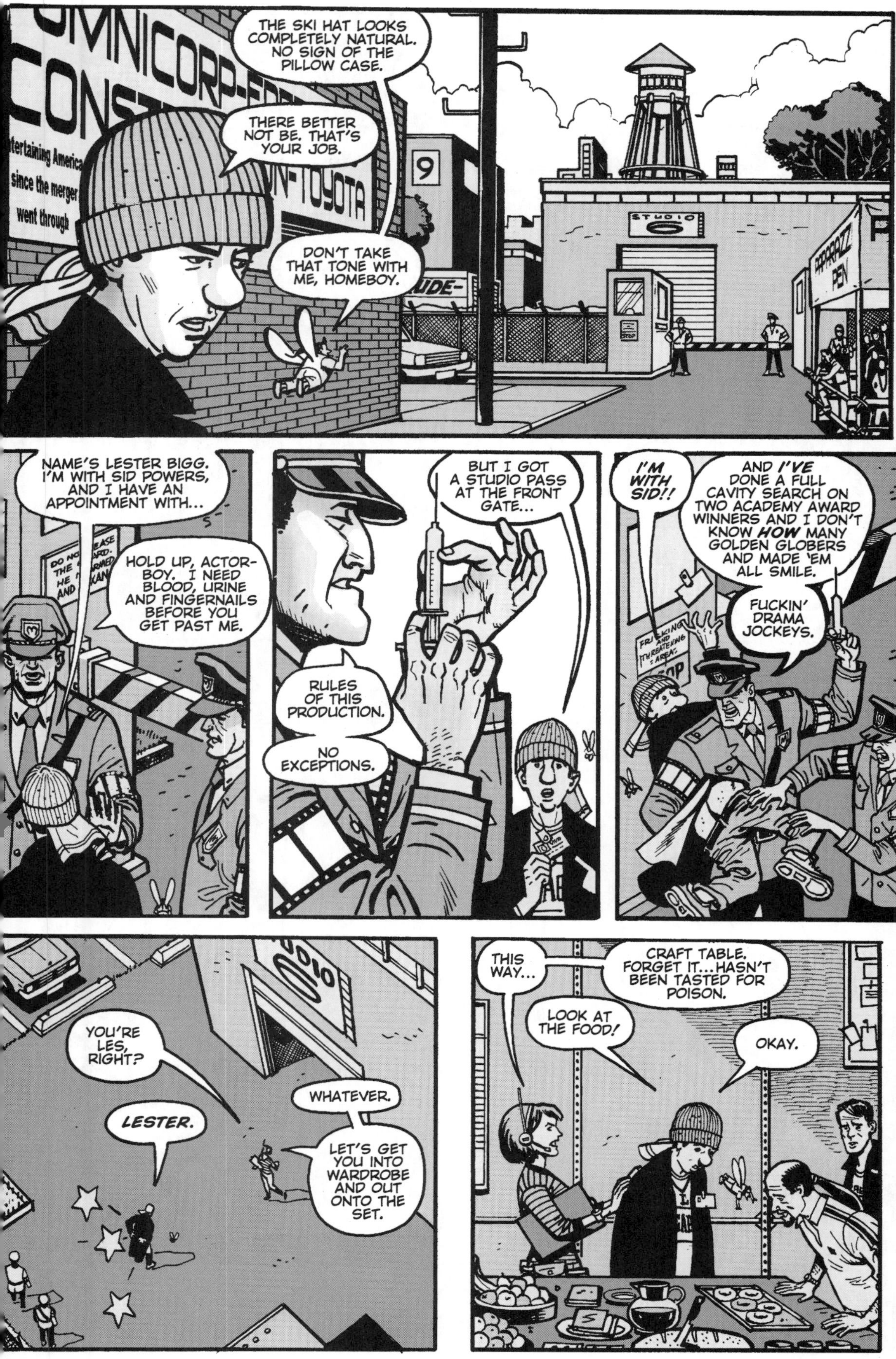
OMNICORP-FORD CONST
Entertaining America since the merger went through
THE SKI HAT LOOKS COMPLETELY NATURAL. NO SIGN OF THE PILLOW CASE.
THERE BETTER NOT BE. THAT'S YOUR JOB.
DON'T TAKE THAT TONE WITH ME, HOMEBOY.
9
STUDIO 6
PAPARAZZI PEN
STOP
NAME'S LESTER BIGG. I'M WITH SID POWERS, AND I HAVE AN APPOINTMENT WITH...
HOLD UP, ACTOR-BOY. I NEED BLOOD, URINE AND FINGERNAILS BEFORE YOU GET PAST ME.
BUT I GOT A STUDIO PASS AT THE FRONT GATE...
RULES OF THIS PRODUCTION.
NO EXCEPTIONS.
I'M WITH SID!!
AND I'VE DONE A FULL CAVITY SEARCH ON TWO ACADEMY AWARD WINNERS AND I DON'T KNOW HOW MANY GOLDEN GLOBERS AND MADE 'EM ALL SMILE.
FUCKIN' DRAMA JOCKEYS.
FRISKING AND THREATENING AREA
STOP
STUDIO 6
YOU'RE LES, RIGHT?
LESTER.
WHATEVER.
LET'S GET YOU INTO WARDROBE AND OUT ONTO THE SET.
THIS WAY...
CRAFT TABLE. FORGET IT... HASN'T BEEN TASTED FOR POISON.
LOOK AT THE FOOD!
OKAY.

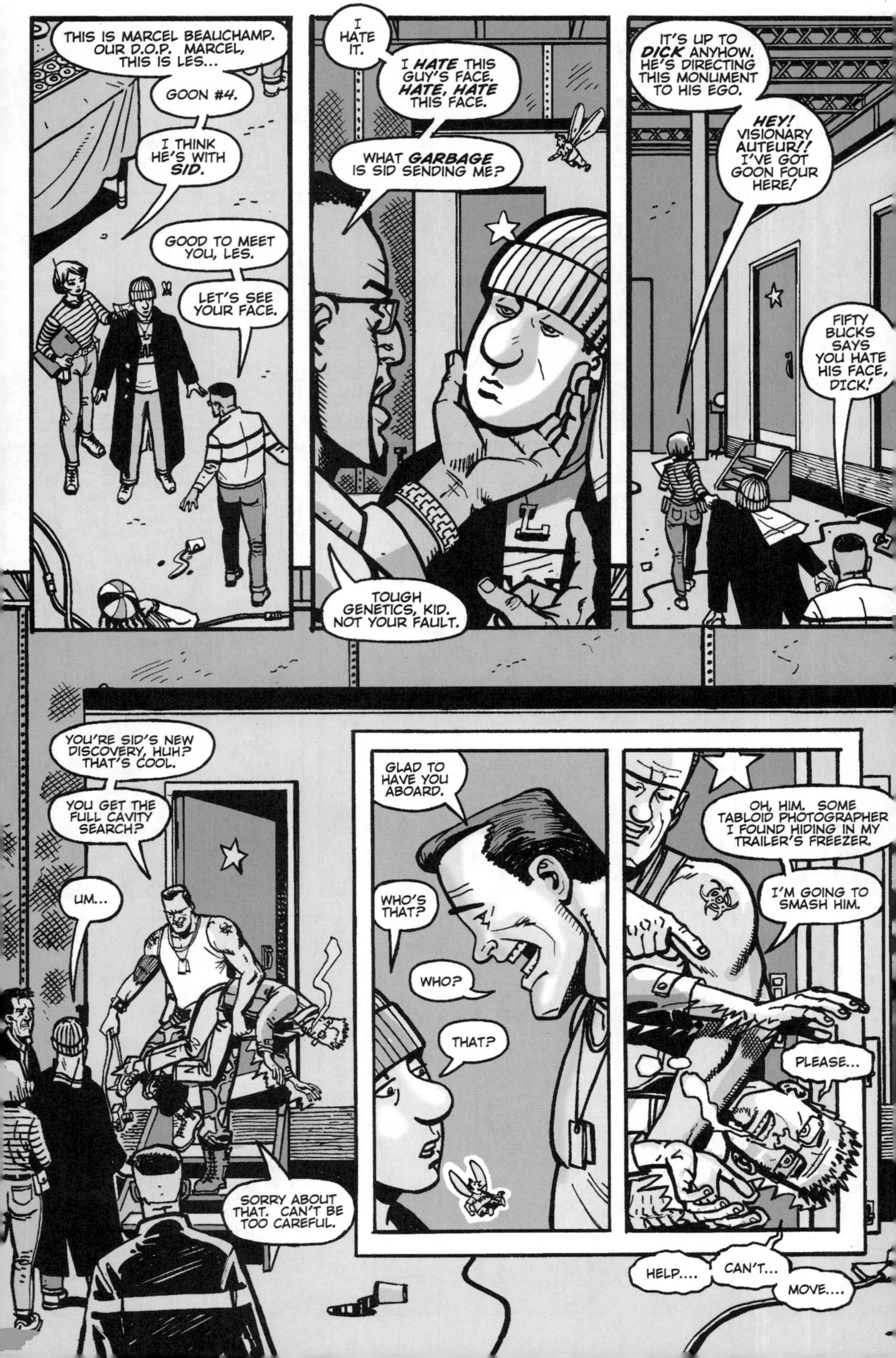

THIS IS MARCEL BEAUCHAMP. OUR D.O.P. MARCEL, THIS IS LES...
GOON #4.
I THINK HE'S WITH **SID.**
GOOD TO MEET YOU, LES.
LET'S SEE YOUR FACE.
I HATE IT.
I **HATE** THIS GUY'S FACE. **HATE, HATE** THIS FACE.
WHAT **GARBAGE** IS SID SENDING ME?
TOUGH GENETICS, KID. NOT YOUR FAULT.
IT'S UP TO **DICK** ANYHOW. HE'S DIRECTING THIS MONUMENT TO HIS EGO.
HEY! VISIONARY **AUTEUR!!** I'VE GOT GOON FOUR HERE!
FIFTY BUCKS SAYS YOU HATE HIS FACE, DICK!
YOU'RE SID'S NEW DISCOVERY, HUH? THAT'S COOL.
YOU GET THE FULL CAVITY SEARCH?
UM...
SORRY ABOUT THAT. CAN'T BE TOO CAREFUL.
GLAD TO HAVE YOU ABOARD.
WHO'S THAT?
WHO?
THAT?
OH, HIM. SOME TABLOID PHOTOGRAPHER I FOUND HIDING IN MY TRAILER'S FREEZER.
I'M GOING TO SMASH HIM.
PLEASE...
HELP....
CAN'T...
MOVE....

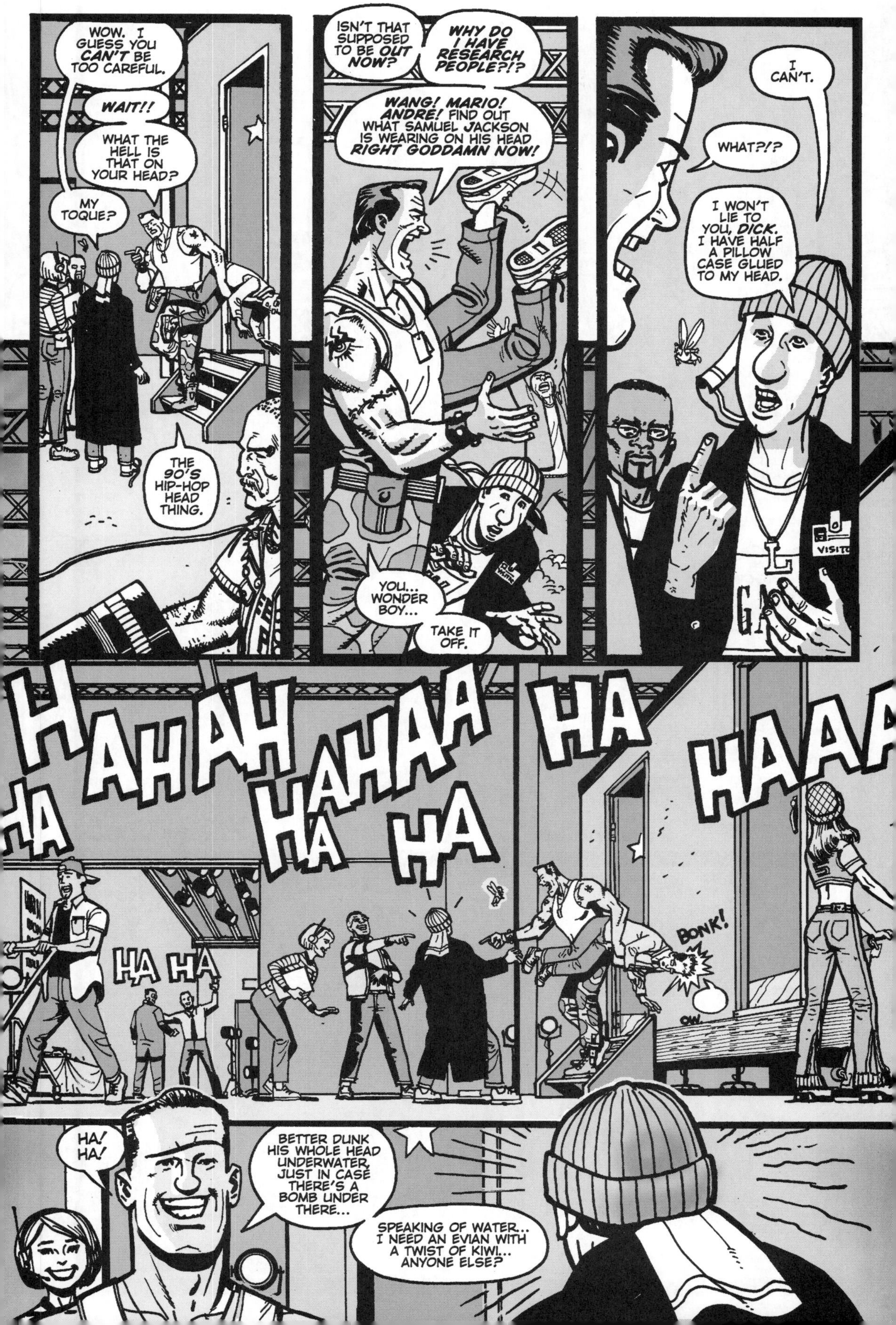

WOW. I GUESS YOU CAN'T BE TOO CAREFUL.
WAIT!!
WHAT THE HELL IS THAT ON YOUR HEAD?
MY TOQUE?
THE 90'S HIP-HOP HEAD THING.
ISN'T THAT SUPPOSED TO BE OUT NOW?
WHY DO I HAVE RESEARCH PEOPLE?!?
WANG! MARIO! ANDRE! FIND OUT WHAT SAMUEL JACKSON IS WEARING ON HIS HEAD RIGHT GODDAMN NOW!
YOU... WONDER BOY...
TAKE IT OFF.
I CAN'T.
WHAT?!?
I WON'T LIE TO YOU, DICK. I HAVE HALF A PILLOW CASE GLUED TO MY HEAD.
HAHAH HA
HAHAA HA HA
HA HAAA
HA HA
BONK!
OW.
HA! HA!
BETTER DUNK HIS WHOLE HEAD UNDERWATER, JUST IN CASE THERE'S A BOMB UNDER THERE...
SPEAKING OF WATER... I NEED AN EVIAN WITH A TWIST OF KIWI... ANYONE ELSE?

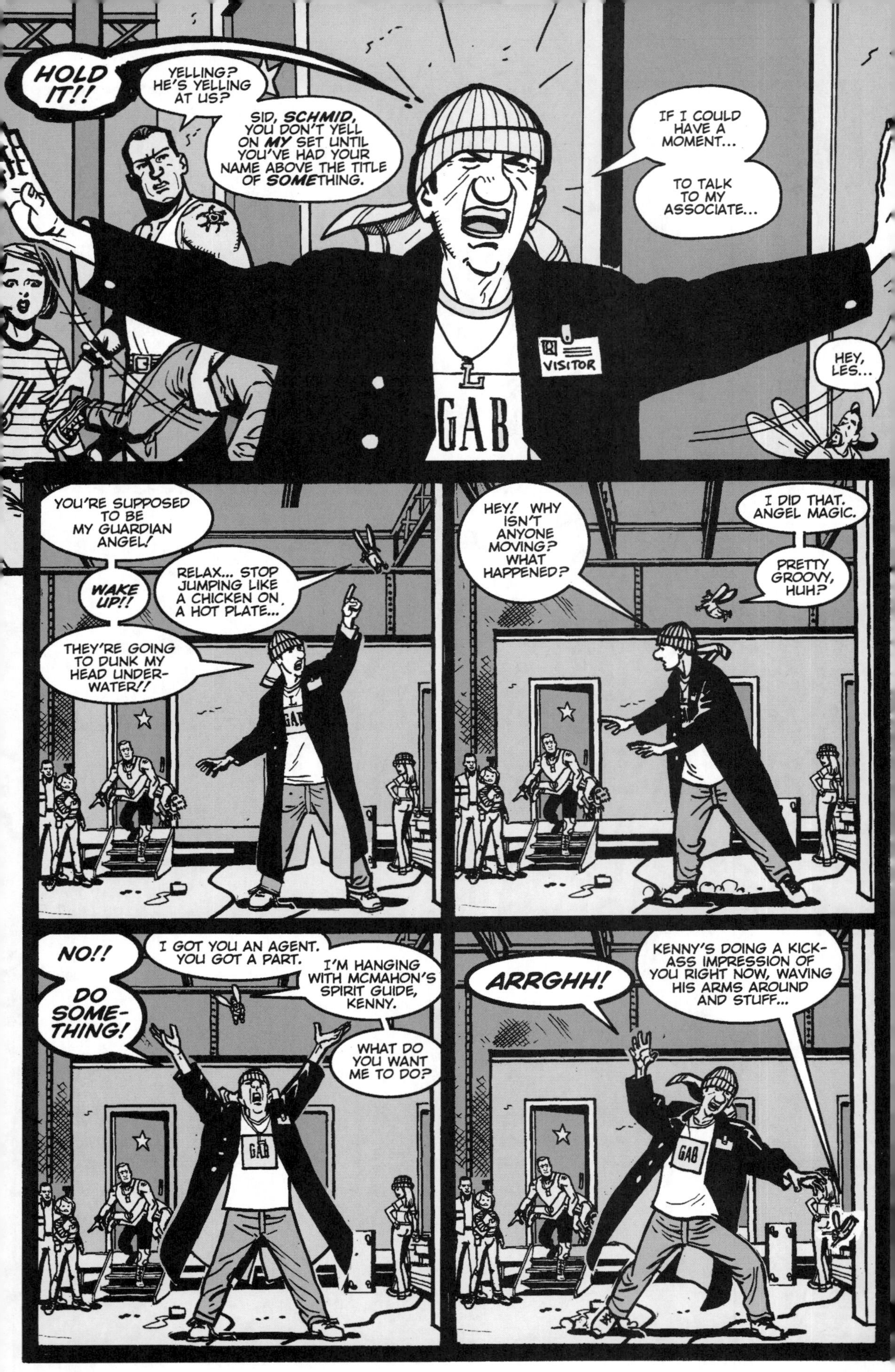
HOLD IT!!
YELLING? HE'S YELLING AT US?
SID, SCHMID, YOU DON'T YELL ON MY SET UNTIL YOU'VE HAD YOUR NAME ABOVE THE TITLE OF SOMETHING.
IF I COULD HAVE A MOMENT...
TO TALK TO MY ASSOCIATE...
VISITOR
GAB
HEY, LES...
YOU'RE SUPPOSED TO BE MY GUARDIAN ANGEL!
WAKE UP!!
THEY'RE GOING TO DUNK MY HEAD UNDER-WATER!!
RELAX... STOP JUMPING LIKE A CHICKEN ON A HOT PLATE...
HEY! WHY ISN'T ANYONE MOVING? WHAT HAPPENED?
I DID THAT. ANGEL MAGIC.
PRETTY GROOVY, HUH?
NO!!
DO SOME-THING!
I GOT YOU AN AGENT. YOU GOT A PART.
I'M HANGING WITH MCMAHON'S SPIRIT GUIDE, KENNY.
WHAT DO YOU WANT ME TO DO?
ARRGHH!
KENNY'S DOING A KICK-ASS IMPRESSION OF YOU RIGHT NOW, WAVING HIS ARMS AROUND AND STUFF...

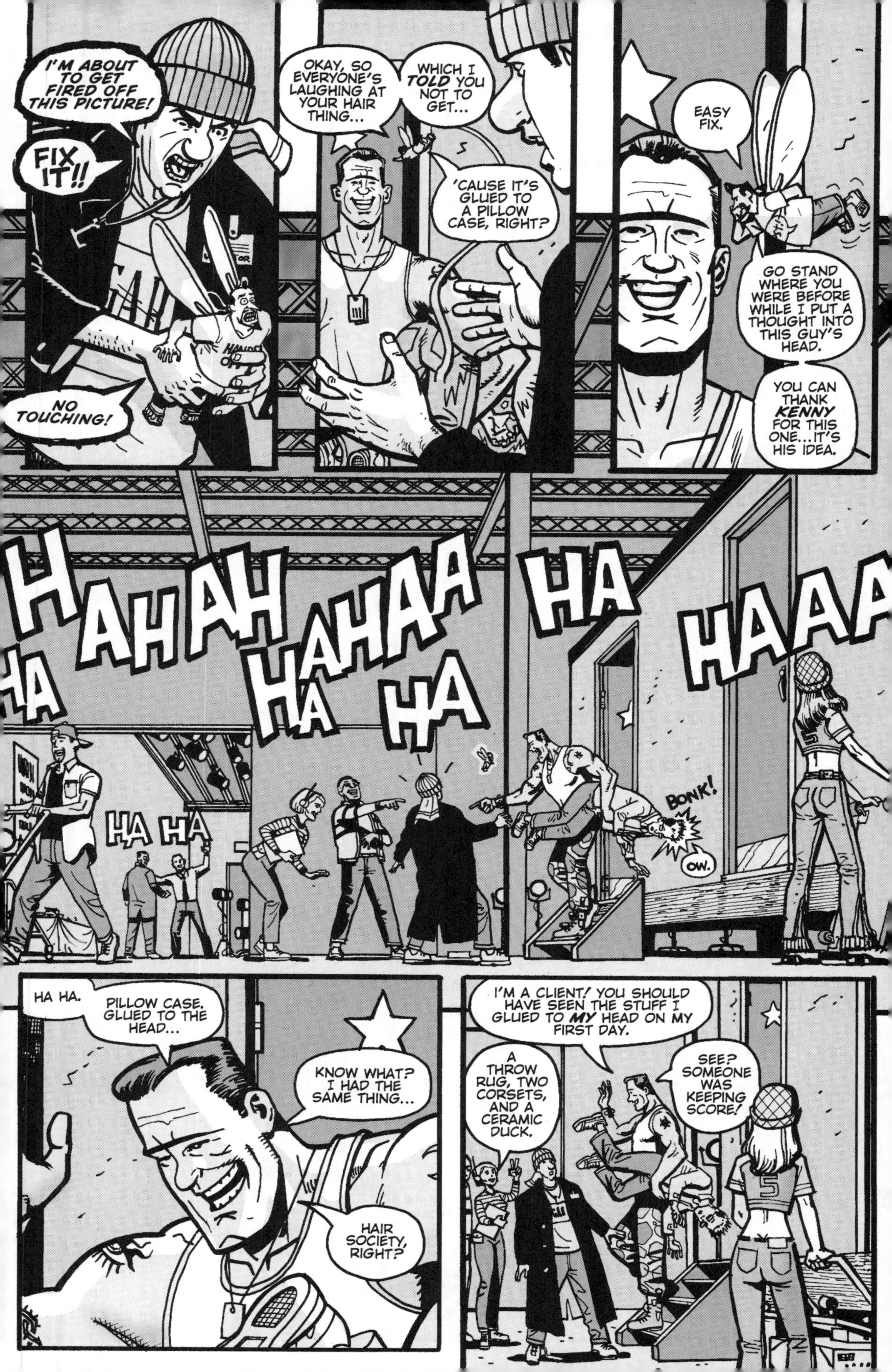
I'M ABOUT TO GET FIRED OFF THIS PICTURE!
FIX IT!!
NO TOUCHING!
OKAY, SO EVERYONE'S LAUGHING AT YOUR HAIR THING...
WHICH I TOLD YOU NOT TO GET...
'CAUSE IT'S GLUED TO A PILLOW CASE, RIGHT?
EASY FIX.
GO STAND WHERE YOU WERE BEFORE WHILE I PUT A THOUGHT INTO THIS GUY'S HEAD.
YOU CAN THANK KENNY FOR THIS ONE...IT'S HIS IDEA.
HA HAH HAH HAHAA HA HA
HA HA
HA HAAA
BONK!
OW.
HA HA.
PILLOW CASE. GLUED TO THE HEAD...
KNOW WHAT? I HAD THE SAME THING...
HAIR SOCIETY, RIGHT?
I'M A CLIENT! YOU SHOULD HAVE SEEN THE STUFF I GLUED TO MY HEAD ON MY FIRST DAY.
A THROW RUG, TWO CORSETS, AND A CERAMIC DUCK.
SEE? SOMEONE WAS KEEPING SCORE!

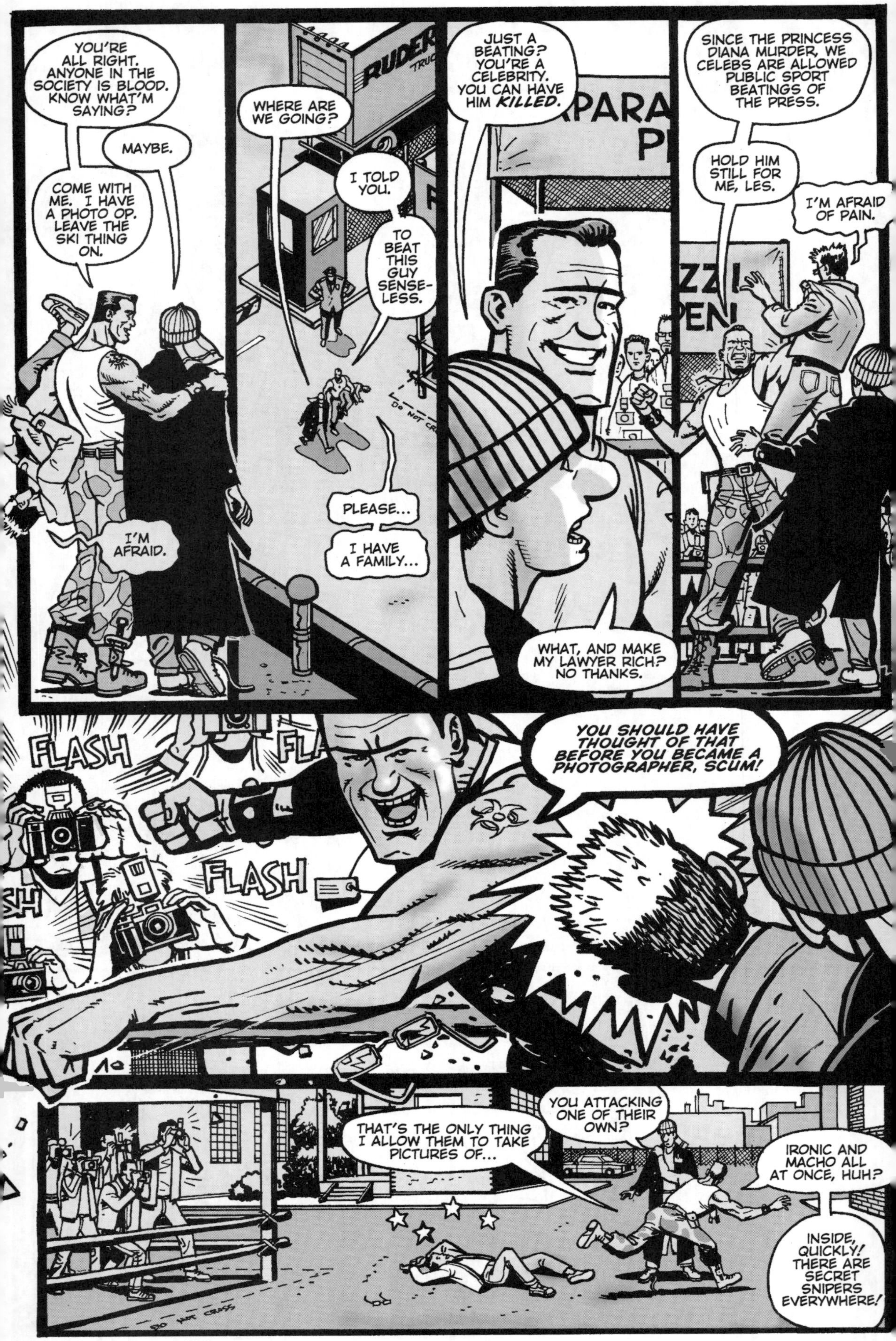
YOU'RE ALL RIGHT. ANYONE IN THE SOCIETY IS BLOOD. KNOW WHAT'M SAYING?
MAYBE.
COME WITH ME. I HAVE A PHOTO OP. LEAVE THE SKI THING ON.
I'M AFRAID.
WHERE ARE WE GOING?
I TOLD YOU.
TO BEAT THIS GUY SENSELESS.
PLEASE...
I HAVE A FAMILY...
JUST A BEATING? YOU'RE A CELEBRITY. YOU CAN HAVE HIM *KILLED*.
WHAT, AND MAKE MY LAWYER RICH? NO THANKS.
SINCE THE PRINCESS DIANA MURDER, WE CELEBS ARE ALLOWED PUBLIC SPORT BEATINGS OF THE PRESS.
HOLD HIM STILL FOR ME, LES.
I'M AFRAID OF PAIN.
FLASH
FLASH
YOU SHOULD HAVE THOUGHT OF THAT BEFORE YOU BECAME A PHOTOGRAPHER, SCUM!
THAT'S THE ONLY THING I ALLOW THEM TO TAKE PICTURES OF...
YOU ATTACKING ONE OF THEIR OWN?
IRONIC AND MACHO ALL AT ONCE, HUH?
INSIDE, QUICKLY! THERE ARE SECRET SNIPERS EVERYWHERE!

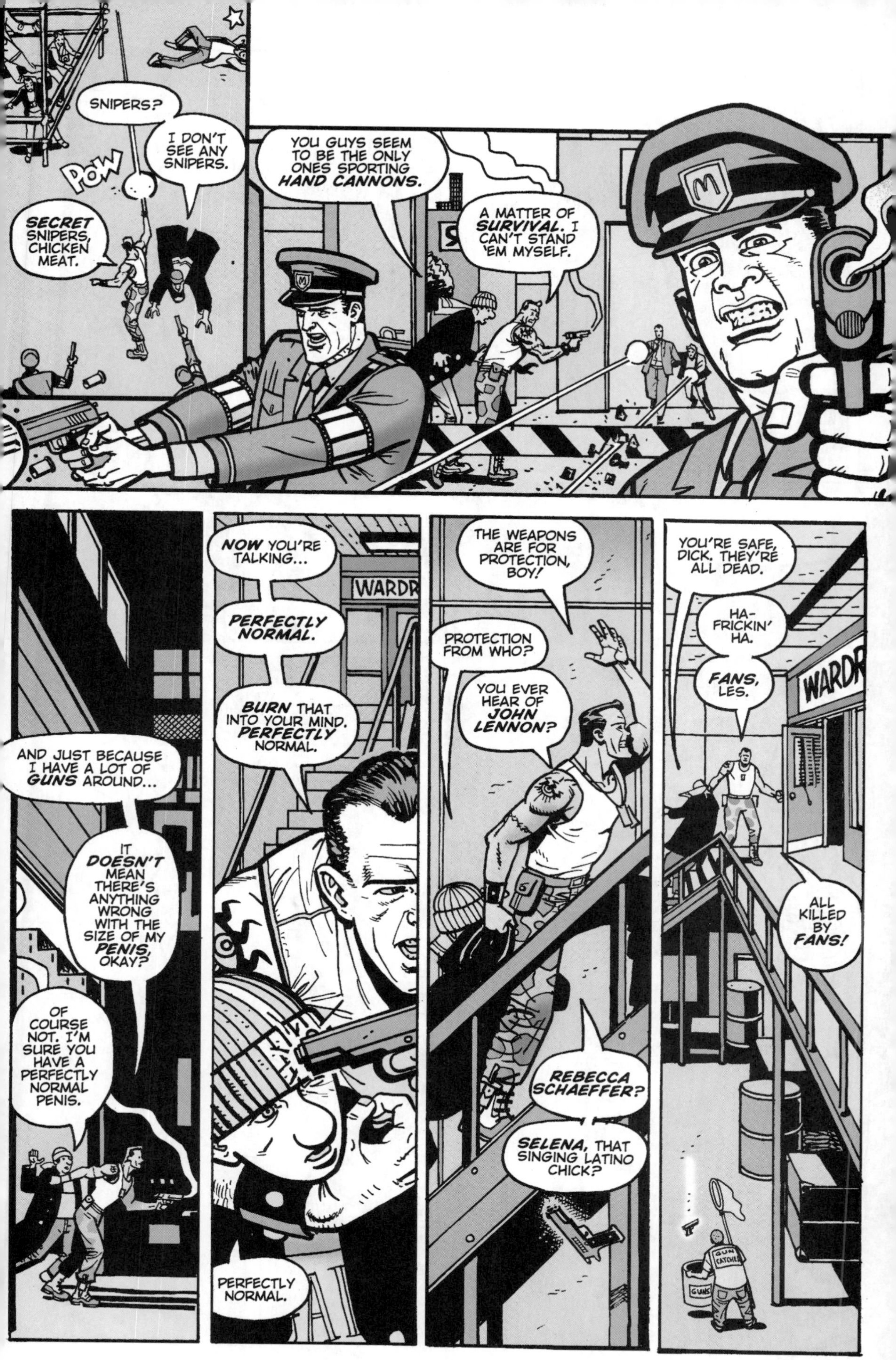
SNIPERS?
I DON'T SEE ANY SNIPERS.
POW
SECRET SNIPERS, CHICKEN MEAT.
YOU GUYS SEEM TO BE THE ONLY ONES SPORTING HAND CANNONS.
A MATTER OF SURVIVAL. I CAN'T STAND 'EM MYSELF.
AND JUST BECAUSE I HAVE A LOT OF GUNS AROUND...
IT DOESN'T MEAN THERE'S ANYTHING WRONG WITH THE SIZE OF MY PENIS, OKAY?
OF COURSE NOT. I'M SURE YOU HAVE A PERFECTLY NORMAL PENIS.
NOW YOU'RE TALKING...
WARDR
PERFECTLY NORMAL.
BURN THAT INTO YOUR MIND. PERFECTLY NORMAL.
PERFECTLY NORMAL.
THE WEAPONS ARE FOR PROTECTION, BOY!
PROTECTION FROM WHO?
YOU EVER HEAR OF JOHN LENNON?
REBECCA SCHAEFFER?
SELENA, THAT SINGING LATINO CHICK?
YOU'RE SAFE, DICK. THEY'RE ALL DEAD.
HA-FRICKIN' HA.
FANS, LES.
WARDR
ALL KILLED BY FANS!
GUN CATCHER
GUNS

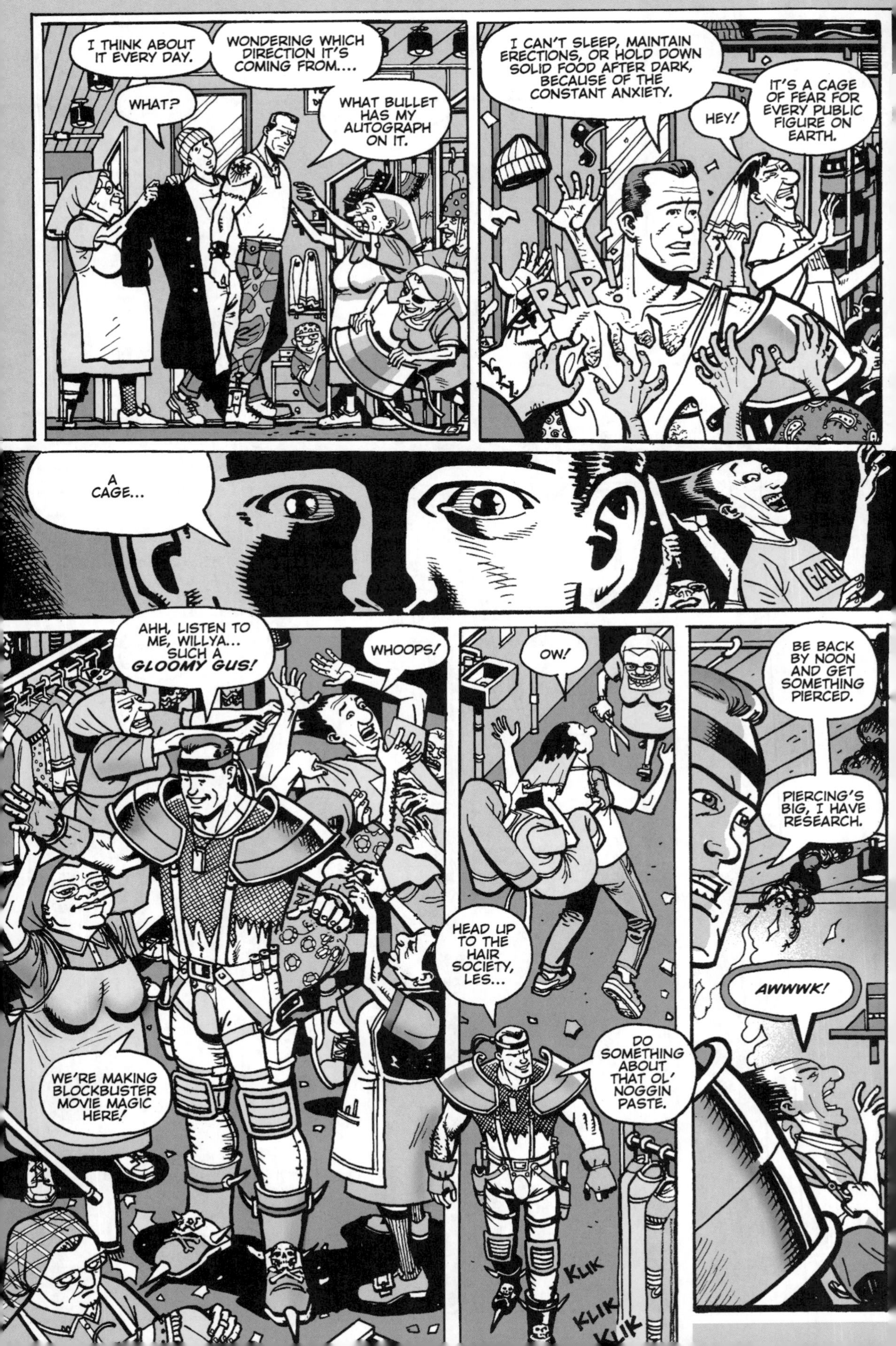
I THINK ABOUT IT EVERY DAY.
WONDERING WHICH DIRECTION IT'S COMING FROM....
WHAT?
WHAT BULLET HAS MY AUTOGRAPH ON IT.
I CAN'T SLEEP, MAINTAIN ERECTIONS, OR HOLD DOWN SOLID FOOD AFTER DARK, BECAUSE OF THE CONSTANT ANXIETY.
HEY!
IT'S A CAGE OF FEAR FOR EVERY PUBLIC FIGURE ON EARTH.
RIP!
A CAGE...
GAB
AHH, LISTEN TO ME, WILLYA... SUCH A *GLOOMY GUS!*
WHOOPS!
WE'RE MAKING BLOCKBUSTER MOVIE MAGIC HERE!
OW!
HEAD UP TO THE HAIR SOCIETY, LES...
DO SOMETHING ABOUT THAT OL' NOGGIN PASTE.
KLIK
KLIK
KLIK
BE BACK BY NOON AND GET SOMETHING PIERCED.
PIERCING'S BIG, I HAVE RESEARCH.
AWWWK!

YEAH, THE *PILLOWCASE* THING. WE *FIX* THAT WITH AN INDUSTRIAL SOLVENT THAT WILL PERMANENTLY DAMAGE YOUR SCALP.

BUT IT'S OKAY, 'CAUSE YOUR HAIR PROSTHETIC COVERS THE SCARRING.

IF YOU THINK IT'S BEST.

SO...SHELLY...? WHAT DO YOU DO WHEN YOU'RE NOT TIGHTENING HAIR WEAVES?

I STEER CLEAR OF HEADSKINS ON MY OWN TIME.

GET IT OUT OF YOUR MIND.

YOU SEEMED ATTRACTED TO ME YESTERDAY...

WHERE ARE YOU *FROM*, COUNTRY MOUSE?!?

I WAS PLAYING YOU TO CLOSE A DEAL.

YOU'RE BALD. IT'S JUST BUSINESS.

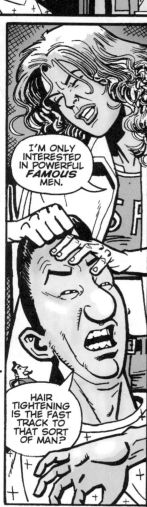

I'M ONLY INTERESTED IN POWERFUL *FAMOUS* MEN.

HAIR TIGHTENING IS THE FAST TRACK TO THAT SORT OF MAN?

THIS IS HOW YOU *FLIRT*?

SPOK

YOU MOCK MY JOB?

START AGAIN, DON JUAN.

TRY TELLING ME ABOUT YOURSELF.

WHAT YOU DO FOR A LIVING.

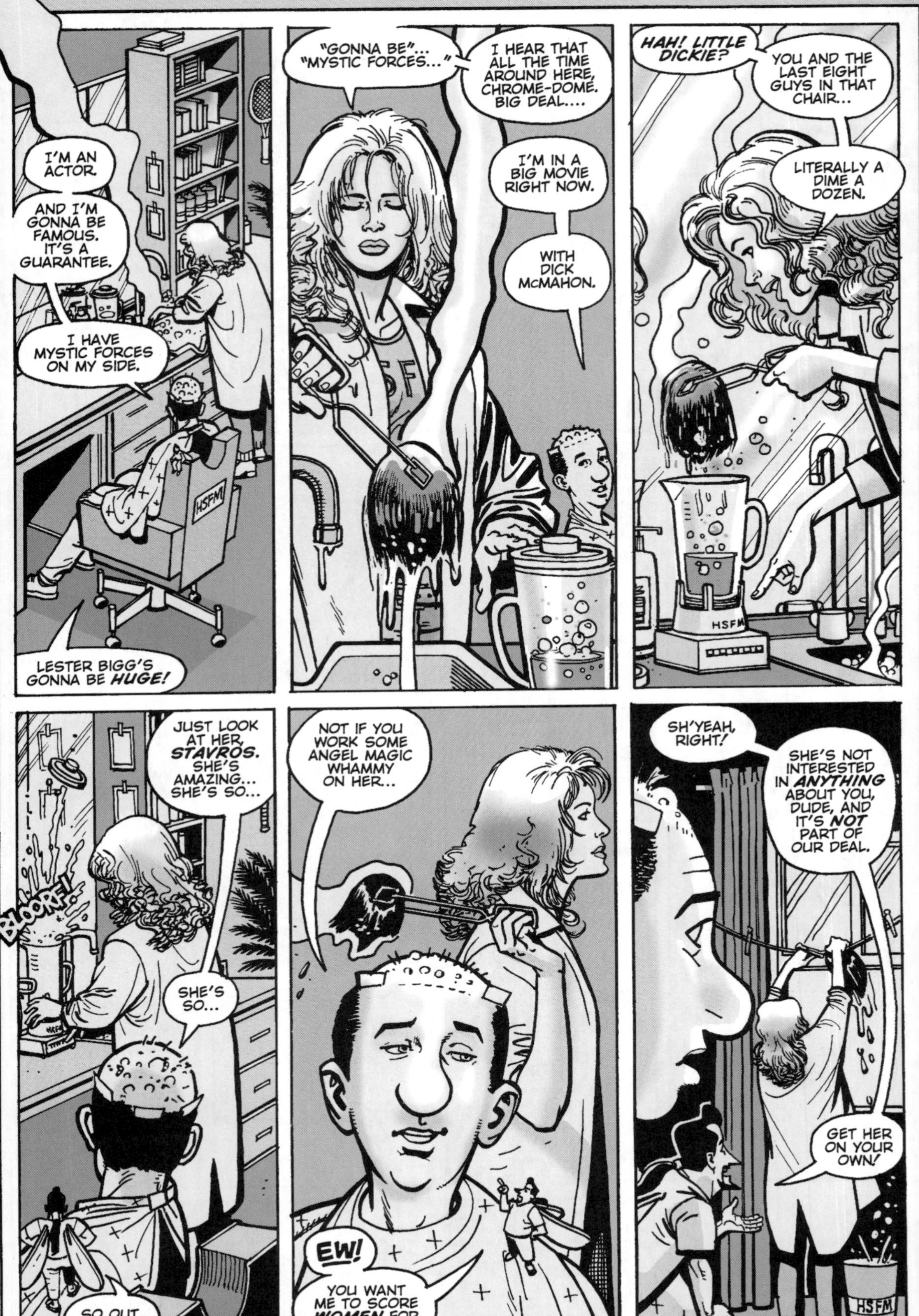

I'M AN ACTOR.
AND I'M GONNA BE FAMOUS. IT'S A GUARANTEE.
I HAVE MYSTIC FORCES ON MY SIDE.
LESTER BIGG'S GONNA BE HUGE!
"GONNA BE"... "MYSTIC FORCES..."
I HEAR THAT ALL THE TIME AROUND HERE, CHROME-DOME. BIG DEAL....
I'M IN A BIG MOVIE RIGHT NOW.
WITH DICK McMAHON.
HAH! LITTLE DICKIE?
YOU AND THE LAST EIGHT GUYS IN THAT CHAIR...
LITERALLY A DIME A DOZEN.
HSFM
JUST LOOK AT HER, STAVROS. SHE'S AMAZING... SHE'S SO...
BLOORF!
SHE'S SO...
SO OUT OF YOUR LEAGUE.
NOT IF YOU WORK SOME ANGEL MAGIC WHAMMY ON HER...
EW!
YOU WANT ME TO SCORE WOMEN FOR YOU?!?
HSFM
SH'YEAH, RIGHT!
SHE'S NOT INTERESTED IN ANYTHING ABOUT YOU, DUDE, AND IT'S NOT PART OF OUR DEAL.
GET HER ON YOUR OWN!
HSFM

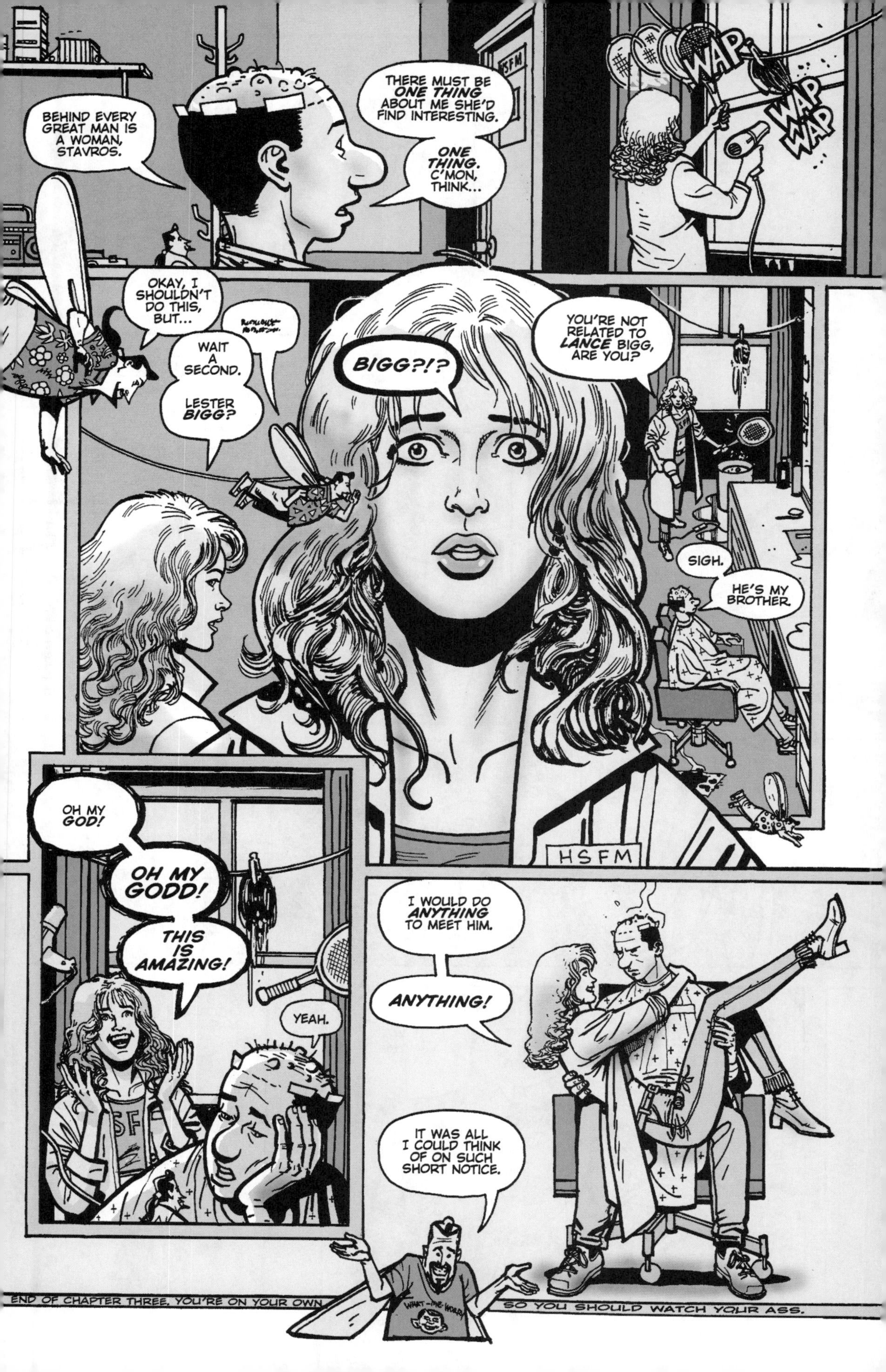

BEHIND EVERY GREAT MAN IS A WOMAN, STAVROS.
THERE MUST BE ONE THING ABOUT ME SHE'D FIND INTERESTING.
ONE THING. C'MON, THINK...
WAP
WAP
WAP
OKAY, I SHOULDN'T DO THIS, BUT...
WAIT A SECOND.
LESTER BIGG?
BIGG?!?
YOU'RE NOT RELATED TO LANCE BIGG, ARE YOU?
SIGH.
HE'S MY BROTHER.
HSFM
OH MY GOD!
OH MY GODD!
THIS IS AMAZING!
YEAH.
I WOULD DO ANYTHING TO MEET HIM.
ANYTHING!
IT WAS ALL I COULD THINK OF ON SUCH SHORT NOTICE.
END OF CHAPTER THREE. YOU'RE ON YOUR OWN
SO YOU SHOULD WATCH YOUR ASS.

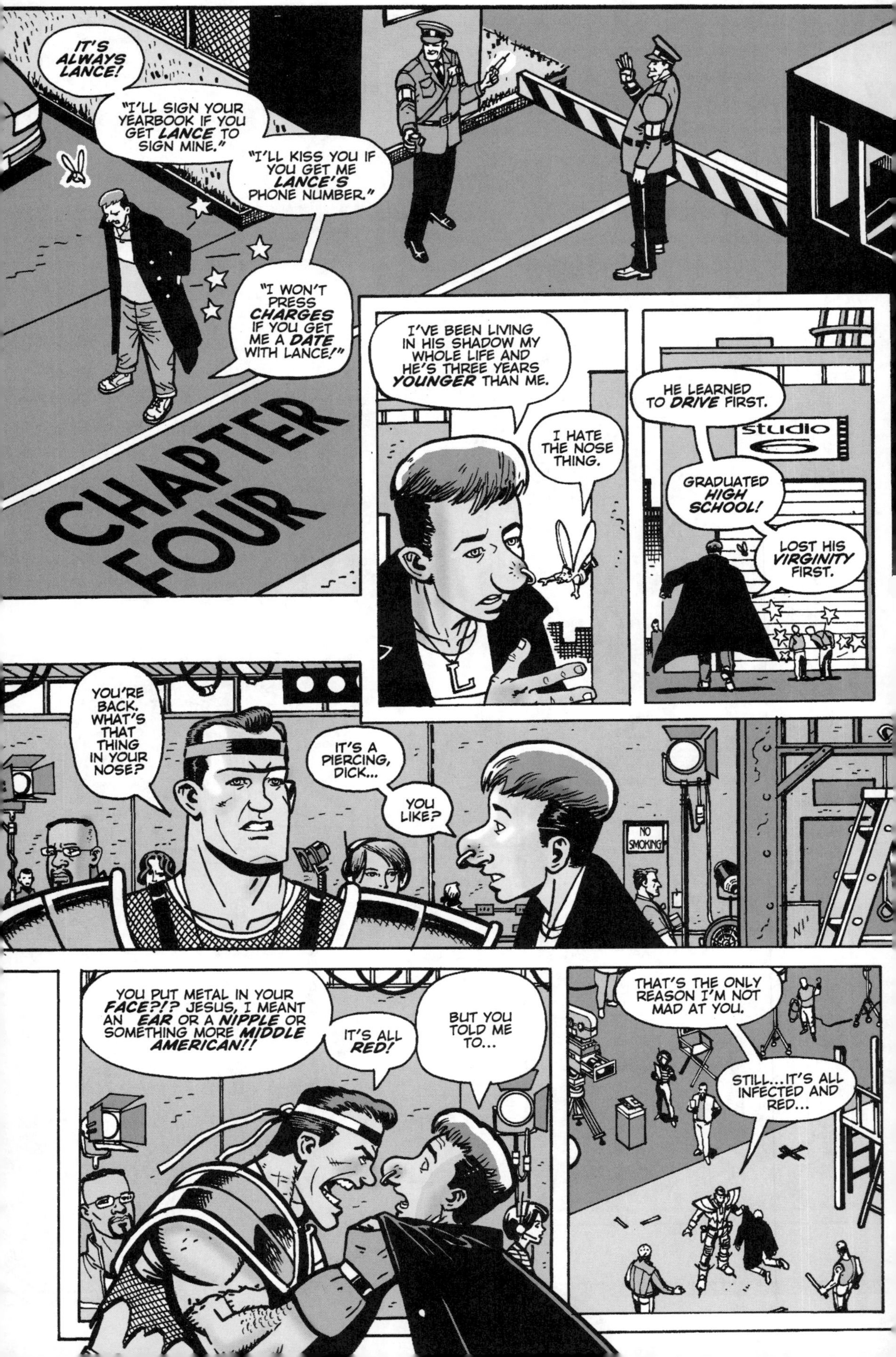

IT'S ALWAYS LANCE!
"I'LL SIGN YOUR YEARBOOK IF YOU GET LANCE TO SIGN MINE."
"I'LL KISS YOU IF YOU GET ME LANCE'S PHONE NUMBER."
"I WON'T PRESS CHARGES IF YOU GET ME A DATE WITH LANCE!"
CHAPTER FOUR
I'VE BEEN LIVING IN HIS SHADOW MY WHOLE LIFE AND HE'S THREE YEARS YOUNGER THAN ME.
I HATE THE NOSE THING.
HE LEARNED TO DRIVE FIRST.
studio 6
GRADUATED HIGH SCHOOL!
LOST HIS VIRGINITY FIRST.
YOU'RE BACK. WHAT'S THAT THING IN YOUR NOSE?
IT'S A PIERCING, DICK...
YOU LIKE?
NO SMOKING
YOU PUT METAL IN YOUR FACE?!? JESUS, I MEANT AN EAR OR A NIPPLE OR SOMETHING MORE MIDDLE AMERICAN!!
IT'S ALL RED!
BUT YOU TOLD ME TO...
THAT'S THE ONLY REASON I'M NOT MAD AT YOU.
STILL...IT'S ALL INFECTED AND RED...

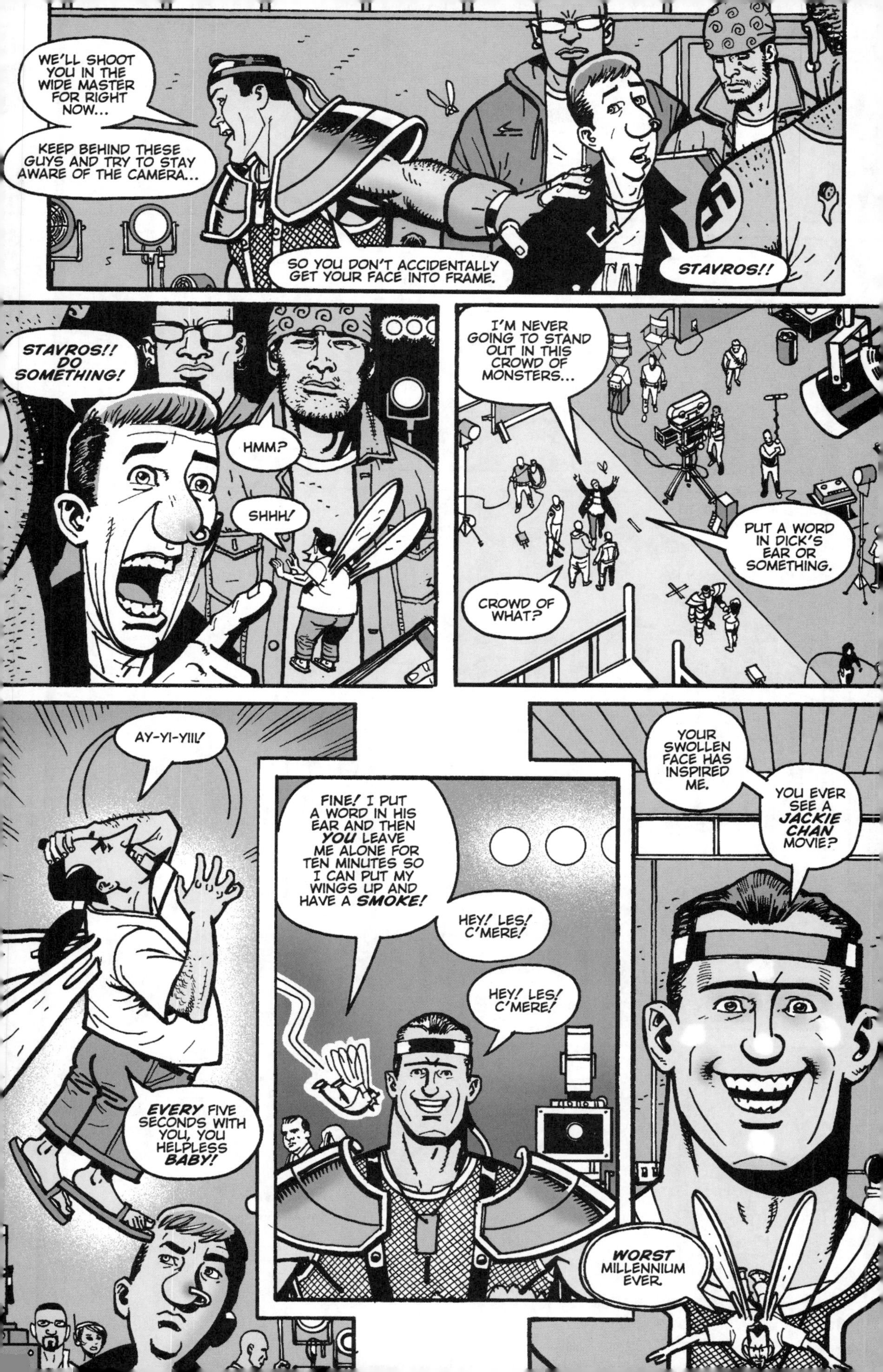
WE'LL SHOOT YOU IN THE WIDE MASTER FOR RIGHT NOW...
KEEP BEHIND THESE GUYS AND TRY TO STAY AWARE OF THE CAMERA...
SO YOU DON'T ACCIDENTALLY GET YOUR FACE INTO FRAME.
STAVROS!!
STAVROS!! DO SOMETHING!
HMM?
SHHH!
I'M NEVER GOING TO STAND OUT IN THIS CROWD OF MONSTERS...
PUT A WORD IN DICK'S EAR OR SOMETHING.
CROWD OF WHAT?
AY-YI-YIII!
EVERY FIVE SECONDS WITH YOU, YOU HELPLESS BABY!
FINE! I PUT A WORD IN HIS EAR AND THEN YOU LEAVE ME ALONE FOR TEN MINUTES SO I CAN PUT MY WINGS UP AND HAVE A SMOKE!
HEY! LES! C'MERE!
HEY! LES! C'MERE!
YOUR SWOLLEN FACE HAS INSPIRED ME.
YOU EVER SEE A JACKIE CHAN MOVIE?
WORST MILLENNIUM EVER.

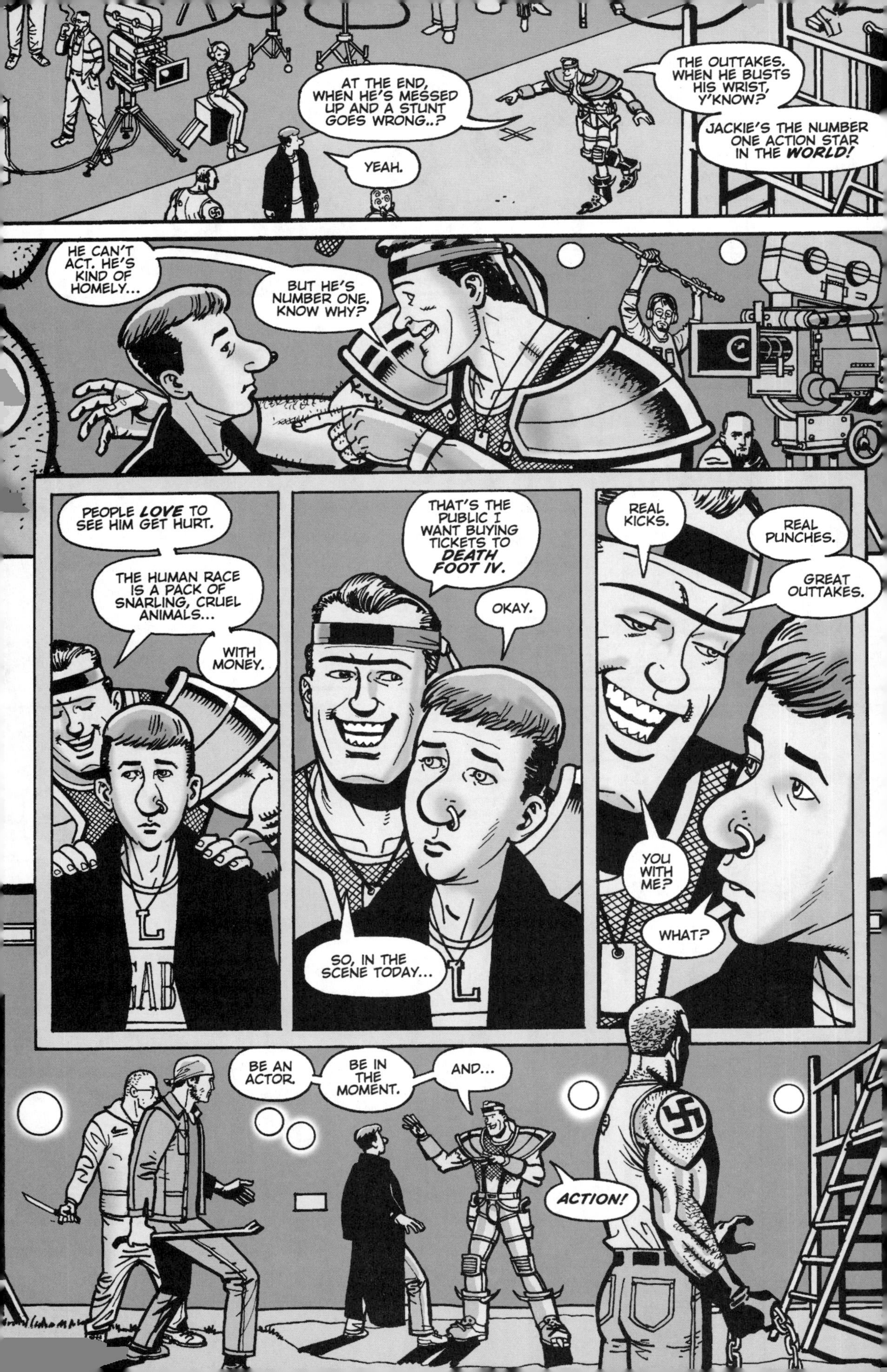
AT THE END, WHEN HE'S MESSED UP AND A STUNT GOES WRONG..?
YEAH.
THE OUTTAKES. WHEN HE BUSTS HIS WRIST, Y'KNOW?
JACKIE'S THE NUMBER ONE ACTION STAR IN THE *WORLD!*
HE CAN'T ACT. HE'S KIND OF HOMELY...
BUT HE'S NUMBER ONE. KNOW WHY?
PEOPLE *LOVE* TO SEE HIM GET HURT.
THE HUMAN RACE IS A PACK OF SNARLING, CRUEL ANIMALS...
WITH MONEY.
THAT'S THE PUBLIC I WANT BUYING TICKETS TO *DEATH FOOT IV*.
OKAY.
SO, IN THE SCENE TODAY...
REAL KICKS.
REAL PUNCHES.
GREAT OUTTAKES.
YOU WITH ME?
WHAT?
BE AN ACTOR.
BE IN THE MOMENT.
AND...
ACTION!

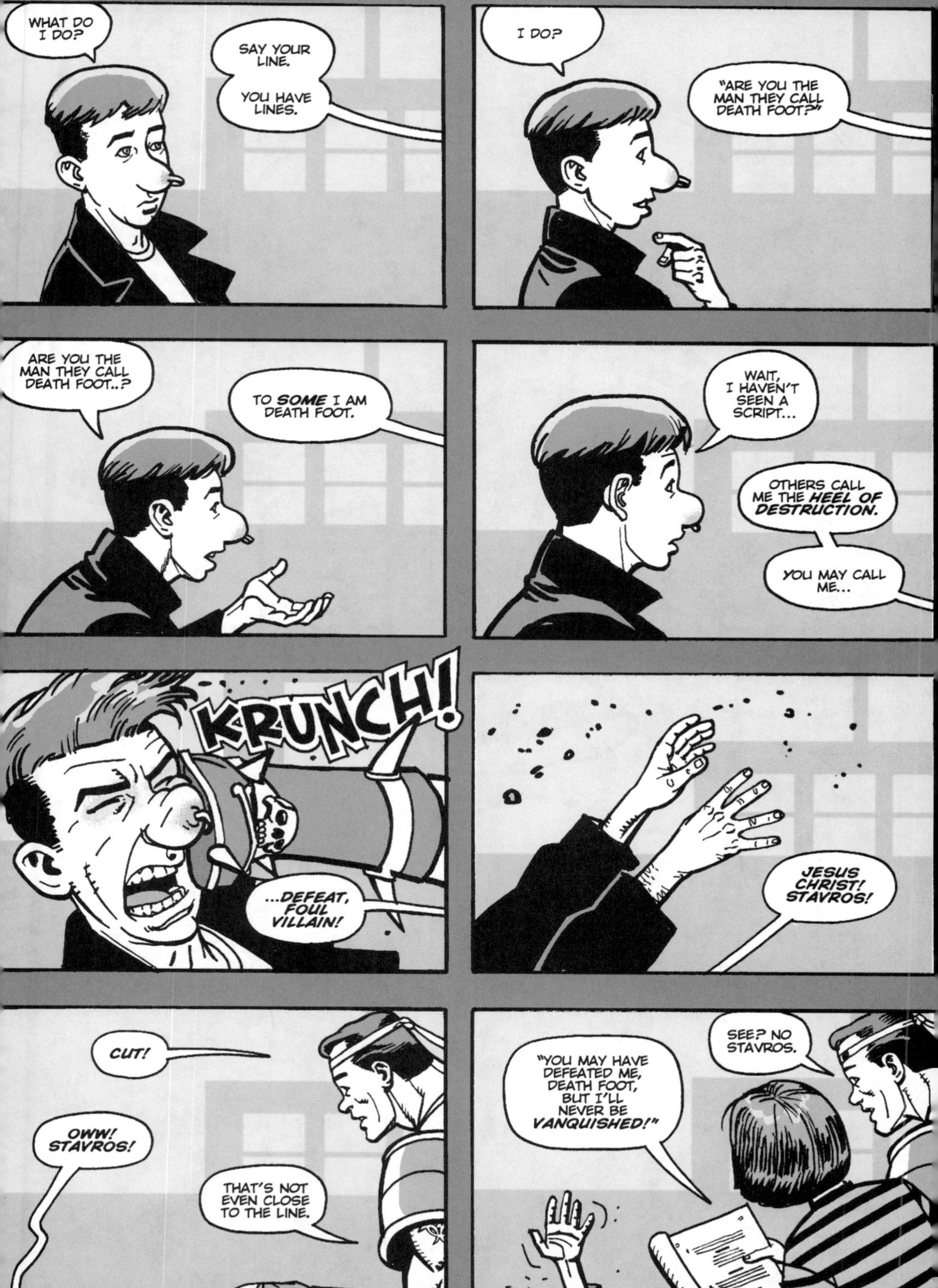
WHAT DO I DO?
SAY YOUR LINE.
YOU HAVE LINES.
I DO?
"ARE YOU THE MAN THEY CALL DEATH FOOT?"
ARE YOU THE MAN THEY CALL DEATH FOOT..?
TO **SOME** I AM DEATH FOOT.
WAIT, I HAVEN'T SEEN A SCRIPT...
OTHERS CALL ME THE ***HEEL OF DESTRUCTION.***
YOU MAY CALL ME...
KRUNCH!
...DEFEAT, FOUL VILLAIN!
JESUS CHRIST! STAVROS!
CUT!
OWW! STAVROS!
THAT'S NOT EVEN CLOSE TO THE LINE.
SEE? NO STAVROS.
"YOU MAY HAVE DEFEATED ME, DEATH FOOT, BUT I'LL NEVER BE ***VANQUISHED!"***

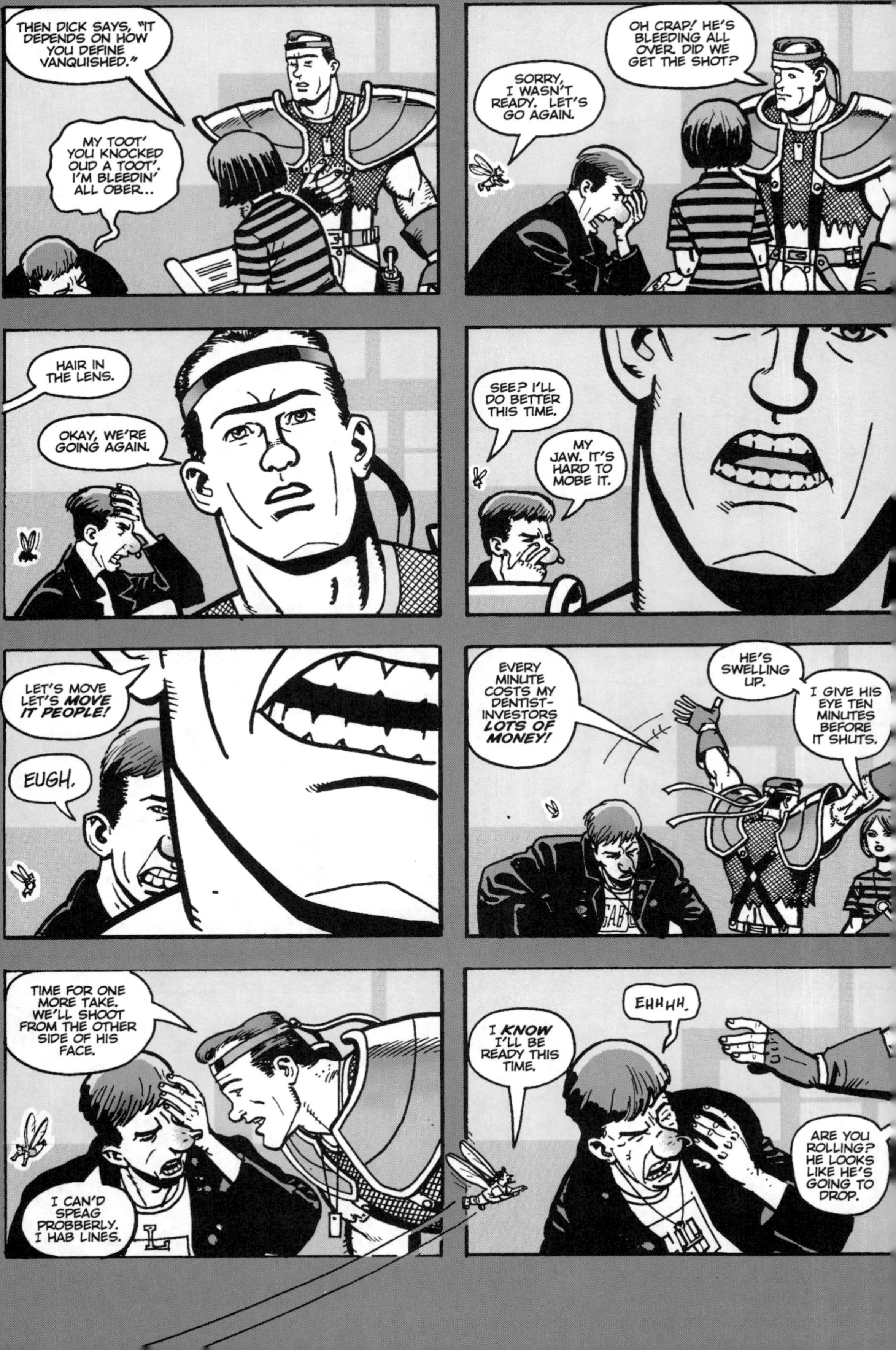
THEN DICK SAYS, "IT DEPENDS ON HOW YOU DEFINE VANQUISHED."
MY TOOT' YOU KNOCKED OUD A TOOT'. I'M BLEEDIN' ALL OBER...
OH CRAP! HE'S BLEEDING ALL OVER. DID WE GET THE SHOT?
SORRY, I WASN'T READY. LET'S GO AGAIN.
HAIR IN THE LENS.
OKAY, WE'RE GOING AGAIN.
SEE? I'LL DO BETTER THIS TIME.
MY JAW. IT'S HARD TO MOBE IT.
LET'S MOVE LET'S MOVE IT PEOPLE!
EUGH.
EVERY MINUTE COSTS MY DENTIST-INVESTORS LOTS OF MONEY!
HE'S SWELLING UP.
I GIVE HIS EYE TEN MINUTES BEFORE IT SHUTS.
TIME FOR ONE MORE TAKE. WE'LL SHOOT FROM THE OTHER SIDE OF HIS FACE.
I CAN'D SPEAG PROBBERLY. I HAB LINES.
EHHHH.
I KNOW I'LL BE READY THIS TIME.
ARE YOU ROLLING? HE LOOKS LIKE HE'S GOING TO DROP.

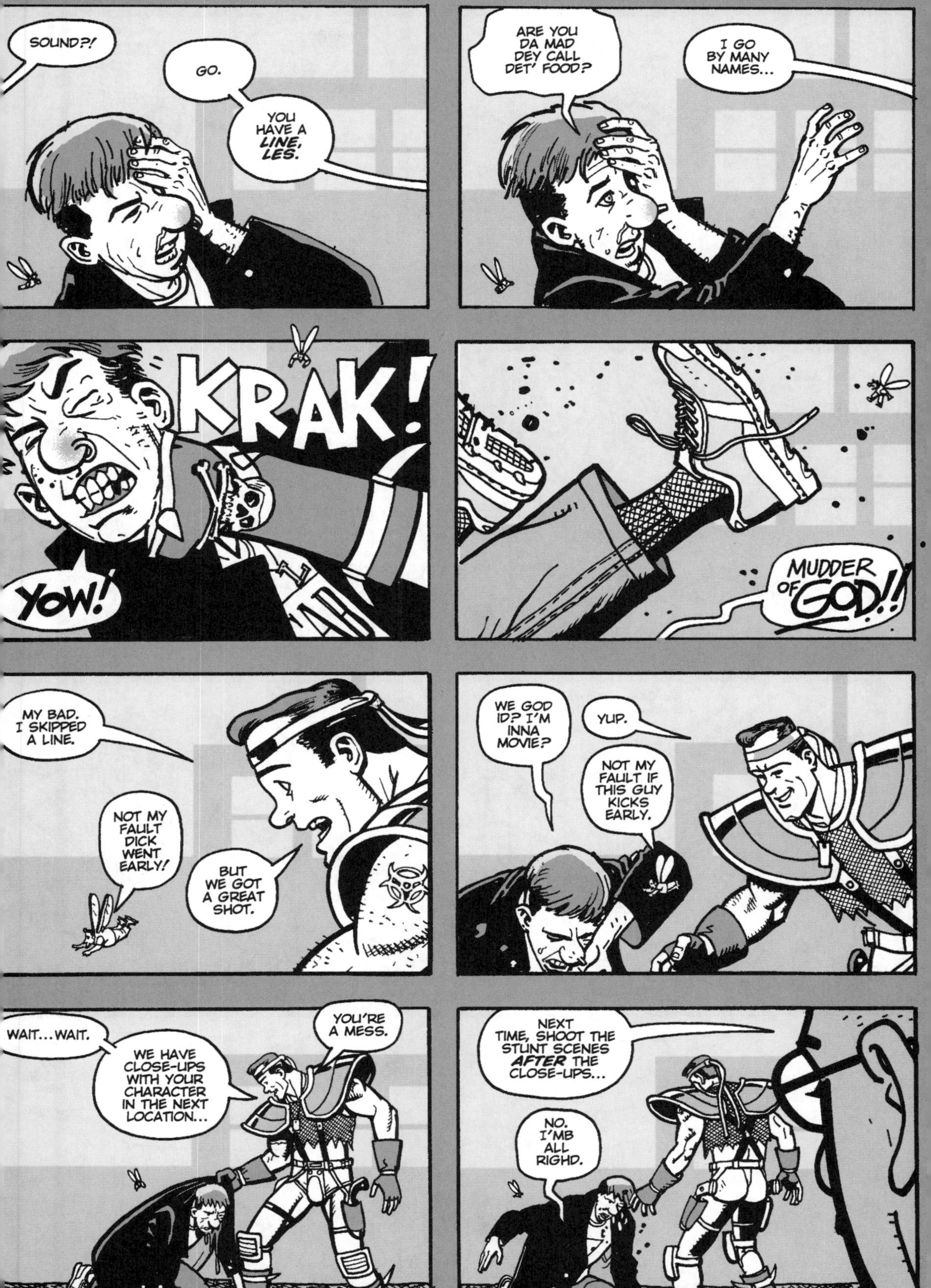
SOUND?!
GO.
YOU HAVE A LINE, LES.
ARE YOU DA MAD DEY CALL DET' FOOD?
I GO BY MANY NAMES...
KRAK!
YOW!
MUDDER OF GOD!!
MY BAD. I SKIPPED A LINE.
NOT MY FAULT DICK WENT EARLY!
BUT WE GOT A GREAT SHOT.
WE GOD ID? I'M INNA MOVIE?
YUP.
NOT MY FAULT IF THIS GUY KICKS EARLY.
WAIT...WAIT.
WE HAVE CLOSE-UPS WITH YOUR CHARACTER IN THE NEXT LOCATION...
YOU'RE A MESS.
NEXT TIME, SHOOT THE STUNT SCENES AFTER THE CLOSE-UPS...
NO. I'MB ALL RIGHD.

IT'S NOT GOING TO WORK, IS IT? IT'S A *LOVE* SCENE...

What?

AND DID YOU SEE THE LATINO HOTTIE PLAYING HIS GIRLFRIEND?

THE SORT OF WOMAN I'D LEAVE MY WIFE FOR, IF I WASN'T GAY.

MENTAL NOTE. DON'T HIT THE DAY PLAYERS UNTIL JUST BEFORE WE WRAP.

LIVE AND LEARN.

ehhhh..

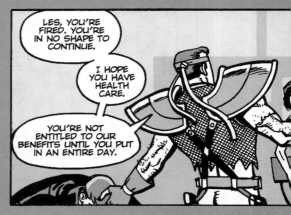

LES, YOU'RE FIRED. YOU'RE IN NO SHAPE TO CONTINUE.

I HOPE YOU HAVE HEALTH CARE.

YOU'RE NOT ENTITLED TO OUR BENEFITS UNTIL YOU PUT IN AN ENTIRE DAY.

WE CAN HIRE HIM AS A FOOD TASTER...

SLAM

THIS MAN NEEDS A HOSPITAL, YOU MONSTER.

OFF YOU GO. THE HOSPITAL IS THAT-AWAY, ABOUT A MILE.

YOU DID DIS. ISS ALL YER FAULD.

OH, CHIN UP, LESTER. YOU SHOWED ME SOME *STONES* IN THERE.

YOU TOOK A PUNCH WITH A SMILE. IT SHOWS A CERTAIN UNDERSTANDING OF THE GAME FOR ONCE.

YOU IMPRESSED ME.

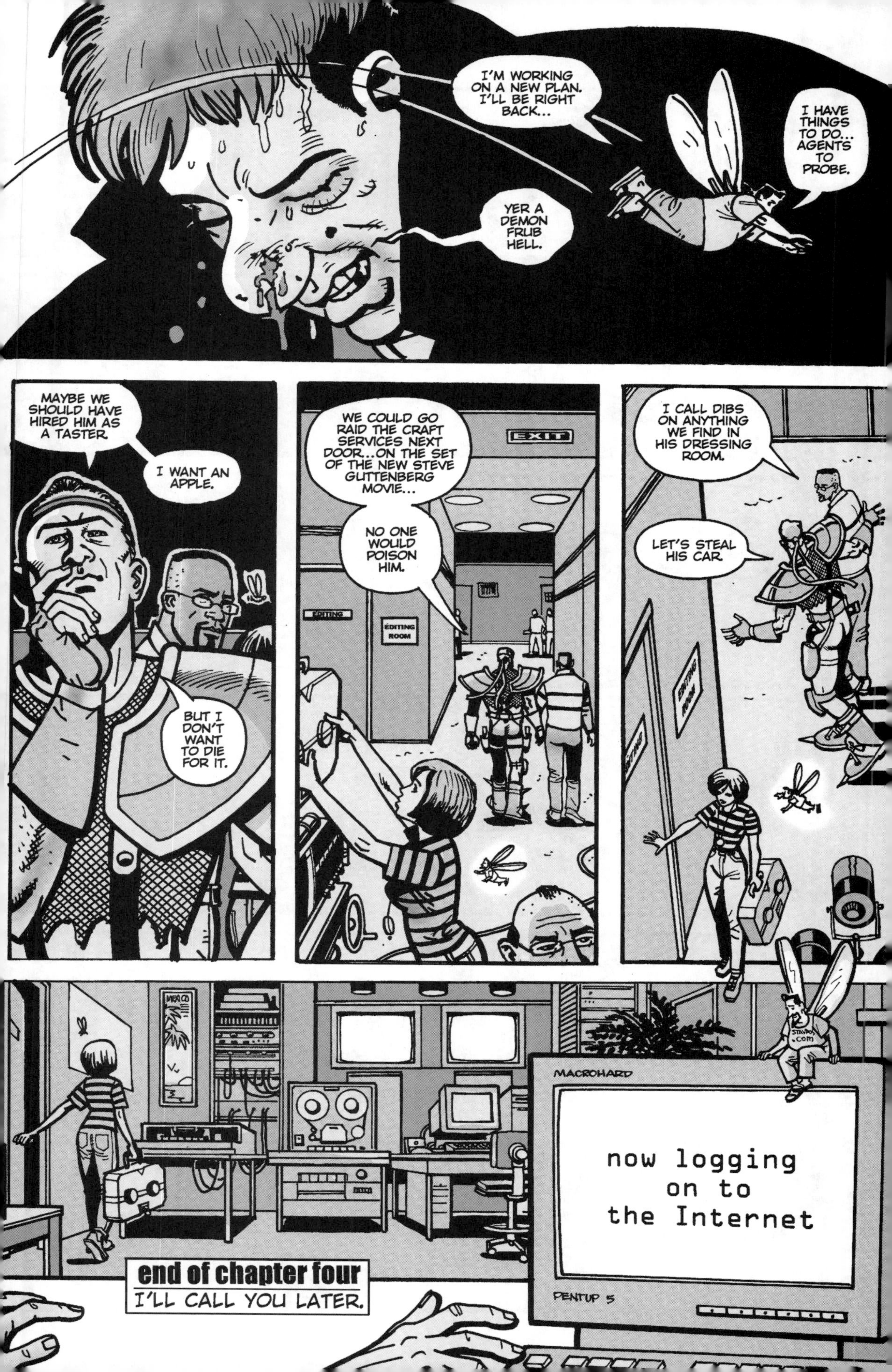
I'M WORKING ON A NEW PLAN. I'LL BE RIGHT BACK...
I HAVE THINGS TO DO... AGENTS TO PROBE.
YER A DEMON FRUB HELL.
MAYBE WE SHOULD HAVE HIRED HIM AS A TASTER.
I WANT AN APPLE.
BUT I DON'T WANT TO DIE FOR IT.
WE COULD GO RAID THE CRAFT SERVICES NEXT DOOR...ON THE SET OF THE NEW STEVE GUTTENBERG MOVIE...
NO ONE WOULD POISON HIM.
EXIT
EDITING
EDITING ROOM
I CALL DIBS ON ANYTHING WE FIND IN HIS DRESSING ROOM.
LET'S STEAL HIS CAR.
EDITING ROOM
MACROHARD
now logging on to the Internet
PENTUP 5
end of chapter four
I'LL CALL YOU LATER.

CHAPTER FIVE

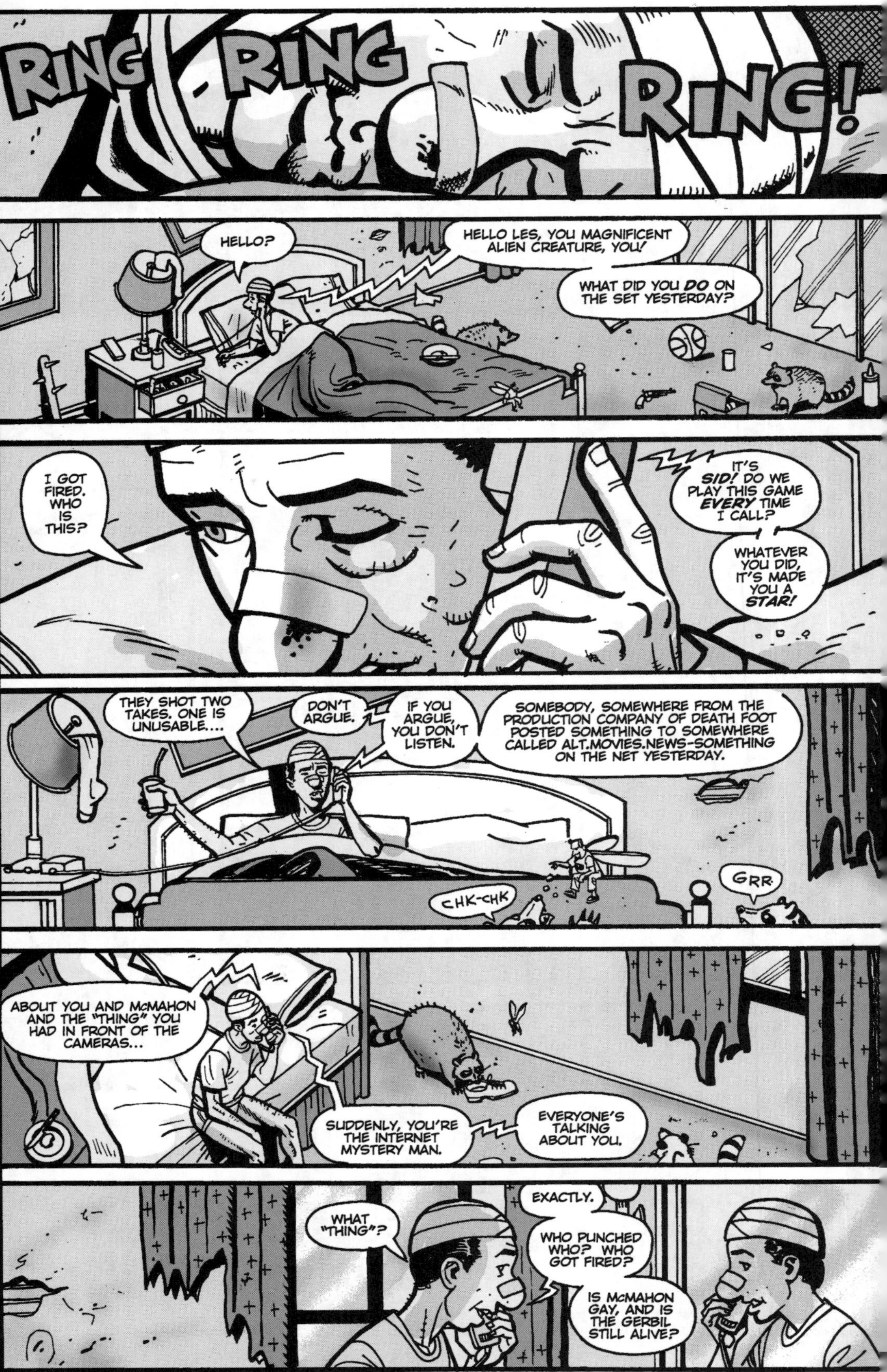
RING RING RING!
HELLO?
HELLO LES, YOU MAGNIFICENT ALIEN CREATURE, YOU!
WHAT DID YOU *DO* ON THE SET YESTERDAY?
I GOT FIRED. WHO IS THIS?
IT'S *SID!* DO WE PLAY THIS GAME *EVERY* TIME I CALL?
WHATEVER YOU DID, IT'S MADE YOU A *STAR!*
THEY SHOT TWO TAKES. ONE IS UNUSABLE....
DON'T ARGUE.
IF YOU ARGUE, YOU DON'T LISTEN.
SOMEBODY, SOMEWHERE FROM THE PRODUCTION COMPANY OF DEATH FOOT POSTED SOMETHING TO SOMEWHERE CALLED ALT.MOVIES.NEWS-SOMETHING ON THE NET YESTERDAY.
CHK-CHK
GRR
ABOUT YOU AND McMAHON AND THE "THING" YOU HAD IN FRONT OF THE CAMERAS...
SUDDENLY, YOU'RE THE INTERNET MYSTERY MAN.
EVERYONE'S TALKING ABOUT YOU.
WHAT "THING"?
EXACTLY.
WHO PUNCHED WHO? WHO GOT FIRED?
IS McMAHON GAY, AND IS THE GERBIL STILL ALIVE?

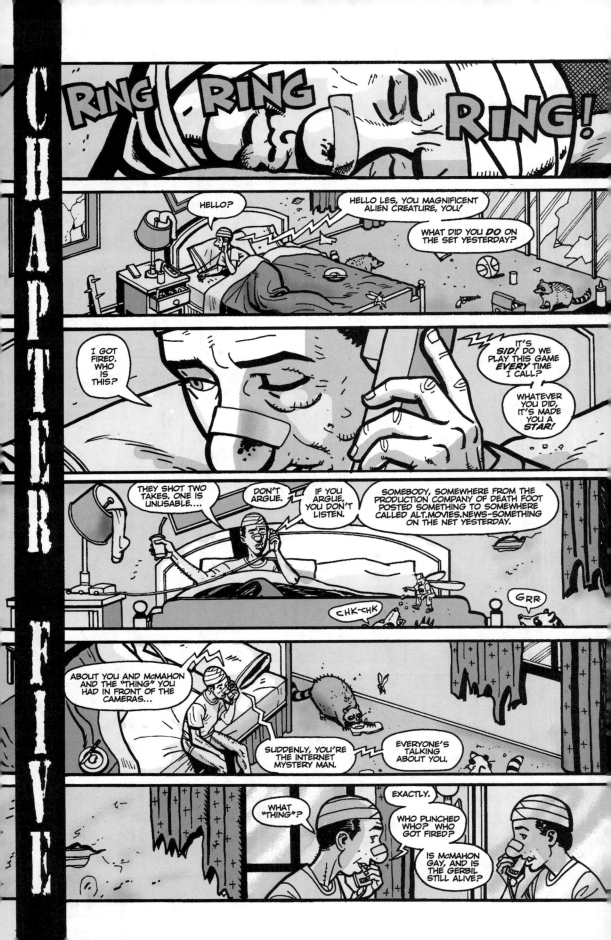

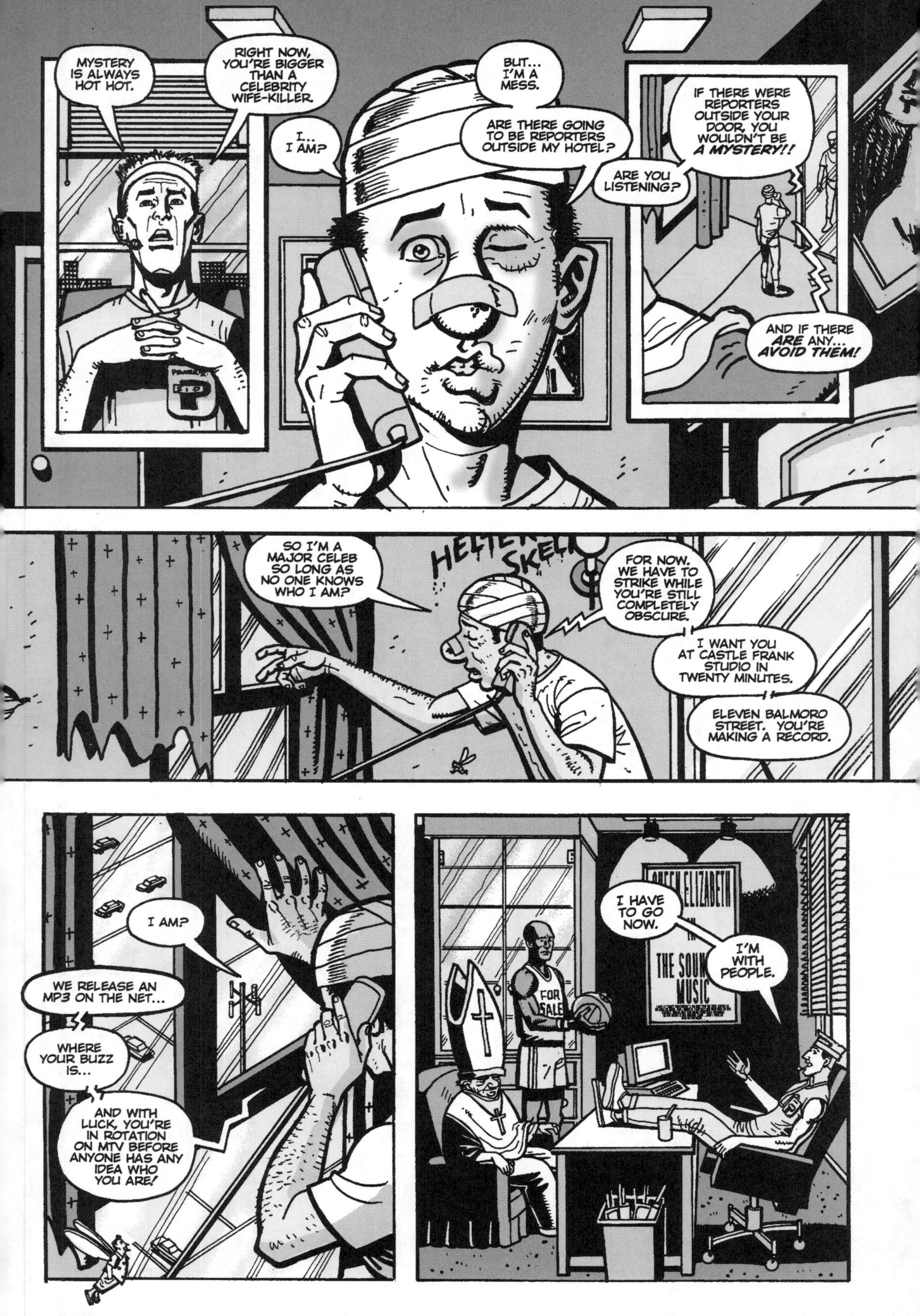
MYSTERY IS ALWAYS HOT HOT.
RIGHT NOW, YOU'RE BIGGER THAN A CELEBRITY WIFE-KILLER.
I... I AM?
BUT... I'M A MESS.
ARE THERE GOING TO BE REPORTERS OUTSIDE MY HOTEL?
ARE YOU LISTENING?
IF THERE WERE REPORTERS OUTSIDE YOUR DOOR, YOU WOULDN'T BE A MYSTERY!!
AND IF THERE ARE ANY... AVOID THEM!
SO I'M A MAJOR CELEB SO LONG AS NO ONE KNOWS WHO I AM?
FOR NOW. WE HAVE TO STRIKE WHILE YOU'RE STILL COMPLETELY OBSCURE.
I WANT YOU AT CASTLE FRANK STUDIO IN TWENTY MINUTES.
ELEVEN BALMORO STREET. YOU'RE MAKING A RECORD.
I AM?
WE RELEASE AN MP3 ON THE NET...
WHERE YOUR BUZZ IS...
AND WITH LUCK, YOU'RE IN ROTATION ON MTV BEFORE ANYONE HAS ANY IDEA WHO YOU ARE!
I HAVE TO GO NOW.
I'M WITH PEOPLE.

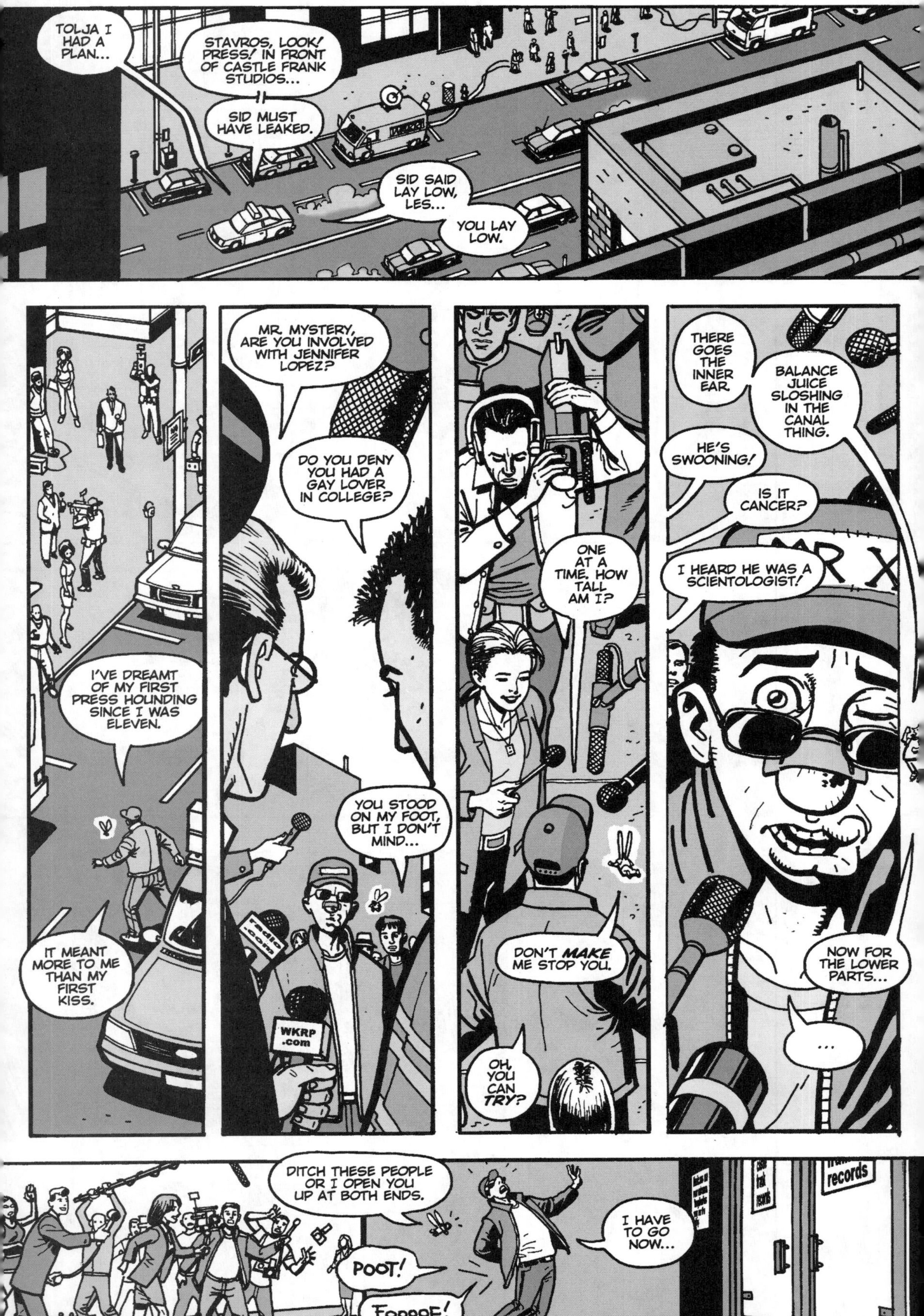
TOLJA I HAD A PLAN...
STAVROS, LOOK! PRESS! IN FRONT OF CASTLE FRANK STUDIOS...
SID MUST HAVE LEAKED.
SID SAID LAY LOW, LES...
YOU LAY LOW.
I'VE DREAMT OF MY FIRST PRESS HOUNDING SINCE I WAS ELEVEN.
IT MEANT MORE TO ME THAN MY FIRST KISS.
MR. MYSTERY, ARE YOU INVOLVED WITH JENNIFER LOPEZ?
DO YOU DENY YOU HAD A GAY LOVER IN COLLEGE?
YOU STOOD ON MY FOOT, BUT I DON'T MIND...
WKRP .com
ONE AT A TIME. HOW TALL AM I?
DON'T MAKE ME STOP YOU.
OH, YOU CAN TRY?
THERE GOES THE INNER EAR.
BALANCE JUICE SLOSHING IN THE CANAL THING.
HE'S SWOONING!
IS IT CANCER?
I HEARD HE WAS A SCIENTOLOGIST!
NOW FOR THE LOWER PARTS...
...
DITCH THESE PEOPLE OR I OPEN YOU UP AT BOTH ENDS.
POOT!
FOOOOF!
I HAVE TO GO NOW...
records

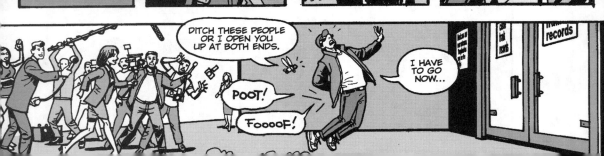

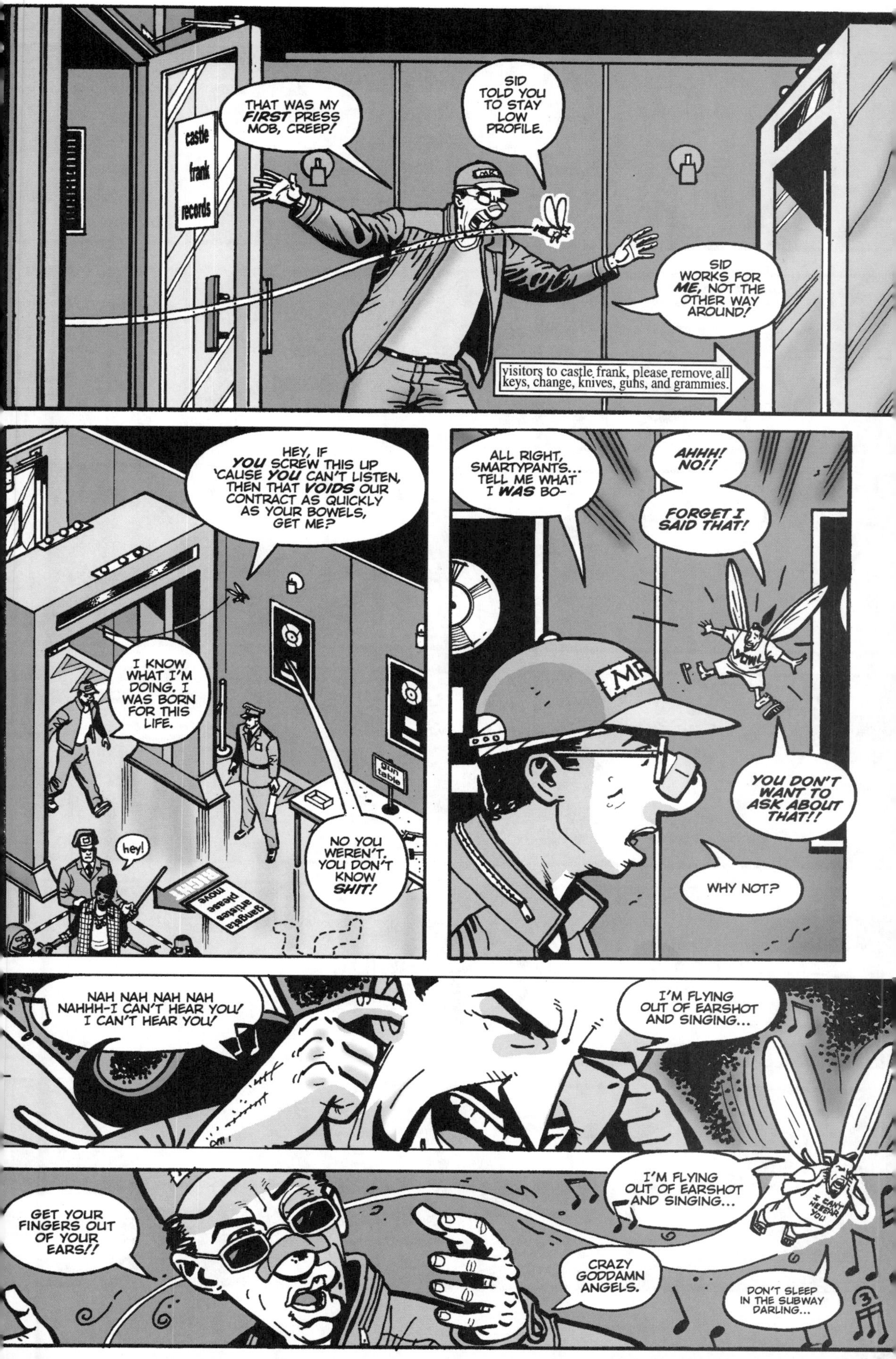
castle frank records
THAT WAS MY *FIRST* PRESS MOB, CREEP!
SID TOLD YOU TO STAY LOW PROFILE.
SID WORKS FOR *ME*, NOT THE OTHER WAY AROUND!
visitors to castle frank, please remove all keys, change, knives, guns, and grammies.
HEY, IF *YOU* SCREW THIS UP 'CAUSE *YOU* CAN'T LISTEN, THEN THAT *VOIDS* OUR CONTRACT AS QUICKLY AS YOUR BOWELS, GET ME?
I KNOW WHAT I'M DOING. I WAS BORN FOR THIS LIFE.
gun table
hey!
gangsta artistes please move RIGHT
NO YOU WEREN'T. YOU DON'T KNOW *SHIT!*
ALL RIGHT, SMARTYPANTS... TELL ME WHAT I *WAS* BO-
AHHH! NO!!
FORGET I SAID THAT!
YOWL
YOU DON'T WANT TO ASK ABOUT THAT!!
WHY NOT?
NAH NAH NAH NAH NAHHH-I CAN'T HEAR YOU! I CAN'T HEAR YOU!
I'M FLYING OUT OF EARSHOT AND SINGING...
GET YOUR FINGERS OUT OF YOUR EARS!!
I'M FLYING OUT OF EARSHOT AND SINGING...
I CAN'T HEEEAR YOU
CRAZY GODDAMN ANGELS.
DON'T SLEEP IN THE SUBWAY DARLING...

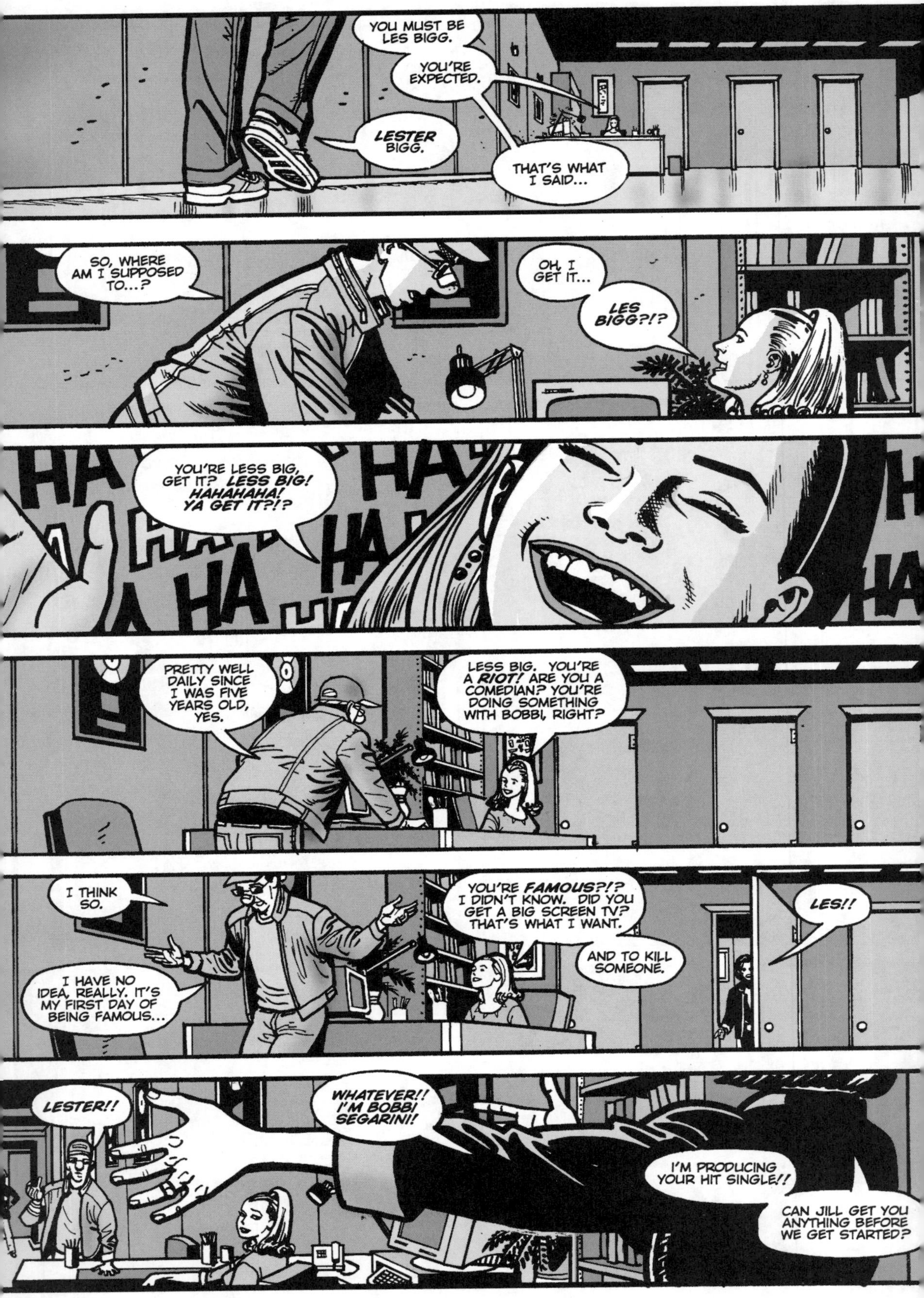
YOU MUST BE LES BIGG.
YOU'RE EXPECTED.
LESTER BIGG.
THAT'S WHAT I SAID...
SO, WHERE AM I SUPPOSED TO...?
OH, I GET IT...
LES BIGG?!?
YOU'RE LESS BIG, GET IT? LESS BIG! HAHAHAHA! YA GET IT?!?
HA HA HA HA HA HA HA
PRETTY WELL DAILY SINCE I WAS FIVE YEARS OLD, YES.
LESS BIG. YOU'RE A RIOT! ARE YOU A COMEDIAN? YOU'RE DOING SOMETHING WITH BOBBI, RIGHT?
I THINK SO.
I HAVE NO IDEA, REALLY. IT'S MY FIRST DAY OF BEING FAMOUS...
YOU'RE FAMOUS?!? I DIDN'T KNOW. DID YOU GET A BIG SCREEN TV? THAT'S WHAT I WANT.
AND TO KILL SOMEONE.
LES!!
LESTER!!
WHATEVER!! I'M BOBBI SEGARINI!
I'M PRODUCING YOUR HIT SINGLE!!
CAN JILL GET YOU ANYTHING BEFORE WE GET STARTED?

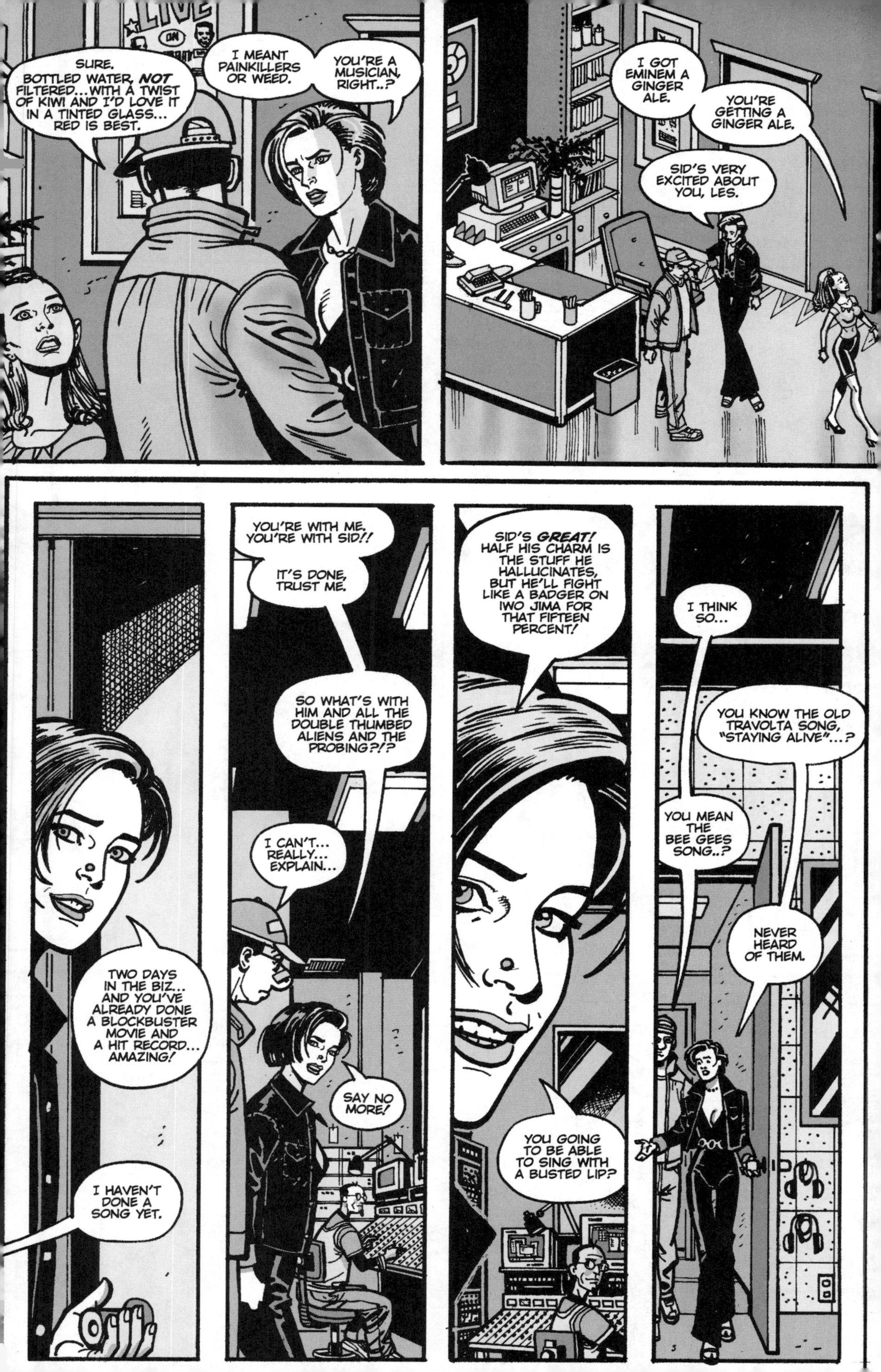
SURE. BOTTLED WATER, ***NOT*** FILTERED...WITH A TWIST OF KIWI AND I'D LOVE IT IN A TINTED GLASS... RED IS BEST.
I MEANT PAINKILLERS OR WEED.
YOU'RE A MUSICIAN, RIGHT..?
I GOT EMINEM A GINGER ALE.
YOU'RE GETTING A GINGER ALE.
SID'S VERY EXCITED ABOUT YOU, LES.
TWO DAYS IN THE BIZ... AND YOU'VE ALREADY DONE A BLOCKBUSTER MOVIE AND A HIT RECORD... AMAZING!
I HAVEN'T DONE A SONG YET.
YOU'RE WITH ME. YOU'RE WITH SID!!
IT'S DONE, TRUST ME.
SO WHAT'S WITH HIM AND ALL THE DOUBLE THUMBED ALIENS AND THE PROBING?!?
I CAN'T... REALLY... EXPLAIN...
SAY NO MORE!
SID'S ***GREAT!*** HALF HIS CHARM IS THE STUFF HE HALLUCINATES, BUT HE'LL FIGHT LIKE A BADGER ON IWO JIMA FOR THAT FIFTEEN PERCENT!
YOU GOING TO BE ABLE TO SING WITH A BUSTED LIP?
I THINK SO...
YOU KNOW THE OLD TRAVOLTA SONG, "STAYING ALIVE"...?
YOU MEAN THE BEE GEES SONG..?
NEVER HEARD OF THEM.

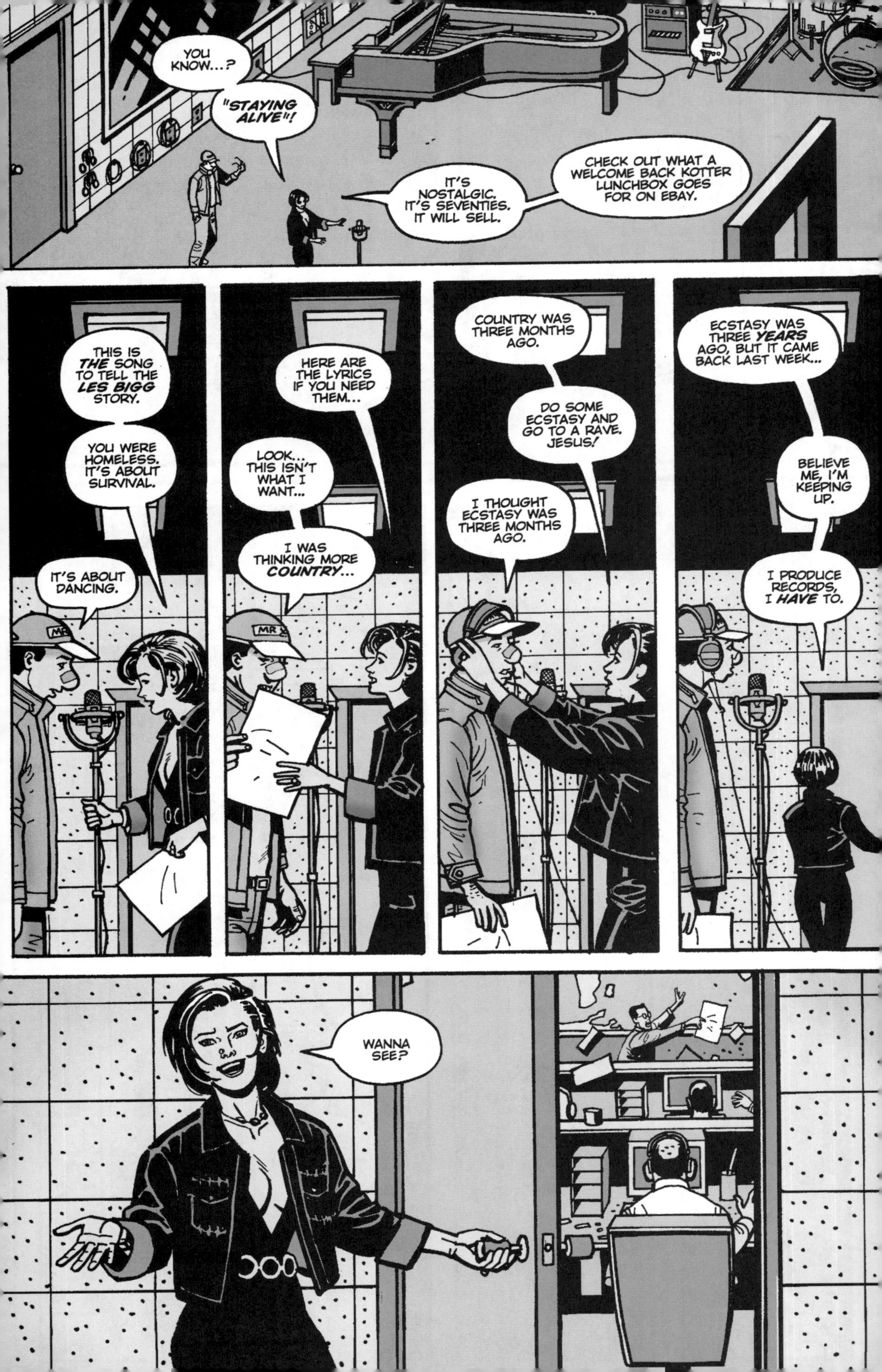
YOU KNOW...?
"STAYING ALIVE"!
IT'S NOSTALGIC. IT'S SEVENTIES. IT WILL SELL.
CHECK OUT WHAT A WELCOME BACK KOTTER LUNCHBOX GOES FOR ON EBAY.
THIS IS THE SONG TO TELL THE LES BIGG STORY.
YOU WERE HOMELESS. IT'S ABOUT SURVIVAL.
IT'S ABOUT DANCING.
HERE ARE THE LYRICS IF YOU NEED THEM...
LOOK... THIS ISN'T WHAT I WANT...
I WAS THINKING MORE COUNTRY...
COUNTRY WAS THREE MONTHS AGO.
DO SOME ECSTASY AND GO TO A RAVE. JESUS!
I THOUGHT ECSTASY WAS THREE MONTHS AGO.
ECSTASY WAS THREE YEARS AGO, BUT IT CAME BACK LAST WEEK...
BELIEVE ME, I'M KEEPING UP.
I PRODUCE RECORDS, I HAVE TO.
WANNA SEE?

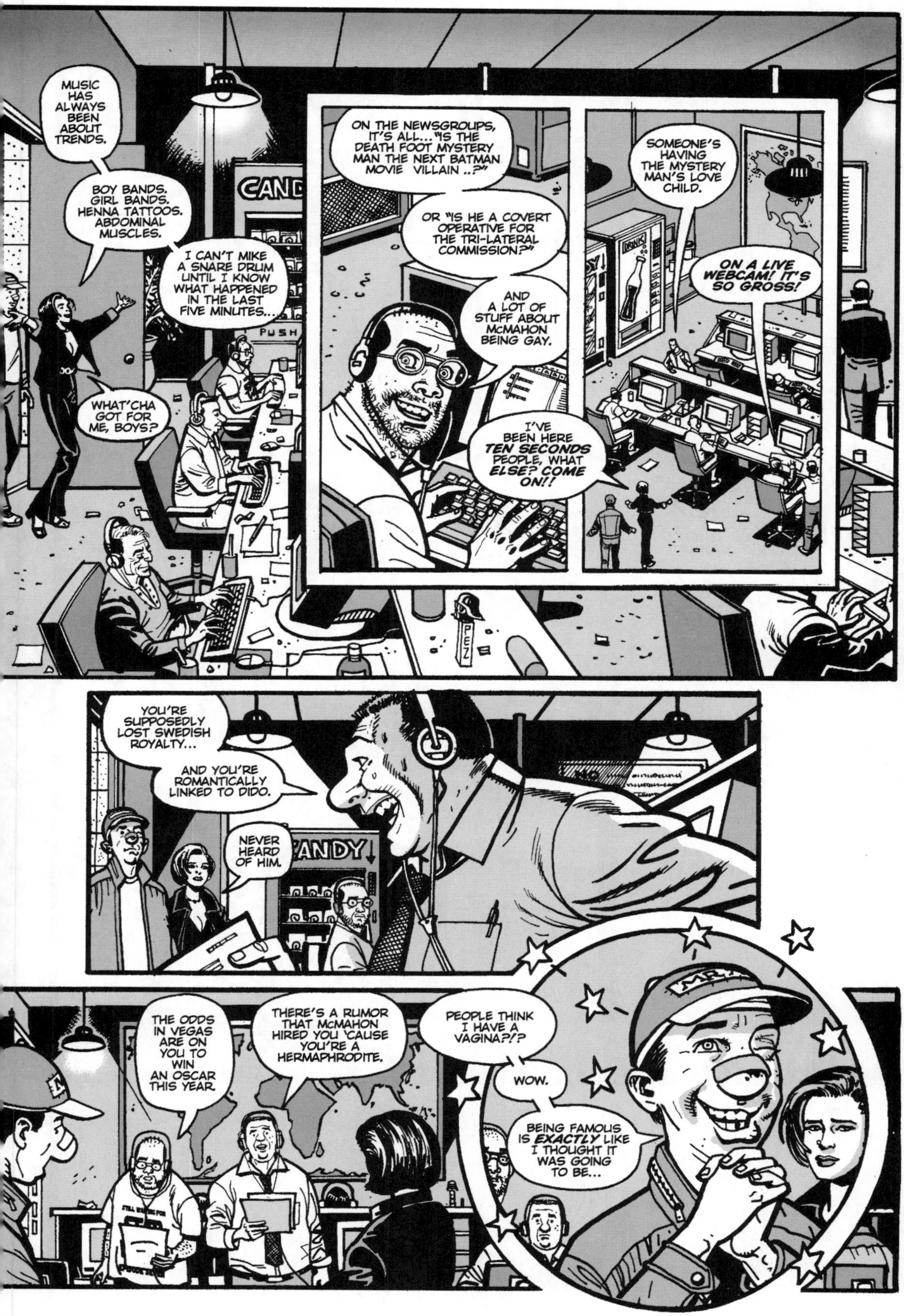
MUSIC HAS ALWAYS BEEN ABOUT TRENDS.
BOY BANDS. GIRL BANDS. HENNA TATTOOS. ABDOMINAL MUSCLES.
I CAN'T MIKE A SNARE DRUM UNTIL I KNOW WHAT HAPPENED IN THE LAST FIVE MINUTES...
WHAT'CHA GOT FOR ME, BOYS?
CANDY
PUSH
ON THE NEWSGROUPS, IT'S ALL... "IS THE DEATH FOOT MYSTERY MAN THE NEXT BATMAN MOVIE VILLAIN ..?"
OR "IS HE A COVERT OPERATIVE FOR THE TRI-LATERAL COMMISSION?"
AND A LOT OF STUFF ABOUT McMAHON BEING GAY.
SOMEONE'S HAVING THE MYSTERY MAN'S LOVE CHILD.
ON A LIVE WEBCAM! IT'S SO GROSS!
DRINK
I'VE BEEN HERE TEN SECONDS PEOPLE, WHAT ELSE? COME ON!!
PEZ
YOU'RE SUPPOSEDLY LOST SWEDISH ROYALTY...
AND YOU'RE ROMANTICALLY LINKED TO DIDO.
NEVER HEARD OF HIM.
CANDY
THE ODDS IN VEGAS ARE ON YOU TO WIN AN OSCAR THIS YEAR.
THERE'S A RUMOR THAT McMAHON HIRED YOU 'CAUSE YOU'RE A HERMAPHRODITE.
PEOPLE THINK I HAVE A VAGINA?!?
WOW.
BEING FAMOUS IS EXACTLY LIKE I THOUGHT IT WAS GOING TO BE...

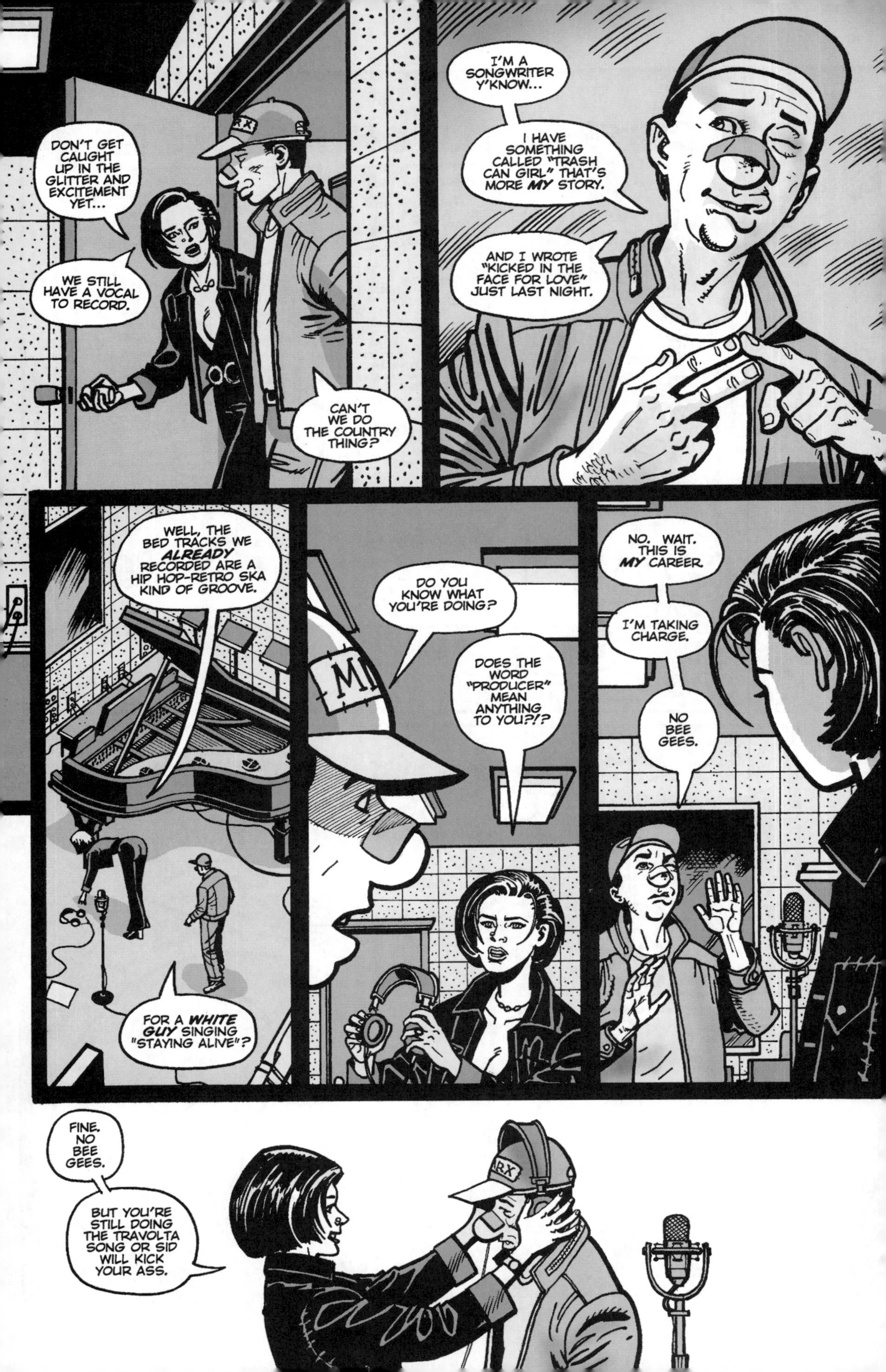
DON'T GET CAUGHT UP IN THE GLITTER AND EXCITEMENT YET...
WE STILL HAVE A VOCAL TO RECORD.
CAN'T WE DO THE COUNTRY THING?
I'M A SONGWRITER Y'KNOW...
I HAVE SOMETHING CALLED "TRASH CAN GIRL" THAT'S MORE *MY* STORY.
AND I WROTE "KICKED IN THE FACE FOR LOVE" JUST LAST NIGHT.
WELL, THE BED TRACKS WE *ALREADY* RECORDED ARE A HIP HOP-RETRO SKA KIND OF GROOVE.
FOR A *WHITE GUY* SINGING "STAYING ALIVE"?
DO YOU KNOW WHAT YOU'RE DOING?
DOES THE WORD "PRODUCER" MEAN ANYTHING TO YOU?!?
NO. WAIT. THIS IS *MY* CAREER.
I'M TAKING CHARGE.
NO BEE GEES.
FINE. NO BEE GEES.
BUT YOU'RE STILL DOING THE TRAVOLTA SONG OR SID WILL KICK YOUR ASS.

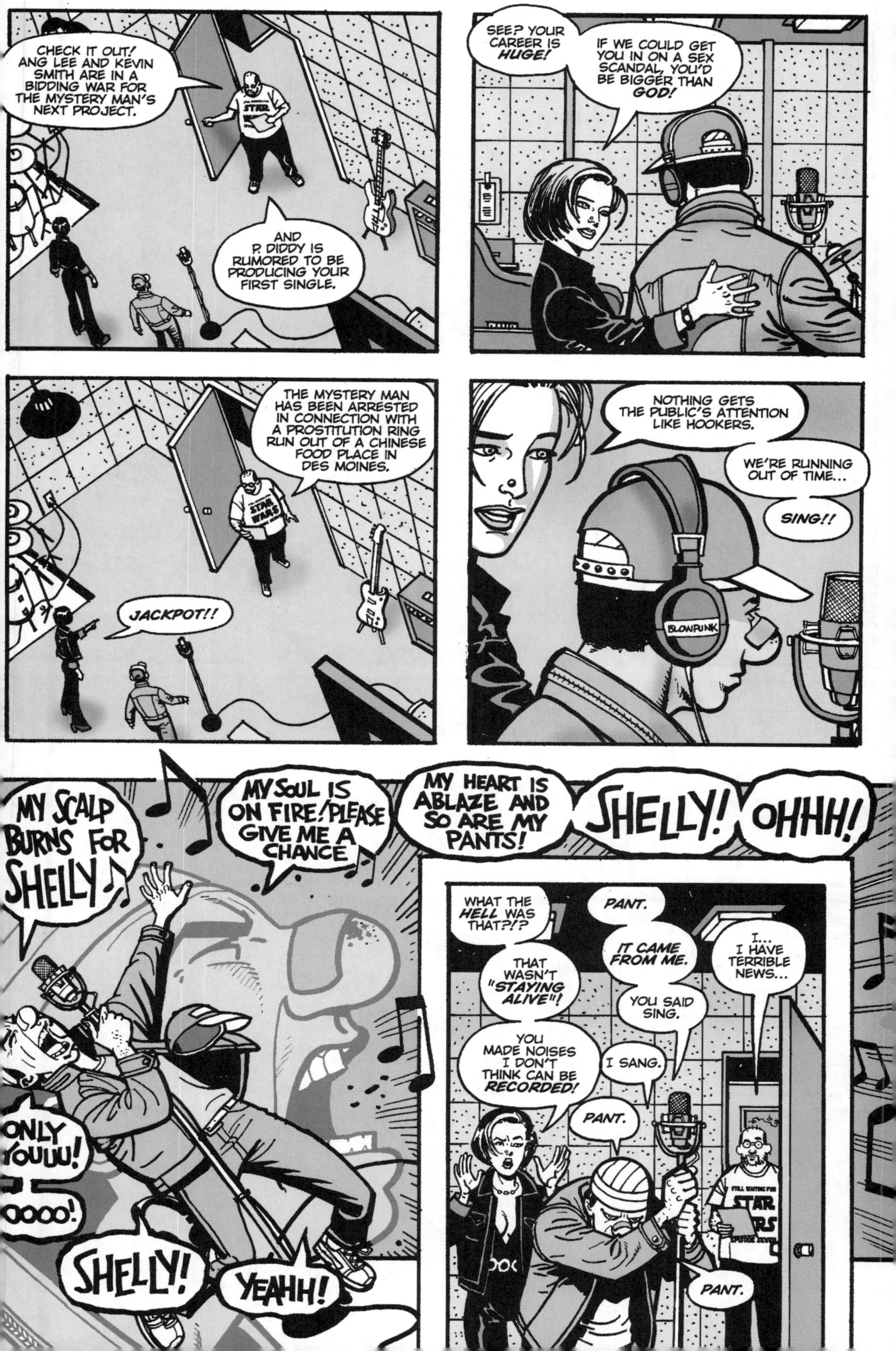
CHECK IT OUT! ANG LEE AND KEVIN SMITH ARE IN A BIDDING WAR FOR THE MYSTERY MAN'S NEXT PROJECT.
AND P. DIDDY IS RUMORED TO BE PRODUCING YOUR FIRST SINGLE.
SEE? YOUR CAREER IS *HUGE!*
IF WE COULD GET YOU IN ON A SEX SCANDAL, YOU'D BE BIGGER THAN *GOD!*
THE MYSTERY MAN HAS BEEN ARRESTED IN CONNECTION WITH A PROSTITUTION RING RUN OUT OF A CHINESE FOOD PLACE IN DES MOINES.
JACKPOT!!
NOTHING GETS THE PUBLIC'S ATTENTION LIKE HOOKERS.
WE'RE RUNNING OUT OF TIME...
SING!!
BLOWPUNK
MY SCALP BURNS FOR SHELLY
MY SOUL IS ON FIRE! PLEASE GIVE ME A CHANCE
MY HEART IS ABLAZE AND SO ARE MY PANTS!
SHELLY!
OHHH!
ONLY YOUUU!
OOOO!
SHELLY!
YEAHH!
WHAT THE *HELL* WAS THAT?!?
PANT.
IT CAME FROM ME.
I... I HAVE TERRIBLE NEWS...
THAT WASN'T *"STAYING ALIVE"*!
YOU SAID SING.
YOU MADE NOISES I DON'T THINK CAN BE *RECORDED!*
I SANG.
PANT.
PANT.

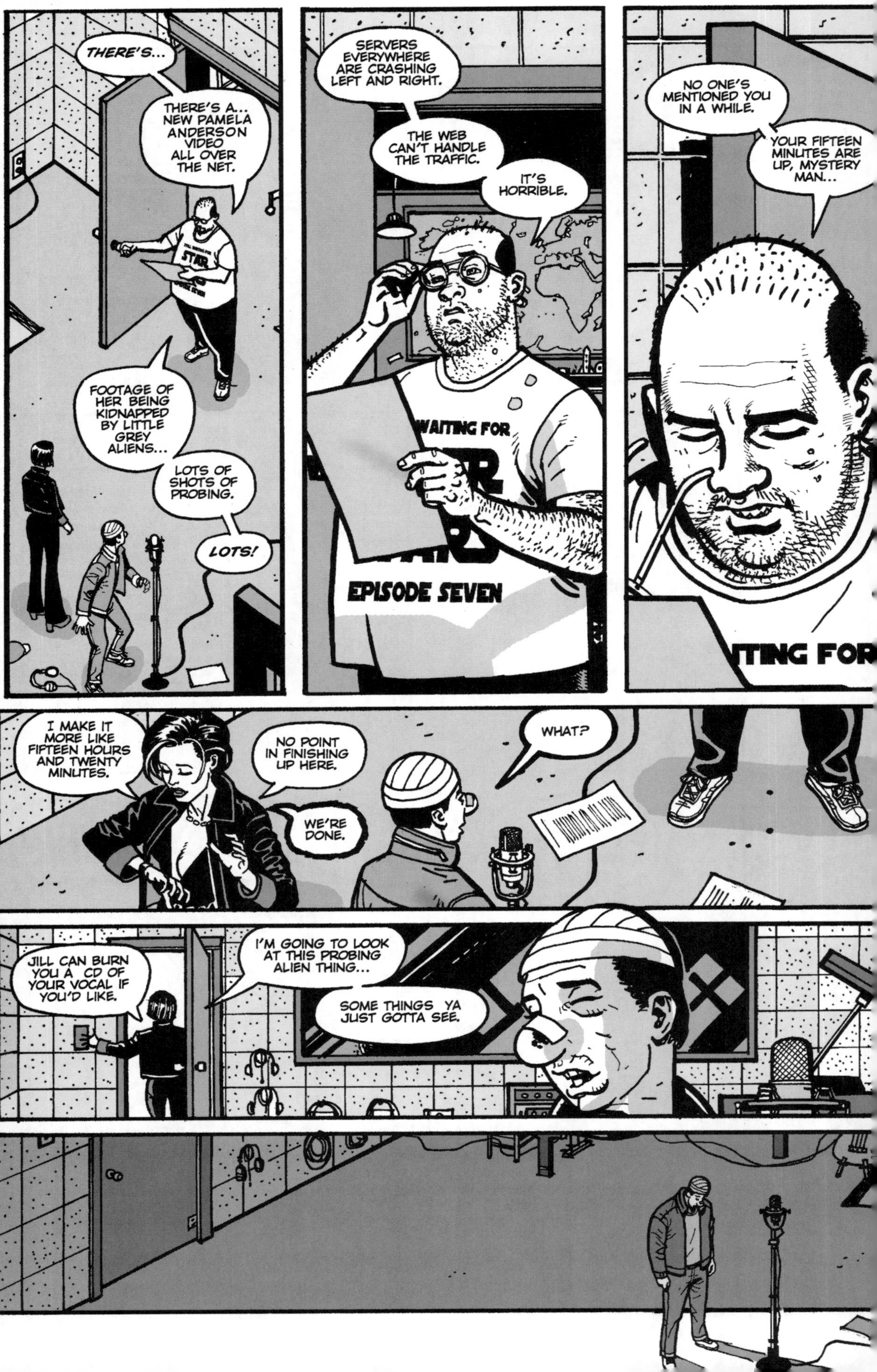
THERE'S...
THERE'S A... NEW PAMELA ANDERSON VIDEO ALL OVER THE NET.
FOOTAGE OF HER BEING KIDNAPPED BY LITTLE GREY ALIENS...
LOTS OF SHOTS OF PROBING.
LOTS!
SERVERS EVERYWHERE ARE CRASHING LEFT AND RIGHT.
THE WEB CAN'T HANDLE THE TRAFFIC.
IT'S HORRIBLE.
WAITING FOR
EPISODE SEVEN
NO ONE'S MENTIONED YOU IN A WHILE.
YOUR FIFTEEN MINUTES ARE UP, MYSTERY MAN...
ITING FOR
I MAKE IT MORE LIKE FIFTEEN HOURS AND TWENTY MINUTES.
NO POINT IN FINISHING UP HERE.
WE'RE DONE.
WHAT?
JILL CAN BURN YOU A CD OF YOUR VOCAL IF YOU'D LIKE.
I'M GOING TO LOOK AT THIS PROBING ALIEN THING...
SOME THINGS YA JUST GOTTA SEE.

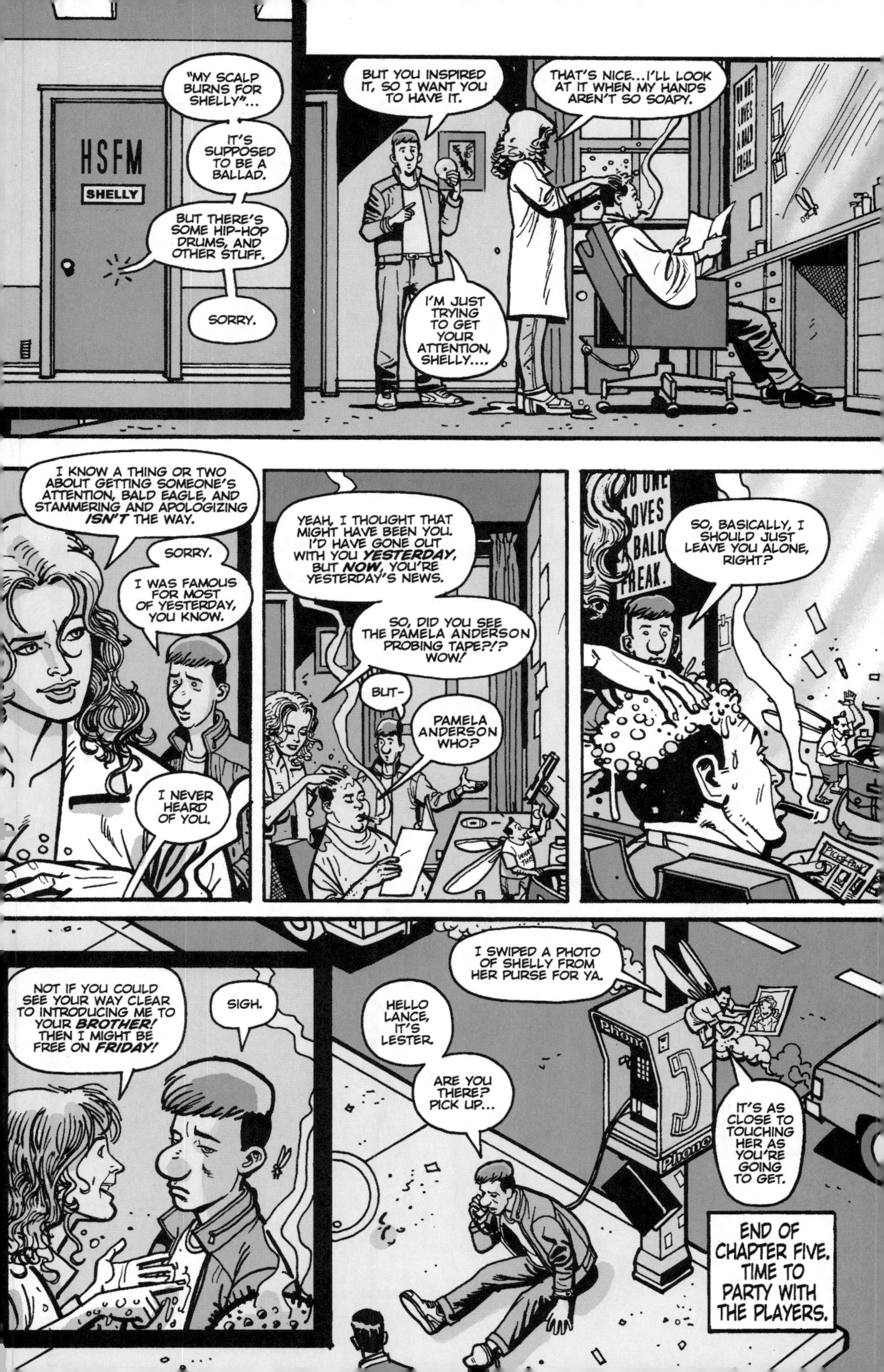
HSFM
SHELLY
"MY SCALP BURNS FOR SHELLY"...
IT'S SUPPOSED TO BE A BALLAD.
BUT THERE'S SOME HIP-HOP DRUMS, AND OTHER STUFF.
SORRY.
BUT YOU INSPIRED IT, SO I WANT YOU TO HAVE IT.
THAT'S NICE...I'LL LOOK AT IT WHEN MY HANDS AREN'T SO SOAPY.
NO ONE LOVES A BALD FREAK.
I'M JUST TRYING TO GET YOUR ATTENTION, SHELLY....
I KNOW A THING OR TWO ABOUT GETTING SOMEONE'S ATTENTION, BALD EAGLE, AND STAMMERING AND APOLOGIZING *ISN'T* THE WAY.
SORRY.
I WAS FAMOUS FOR MOST OF YESTERDAY, YOU KNOW.
I NEVER HEARD OF YOU.
YEAH, I THOUGHT THAT MIGHT HAVE BEEN YOU. I'D HAVE GONE OUT WITH YOU *YESTERDAY,* BUT *NOW,* YOU'RE YESTERDAY'S NEWS.
SO, DID YOU SEE THE PAMELA ANDERSON PROBING TAPE?!? WOW!
BUT-
PAMELA ANDERSON WHO?
SO, BASICALLY, I SHOULD JUST LEAVE YOU ALONE, RIGHT?
NOT IF YOU COULD SEE YOUR WAY CLEAR TO INTRODUCING ME TO YOUR *BROTHER!* THEN I MIGHT BE FREE ON *FRIDAY!*
SIGH.
I SWIPED A PHOTO OF SHELLY FROM HER PURSE FOR YA.
HELLO LANCE, IT'S LESTER.
ARE YOU THERE? PICK UP...
PHONE
IT'S AS CLOSE TO TOUCHING HER AS YOU'RE GOING TO GET.
END OF CHAPTER FIVE. TIME TO PARTY WITH THE PLAYERS.

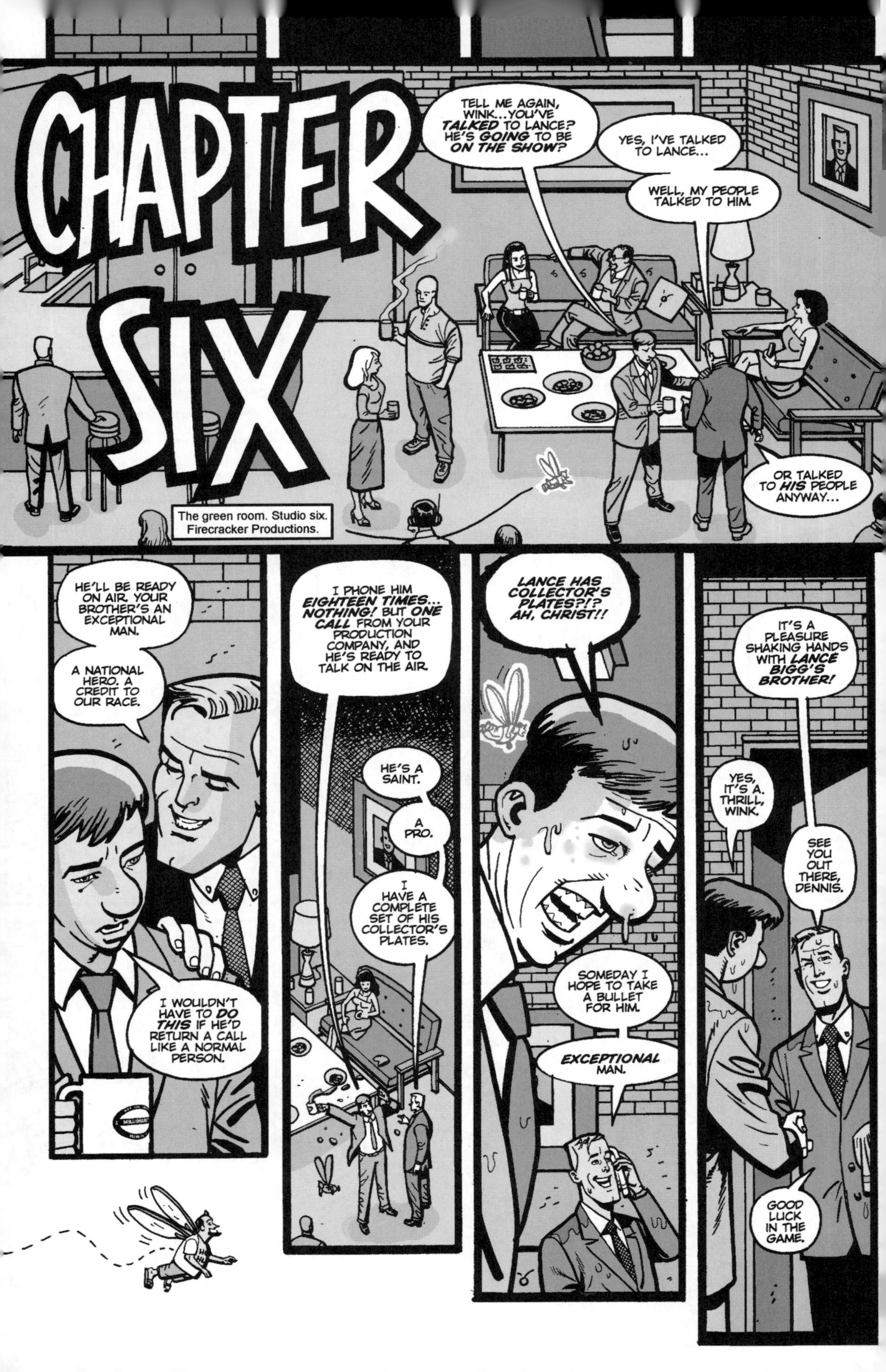
CHAPTER SIX
The green room. Studio six. Firecracker Productions.
TELL ME AGAIN, WINK...YOU'VE TALKED TO LANCE? HE'S GOING TO BE ON THE SHOW?
YES, I'VE TALKED TO LANCE...
WELL, MY PEOPLE TALKED TO HIM.
OR TALKED TO HIS PEOPLE ANYWAY...
HE'LL BE READY ON AIR. YOUR BROTHER'S AN EXCEPTIONAL MAN.
A NATIONAL HERO. A CREDIT TO OUR RACE.
I WOULDN'T HAVE TO DO THIS IF HE'D RETURN A CALL LIKE A NORMAL PERSON.
I PHONE HIM EIGHTEEN TIMES... NOTHING! BUT ONE CALL FROM YOUR PRODUCTION COMPANY, AND HE'S READY TO TALK ON THE AIR.
HE'S A SAINT.
A PRO.
I HAVE A COMPLETE SET OF HIS COLLECTOR'S PLATES.
LANCE HAS COLLECTOR'S PLATES?!? AH, CHRIST!!
SOMEDAY I HOPE TO TAKE A BULLET FOR HIM.
EXCEPTIONAL MAN.
IT'S A PLEASURE SHAKING HANDS WITH LANCE BIGG'S BROTHER!
YES, IT'S A THRILL, WINK.
SEE YOU OUT THERE, DENNIS.
GOOD LUCK IN THE GAME.

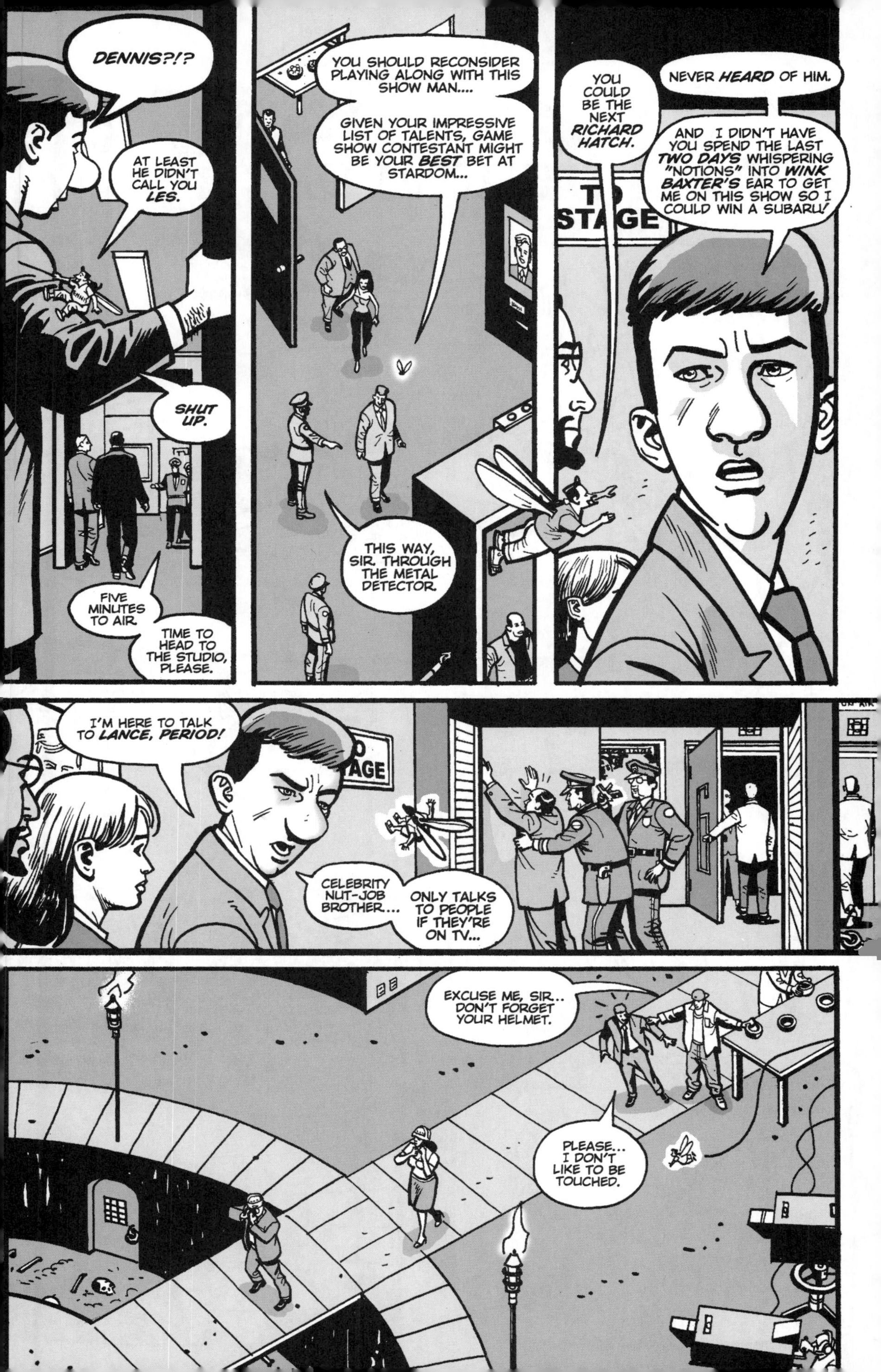

DENNIS?!?
AT LEAST HE DIDN'T CALL YOU *LES.*
SHUT UP.
FIVE MINUTES TO AIR.
TIME TO HEAD TO THE STUDIO, PLEASE.
YOU SHOULD RECONSIDER PLAYING ALONG WITH THIS SHOW MAN....
GIVEN YOUR IMPRESSIVE LIST OF TALENTS, GAME SHOW CONTESTANT MIGHT BE YOUR *BEST* BET AT STARDOM...
THIS WAY, SIR. THROUGH THE METAL DETECTOR.
YOU COULD BE THE NEXT *RICHARD HATCH.*
NEVER *HEARD* OF HIM.
AND I DIDN'T HAVE YOU SPEND THE LAST *TWO DAYS* WHISPERING "NOTIONS" INTO *WINK BAXTER'S* EAR TO GET ME ON THIS SHOW SO I COULD WIN A SUBARU!
TO STAGE
I'M HERE TO TALK TO *LANCE, PERIOD!*
CELEBRITY NUT-JOB BROTHER...
ONLY TALKS TO PEOPLE IF THEY'RE ON TV...
EXCUSE ME, SIR... DON'T FORGET YOUR HELMET.
PLEASE... I DON'T LIKE TO BE TOUCHED.

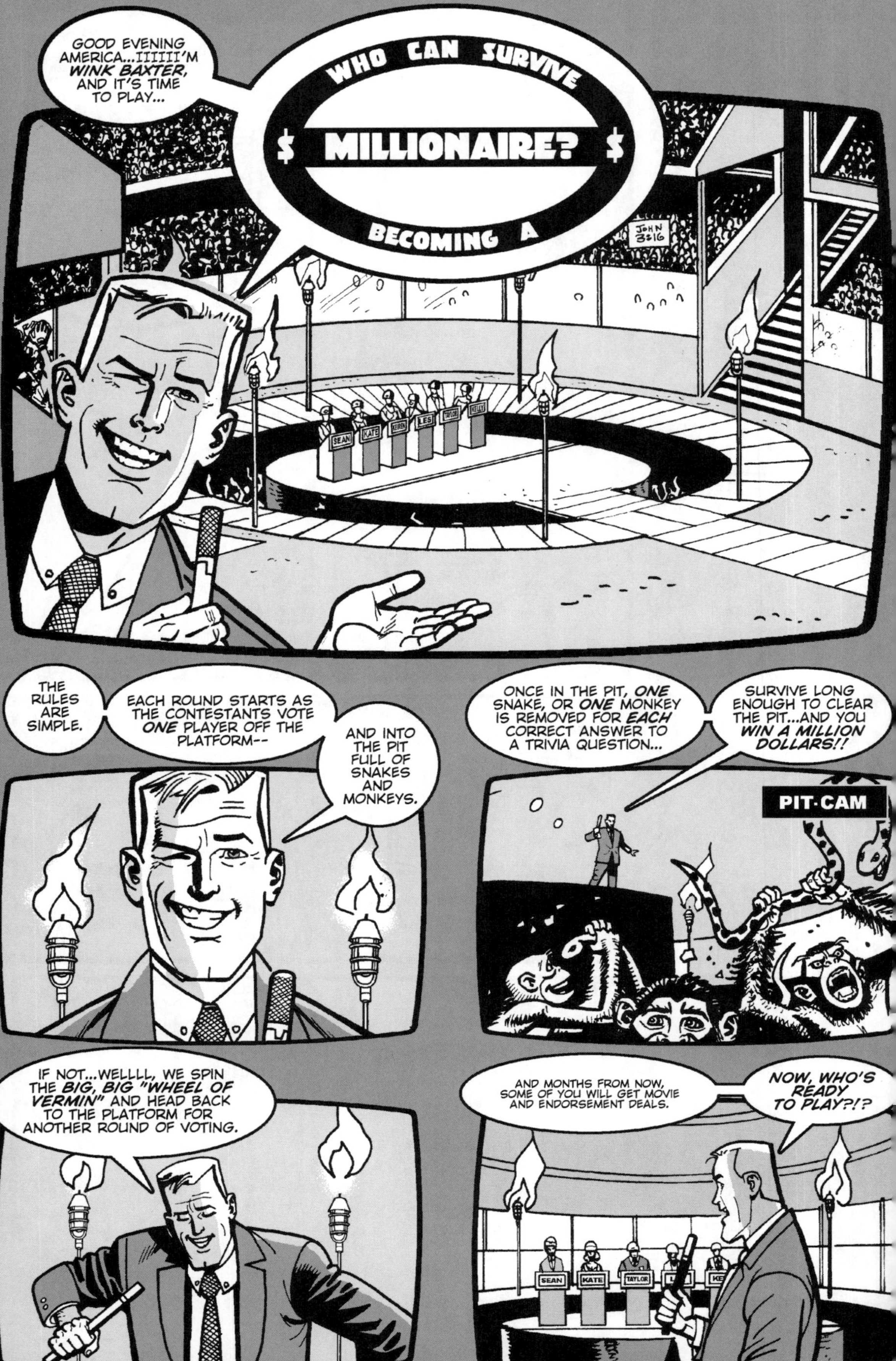
GOOD EVENING AMERICA...IIIIII'M *WINK BAXTER,* AND IT'S TIME TO PLAY...
WHO CAN SURVIVE BECOMING A $ MILLIONAIRE? $
JOHN 3:16
SEAN
KATE
KEIREN
LES
TAYLOR
KELLY
THE RULES ARE SIMPLE.
EACH ROUND STARTS AS THE CONTESTANTS VOTE *ONE* PLAYER OFF THE PLATFORM--
AND INTO THE PIT FULL OF SNAKES AND MONKEYS.
ONCE IN THE PIT, *ONE* SNAKE, OR *ONE* MONKEY IS REMOVED FOR *EACH* CORRECT ANSWER TO A TRIVIA QUESTION...
SURVIVE LONG ENOUGH TO CLEAR THE PIT...AND YOU *WIN A MILLION DOLLARS!!*
PIT-CAM
IF NOT...WELLLL, WE SPIN THE *BIG, BIG "WHEEL OF VERMIN"* AND HEAD BACK TO THE PLATFORM FOR ANOTHER ROUND OF VOTING.
AND MONTHS FROM NOW, SOME OF YOU WILL GET MOVIE AND ENDORSEMENT DEALS.
NOW, WHO'S READY TO PLAY?!?
SEAN
KATE
TAYLOR

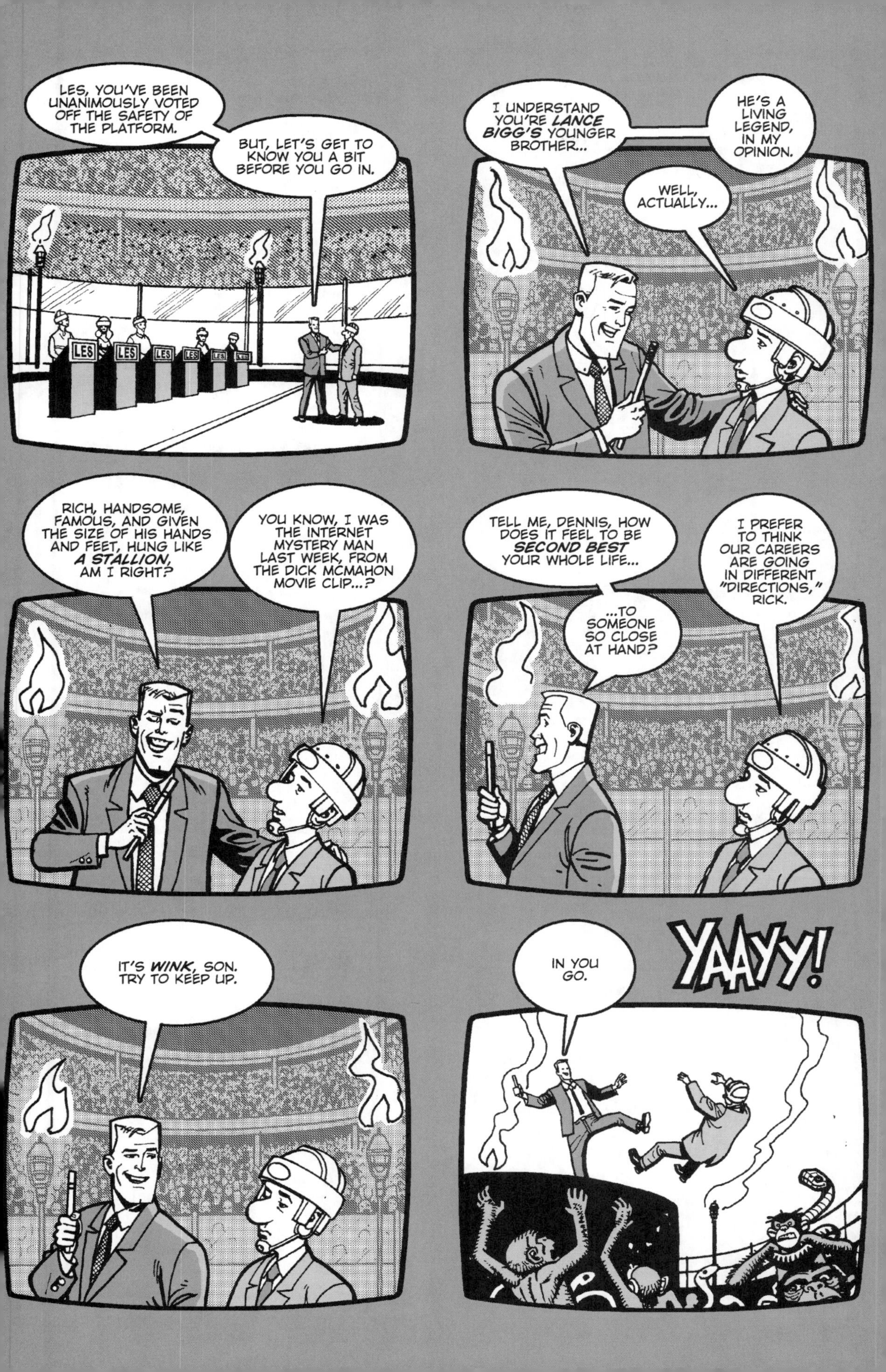
LES, YOU'VE BEEN UNANIMOUSLY VOTED OFF THE SAFETY OF THE PLATFORM.
BUT, LET'S GET TO KNOW YOU A BIT BEFORE YOU GO IN.
LES
I UNDERSTAND YOU'RE LANCE BIGG'S YOUNGER BROTHER...
HE'S A LIVING LEGEND, IN MY OPINION.
WELL, ACTUALLY...
RICH, HANDSOME, FAMOUS, AND GIVEN THE SIZE OF HIS HANDS AND FEET, HUNG LIKE A STALLION, AM I RIGHT?
YOU KNOW, I WAS THE INTERNET MYSTERY MAN LAST WEEK, FROM THE DICK MCMAHON MOVIE CLIP...?
TELL ME, DENNIS, HOW DOES IT FEEL TO BE SECOND BEST YOUR WHOLE LIFE...
...TO SOMEONE SO CLOSE AT HAND?
I PREFER TO THINK OUR CAREERS ARE GOING IN DIFFERENT "DIRECTIONS," RICK.
IT'S WINK, SON. TRY TO KEEP UP.
IN YOU GO.
YAAYY!

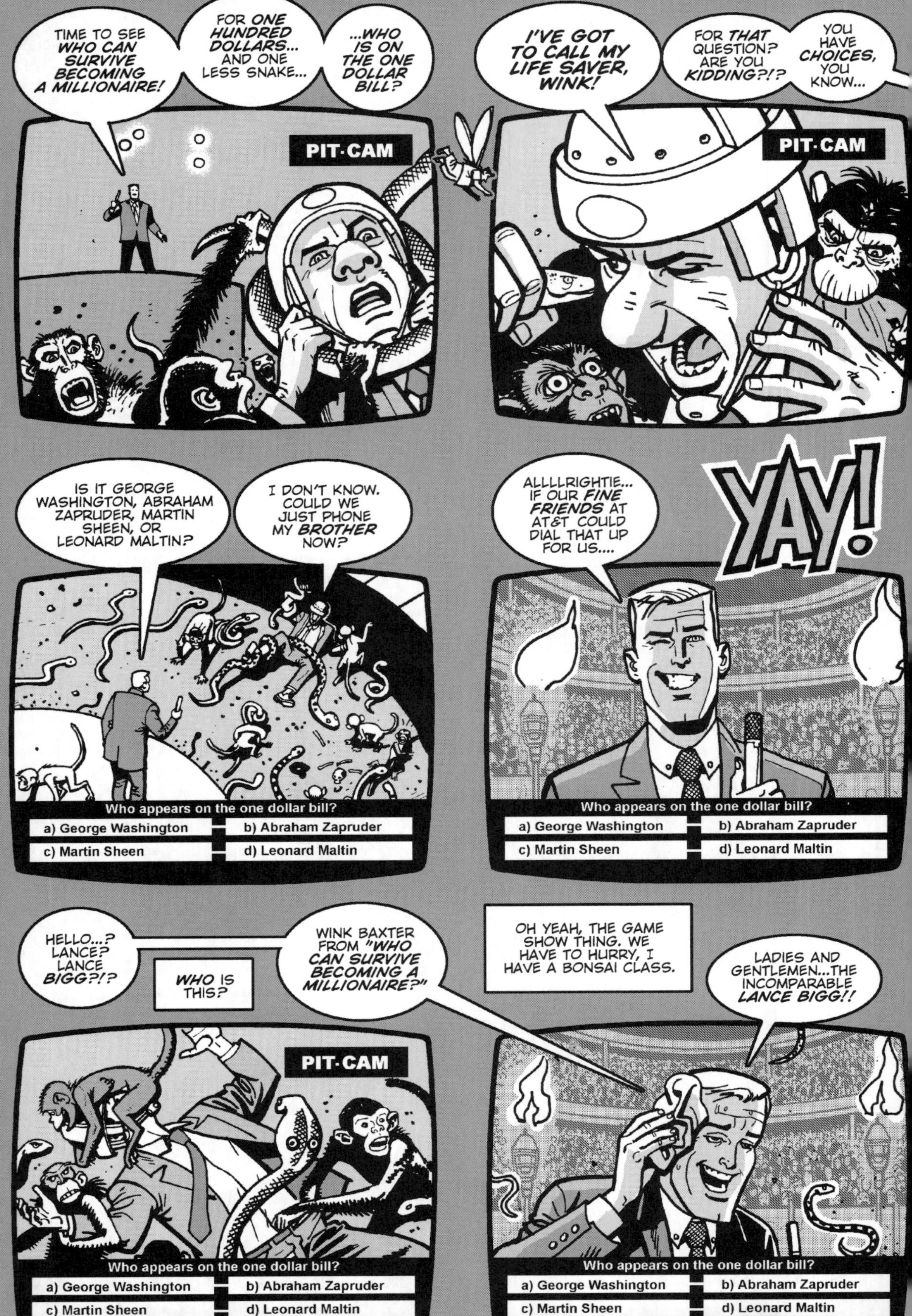
TIME TO SEE WHO CAN SURVIVE BECOMING A MILLIONAIRE!
FOR ONE HUNDRED DOLLARS... AND ONE LESS SNAKE...
...WHO IS ON THE ONE DOLLAR BILL?
PIT·CAM
I'VE GOT TO CALL MY LIFE SAVER, WINK!
FOR THAT QUESTION? ARE YOU KIDDING?!?
YOU HAVE CHOICES, YOU KNOW...
PIT·CAM
IS IT GEORGE WASHINGTON, ABRAHAM ZAPRUDER, MARTIN SHEEN, OR LEONARD MALTIN?
I DON'T KNOW. COULD WE JUST PHONE MY BROTHER NOW?
Who appears on the one dollar bill?
a) George Washington
b) Abraham Zapruder
c) Martin Sheen
d) Leonard Maltin
YAY!
ALLLLRIGHTIE... IF OUR FINE FRIENDS AT AT&T COULD DIAL THAT UP FOR US....
Who appears on the one dollar bill?
a) George Washington
b) Abraham Zapruder
c) Martin Sheen
d) Leonard Maltin
HELLO...? LANCE? LANCE BIGG?!?
WHO IS THIS?
WINK BAXTER FROM "WHO CAN SURVIVE BECOMING A MILLIONAIRE?"
PIT·CAM
Who appears on the one dollar bill?
a) George Washington
b) Abraham Zapruder
c) Martin Sheen
d) Leonard Maltin
OH YEAH, THE GAME SHOW THING. WE HAVE TO HURRY, I HAVE A BONSAI CLASS.
LADIES AND GENTLEMEN...THE INCOMPARABLE LANCE BIGG!!
Who appears on the one dollar bill?
a) George Washington
b) Abraham Zapruder
c) Martin Sheen
d) Leonard Maltin

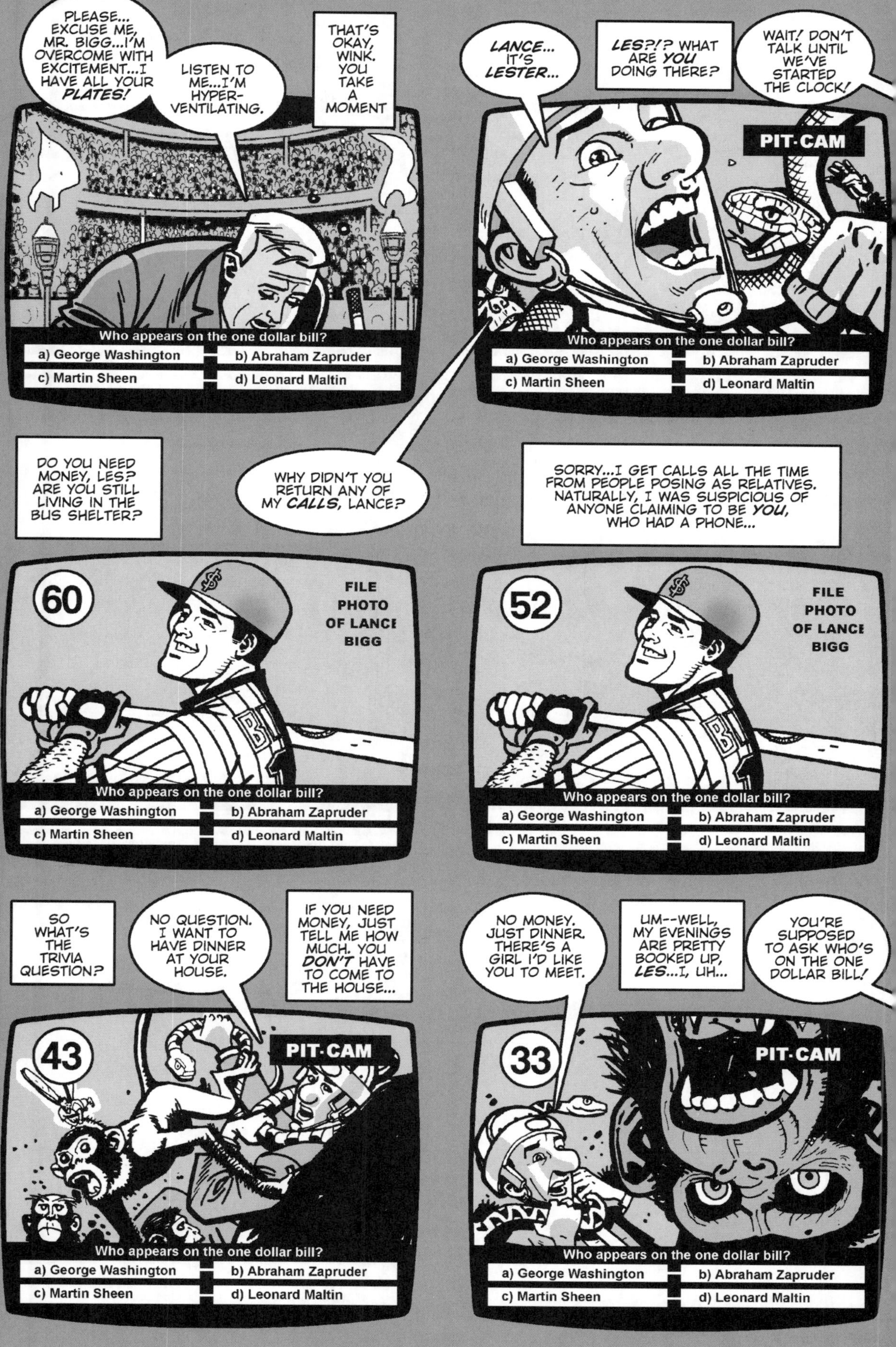

PLEASE... EXCUSE ME, MR. BIGG...I'M OVERCOME WITH EXCITEMENT...I HAVE ALL YOUR PLATES!
LISTEN TO ME...I'M HYPER-VENTILATING.
THAT'S OKAY, WINK. YOU TAKE A MOMENT
Who appears on the one dollar bill?
a) George Washington
b) Abraham Zapruder
c) Martin Sheen
d) Leonard Maltin
LANCE... IT'S LESTER...
LES?!? WHAT ARE YOU DOING THERE?
WAIT! DON'T TALK UNTIL WE'VE STARTED THE CLOCK!
PIT-CAM
Who appears on the one dollar bill?
a) George Washington
b) Abraham Zapruder
c) Martin Sheen
d) Leonard Maltin
DO YOU NEED MONEY, LES? ARE YOU STILL LIVING IN THE BUS SHELTER?
WHY DIDN'T YOU RETURN ANY OF MY CALLS, LANCE?
SORRY...I GET CALLS ALL THE TIME FROM PEOPLE POSING AS RELATIVES. NATURALLY, I WAS SUSPICIOUS OF ANYONE CLAIMING TO BE YOU, WHO HAD A PHONE...
60
FILE PHOTO OF LANCE BIGG
Who appears on the one dollar bill?
a) George Washington
b) Abraham Zapruder
c) Martin Sheen
d) Leonard Maltin
52
FILE PHOTO OF LANCE BIGG
Who appears on the one dollar bill?
a) George Washington
b) Abraham Zapruder
c) Martin Sheen
d) Leonard Maltin
SO WHAT'S THE TRIVIA QUESTION?
NO QUESTION. I WANT TO HAVE DINNER AT YOUR HOUSE.
IF YOU NEED MONEY, JUST TELL ME HOW MUCH. YOU DON'T HAVE TO COME TO THE HOUSE...
43
PIT-CAM
Who appears on the one dollar bill?
a) George Washington
b) Abraham Zapruder
c) Martin Sheen
d) Leonard Maltin
NO MONEY. JUST DINNER. THERE'S A GIRL I'D LIKE YOU TO MEET.
UM--WELL, MY EVENINGS ARE PRETTY BOOKED UP, LES...I, UH...
YOU'RE SUPPOSED TO ASK WHO'S ON THE ONE DOLLAR BILL!
33
PIT-CAM
Who appears on the one dollar bill?
a) George Washington
b) Abraham Zapruder
c) Martin Sheen
d) Leonard Maltin

IT'S BEN FRANKLIN, ISN'T IT? I HAVEN'T SEEN PAPER MONEY IN YEARS!
WHAT ABOUT DINNER, LANCE?
OH, I DON'T PAY FOR DINNERS WITH CASH, LES. I HAVE A CARD!
26
PIT·CAM
Who appears on the one dollar bill?
a) George Washington
b) Abraham Zapruder
c) Martin Sheen
d) Leonard Maltin
PSSST! GET THE AUDIENCE ON YOUR SIDE, AND QUICK! YOU'RE RUNNING OUT OF TIME!
FRANKLIN ISN'T ONE OF THE CHOICES, MR. BIGG...
19
PIT·CAM
Who appears on the one dollar bill?
a) George Washington
b) Abraham Zapruder
c) Martin Sheen
d) Leonard Maltin
HEY AUDIENCE! DO YOU THINK LANCE SHOULD MEET MY GIRLFRIEND ON FRIDAY?
09
PIT·CAM
Who appears on the one dollar bill?
a) George Washington
b) Abraham Zapruder
c) Martin Sheen
d) Leonard Maltin
YAAYY!
HEH-HEH. GOOD ONE, LES...I CAN'T DISAPPOINT THE AUDIENCE, CAN I? I'LL SEE YOU ON FRIDAY, I SUPPOSE.
01
Who appears on the one dollar bill?
a) George Washington
b) Abraham Zapruder
c) Martin Sheen
d) Leonard Maltin
NOT MUCH HELP WITH THE TRIVIA QUESTION...SO WHAT'S YOUR "ULTIMATE ANSWER"? WHO IS ON THE ONE DOLLAR BILL?
I'M GOING WITH LEONARD MALTIN, WINK...
Who appears on the one dollar bill?
a) George Washington
b) Abraham Zapruder
c) Martin Sheen
d) Leonard Maltin
HEY! YOU CAN'T CLIMB OUT OF THE VERMIN PIT! YOU SIGNED A CONTRACT!
THE MONKEYS ARE ALL DEAD. THE SNAKES ARE ASLEEP, AND I'M DONE.
Who appears on the one dollar bill?
a) George Washington
b) Abraham Zapruder
c) Martin Sheen
d) Leonard Maltin

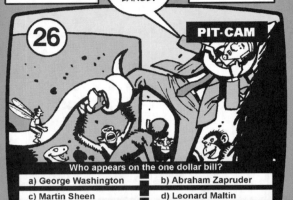

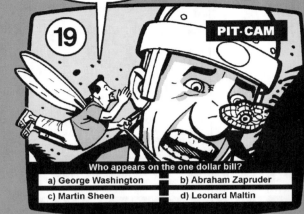

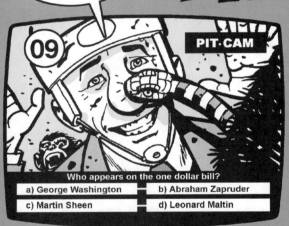

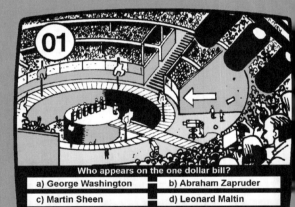

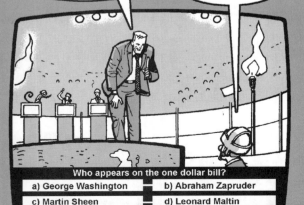

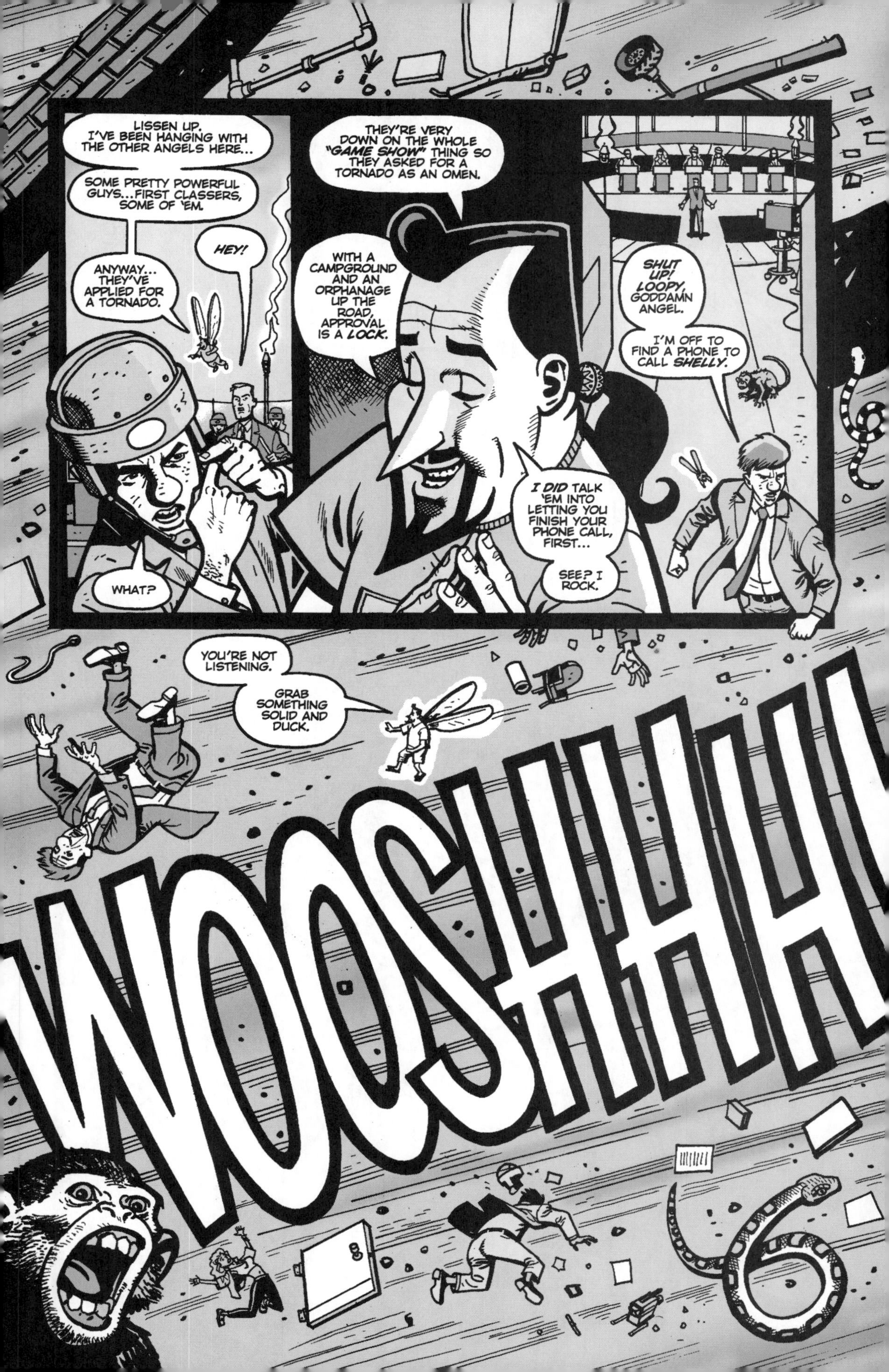
LISSEN UP. I'VE BEEN HANGING WITH THE OTHER ANGELS HERE...
SOME PRETTY POWERFUL GUYS...FIRST CLASSERS, SOME OF 'EM.
HEY!
ANYWAY... THEY'VE APPLIED FOR A TORNADO.
WHAT?
THEY'RE VERY DOWN ON THE WHOLE "GAME SHOW" THING SO THEY ASKED FOR A TORNADO AS AN OMEN.
WITH A CAMPGROUND AND AN ORPHANAGE UP THE ROAD, APPROVAL IS A LOCK.
I DID TALK 'EM INTO LETTING YOU FINISH YOUR PHONE CALL, FIRST...
SEE? I ROCK.
SHUT UP! LOOPY, GODDAMN ANGEL.
I'M OFF TO FIND A PHONE TO CALL SHELLY.
YOU'RE NOT LISTENING.
GRAB SOMETHING SOLID AND DUCK.
WOOSHHHH

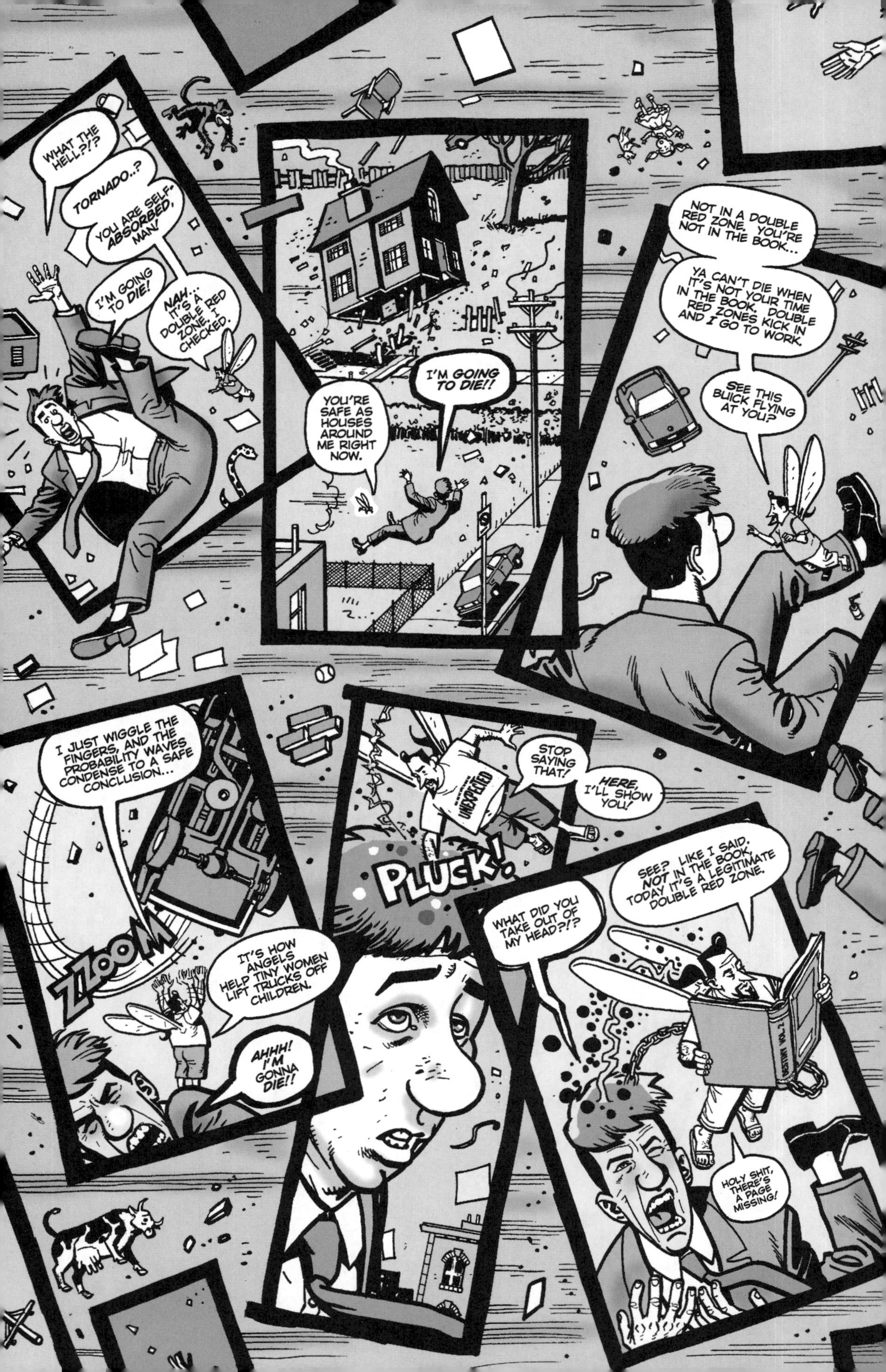
WHAT THE HELL?!?
TORNADO..?
YOU ARE SELF-ABSORBED, MAN!
I'M GOING TO DIE!
NAH... IT'S A DOUBLE RED ZONE. I CHECKED.
I'M GOING TO DIE!!
YOU'RE SAFE AS HOUSES AROUND ME RIGHT NOW.
NOT IN A DOUBLE RED ZONE. YOU'RE NOT IN THE BOOK...
YA CAN'T DIE WHEN IT'S NOT YOUR TIME IN THE BOOK. DOUBLE RED ZONES KICK IN AND I GO TO WORK.
SEE THIS BUICK FLYING AT YOU?
I JUST WIGGLE THE FINGERS, AND THE PROBABILITY WAVES CONDENSE TO A SAFE CONCLUSION...
ZZOOM
IT'S HOW ANGELS HELP TINY WOMEN LIFT TRUCKS OFF CHILDREN.
AHHH! I'M GONNA DIE!!
STOP SAYING THAT!
HERE, I'LL SHOW YOU!
UNEXPECTED
PLUCK!
WHAT DID YOU TAKE OUT OF MY HEAD?!?
SEE? LIKE I SAID. NOT IN THE BOOK. TODAY IT'S A LEGITIMATE DOUBLE RED ZONE.
HOLY SHIT, THERE'S A PAGE MISSING!

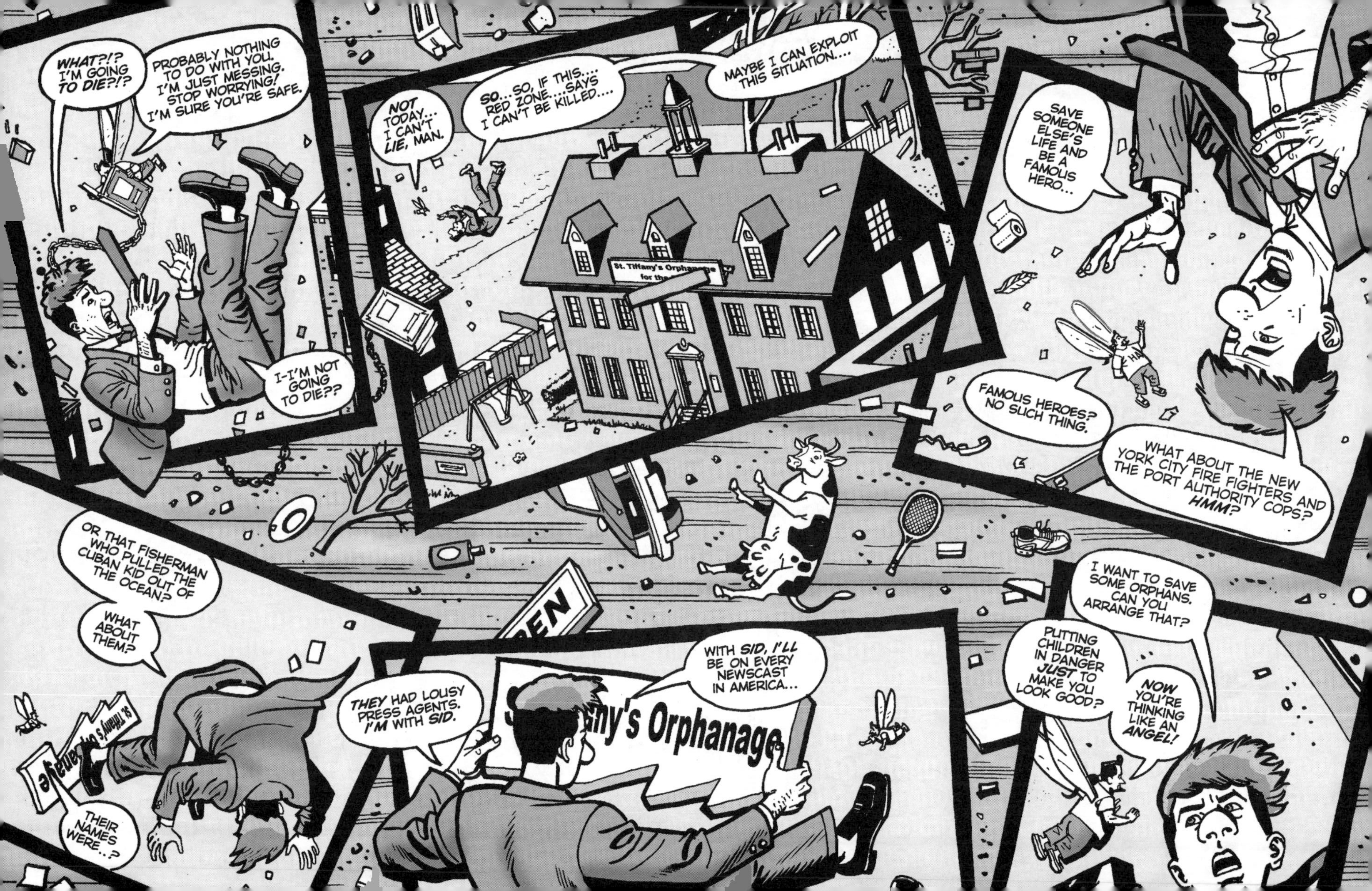
WHAT?!? I'M GOING TO DIE?!?
PROBABLY NOTHING TO DO WITH YOU. I'M JUST MESSING. STOP WORRYING! I'M SURE YOU'RE SAFE.
I-I'M NOT GOING TO DIE??
NOT TODAY... I CAN'T LIE, MAN.
SO...SO, IF THIS.... RED ZONE....SAYS I CAN'T BE KILLED....
MAYBE I CAN EXPLOIT THIS SITUATION....
St. Tiffany's Orphanage
SAVE SOMEONE ELSE'S LIFE AND BE A FAMOUS HERO...
FAMOUS HEROES? NO SUCH THING.
WHAT ABOUT THE NEW YORK CITY FIRE FIGHTERS AND THE PORT AUTHORITY COPS? HMM?
OR THAT FISHERMAN WHO PULLED THE CUBAN KID OUT OF THE OCEAN?
WHAT ABOUT THEM?
THEIR NAMES WERE..?
THEY HAD LOUSY PRESS AGENTS. I'M WITH SID.
WITH SID, I'LL BE ON EVERY NEWSCAST IN AMERICA...
ny's Orphanage
I WANT TO SAVE SOME ORPHANS. CAN YOU ARRANGE THAT?
PUTTING CHILDREN IN DANGER JUST TO MAKE YOU LOOK GOOD?
NOW YOU'RE THINKING LIKE AN ANGEL!

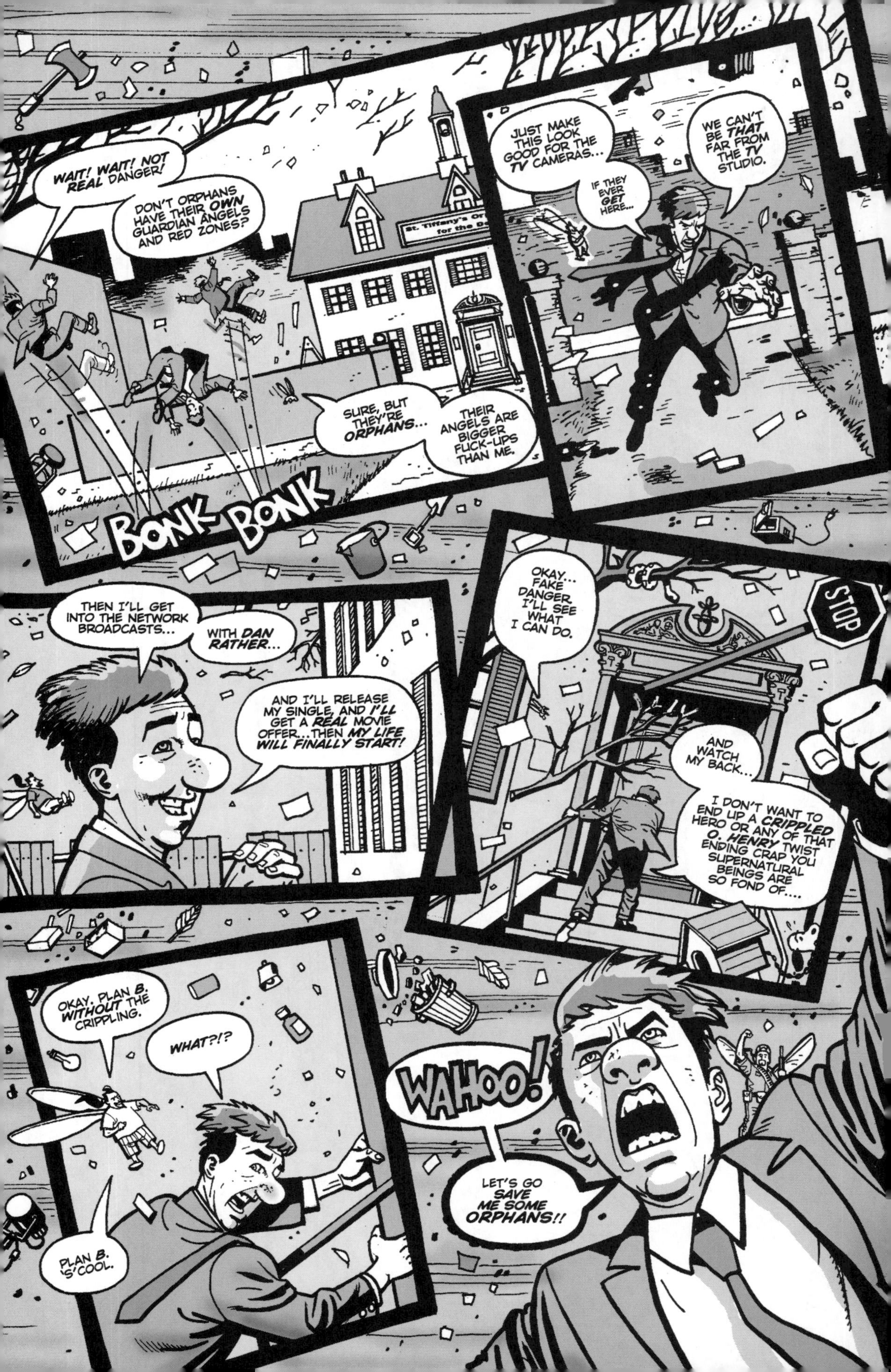
WAIT! WAIT! NOT REAL DANGER!
DON'T ORPHANS HAVE THEIR OWN GUARDIAN ANGELS AND RED ZONES?
SURE, BUT THEY'RE ORPHANS...
THEIR ANGELS ARE BIGGER FUCK-UPS THAN ME.
BONK BONK
JUST MAKE THIS LOOK GOOD FOR THE TV CAMERAS...
IF THEY EVER GET HERE...
WE CAN'T BE THAT FAR FROM THE TV STUDIO.
THEN I'LL GET INTO THE NETWORK BROADCASTS...
WITH DAN RATHER...
AND I'LL RELEASE MY SINGLE, AND I'LL GET A REAL MOVIE OFFER...THEN MY LIFE WILL FINALLY START!
OKAY... FAKE DANGER. I'LL SEE WHAT I CAN DO.
STOP
AND WATCH MY BACK...
I DON'T WANT TO END UP A CRIPPLED HERO OR ANY OF THAT O. HENRY TWIST ENDING CRAP YOU SUPERNATURAL BEINGS ARE SO FOND OF....
OKAY. PLAN B. WITHOUT THE CRIPPLING.
WHAT?!?
PLAN B. 'S'COOL.
WAHOO!
LET'S GO SAVE ME SOME ORPHANS!!

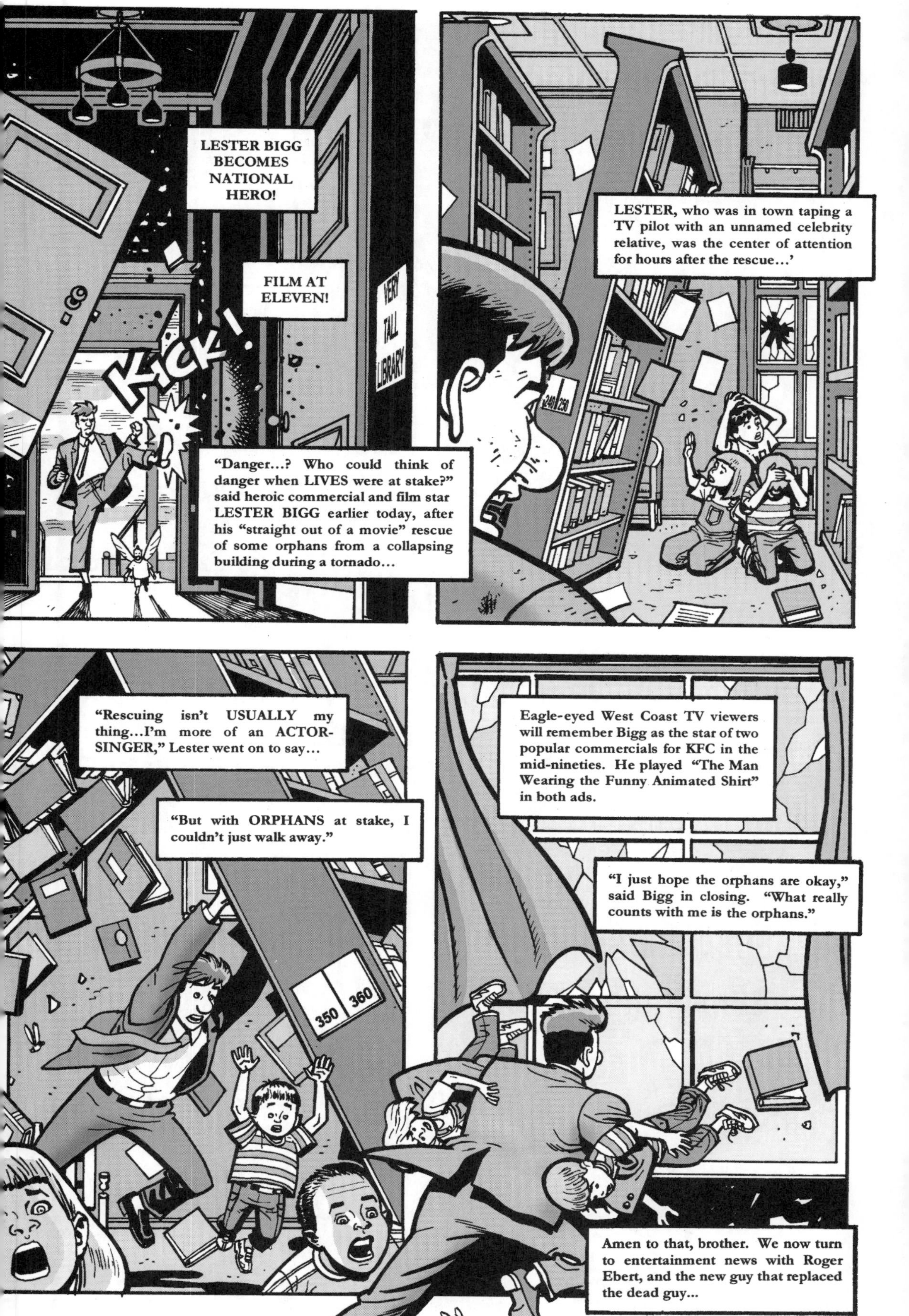
LESTER BIGG BECOMES NATIONAL HERO!
FILM AT ELEVEN!
VERY TALL LIBRARY
KICK!
"Danger...? Who could think of danger when LIVES were at stake?" said heroic commercial and film star LESTER BIGG earlier today, after his "straight out of a movie" rescue of some orphans from a collapsing building during a tornado...
LESTER, who was in town taping a TV pilot with an unnamed celebrity relative, was the center of attention for hours after the rescue...'
240
250
"Rescuing isn't USUALLY my thing...I'm more of an ACTOR-SINGER," Lester went on to say...
"But with ORPHANS at stake, I couldn't just walk away."
350
360
Eagle-eyed West Coast TV viewers will remember Bigg as the star of two popular commercials for KFC in the mid-nineties. He played "The Man Wearing the Funny Animated Shirt" in both ads.
"I just hope the orphans are okay," said Bigg in closing. "What really counts with me is the orphans."
Amen to that, brother. We now turn to entertainment news with Roger Ebert, and the new guy that replaced the dead guy...

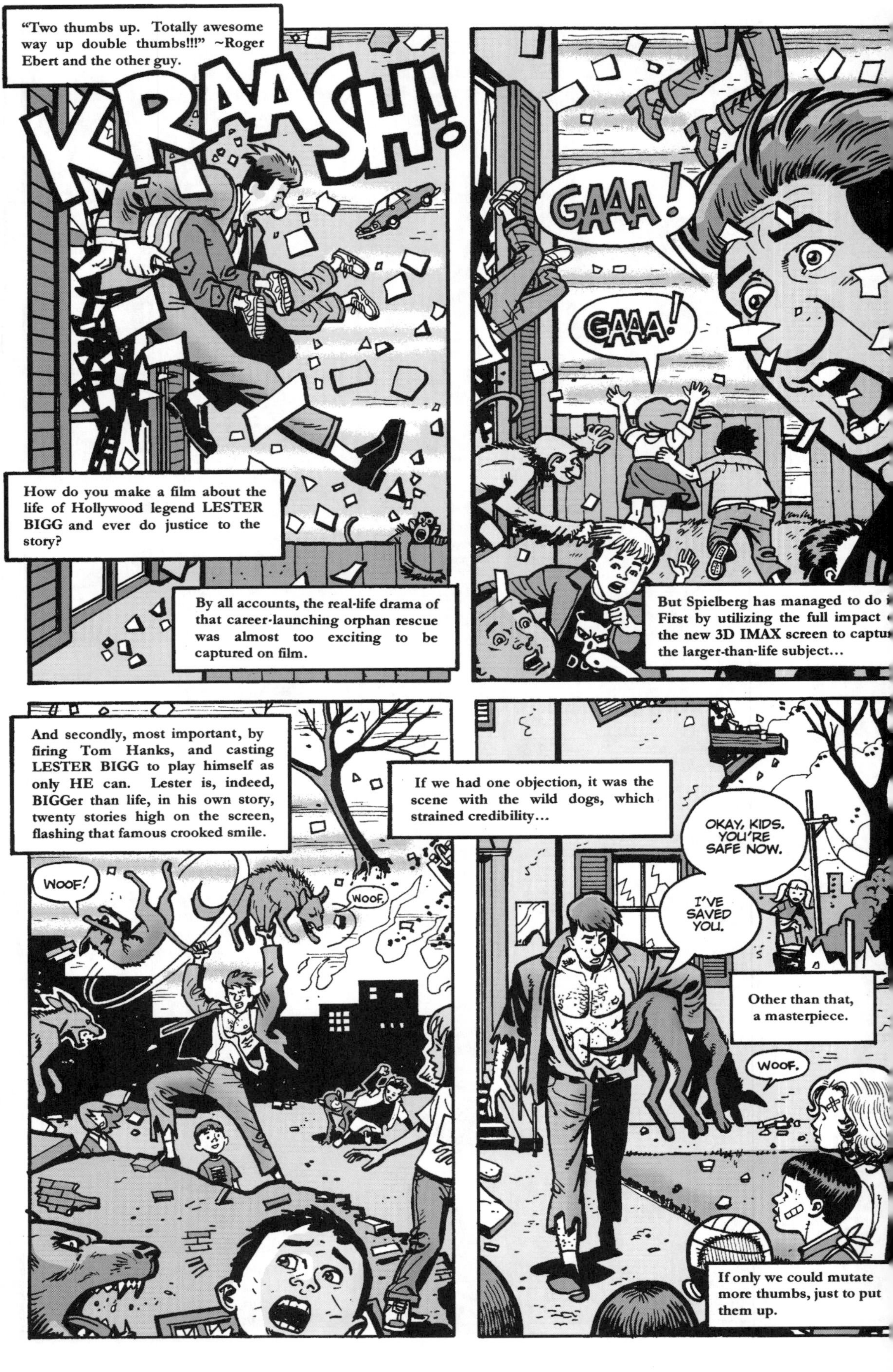
"Two thumbs up. Totally awesome way up double thumbs!!!" ~Roger Ebert and the other guy.
KRAASH!
How do you make a film about the life of Hollywood legend LESTER BIGG and ever do justice to the story?
By all accounts, the real-life drama of that career-launching orphan rescue was almost too exciting to be captured on film.
GAAA!
GAAA!
But Spielberg has managed to do i
First by utilizing the full impact
the new 3D IMAX screen to captu
the larger-than-life subject…
And secondly, most important, by firing Tom Hanks, and casting LESTER BIGG to play himself as only HE can. Lester is, indeed, BIGGer than life, in his own story, twenty stories high on the screen, flashing that famous crooked smile.
WOOF!
WOOF.
If we had one objection, it was the scene with the wild dogs, which strained credibility…
OKAY, KIDS. YOU'RE SAFE NOW.
I'VE SAVED YOU.
Other than that, a masterpiece.
WOOF.
If only we could mutate more thumbs, just to put them up.

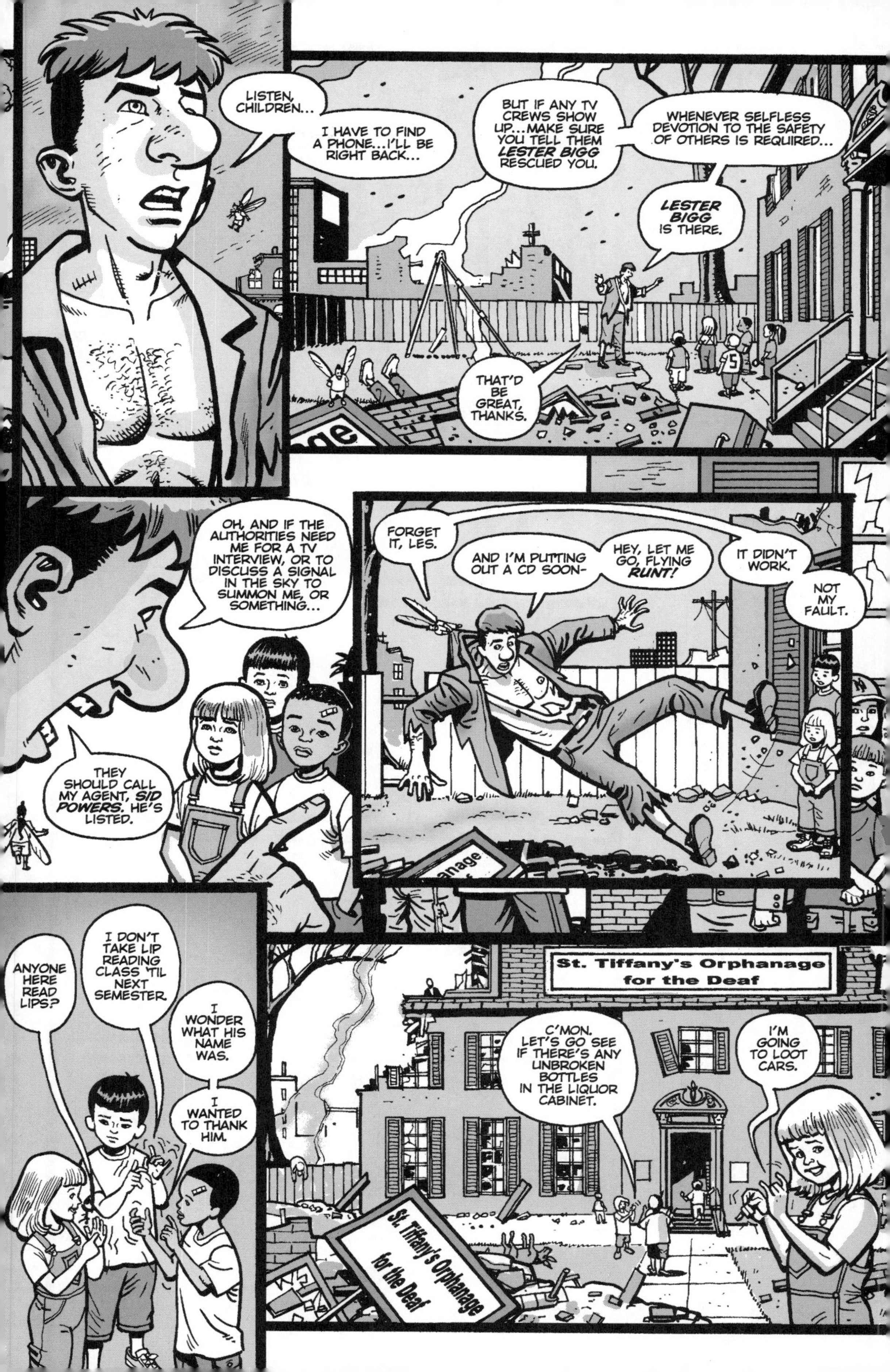
LISTEN, CHILDREN...
I HAVE TO FIND A PHONE...I'LL BE RIGHT BACK...
BUT IF ANY TV CREWS SHOW UP...MAKE SURE YOU TELL THEM LESTER BIGG RESCUED YOU.
WHENEVER SELFLESS DEVOTION TO THE SAFETY OF OTHERS IS REQUIRED...
LESTER BIGG IS THERE.
THAT'D BE GREAT, THANKS.
OH, AND IF THE AUTHORITIES NEED ME FOR A TV INTERVIEW, OR TO DISCUSS A SIGNAL IN THE SKY TO SUMMON ME, OR SOMETHING...
THEY SHOULD CALL MY AGENT, SID POWERS. HE'S LISTED.
FORGET IT, LES.
AND I'M PUTTING OUT A CD SOON-
HEY, LET ME GO, FLYING RUNT!
IT DIDN'T WORK.
NOT MY FAULT.
ANYONE HERE READ LIPS?
I DON'T TAKE LIP READING CLASS 'TIL NEXT SEMESTER.
I WONDER WHAT HIS NAME WAS.
I WANTED TO THANK HIM.
St. Tiffany's Orphanage for the Deaf
C'MON. LET'S GO SEE IF THERE'S ANY UNBROKEN BOTTLES IN THE LIQUOR CABINET.
I'M GOING TO LOOT CARS.
St. Tiffany's Orphanage for the Deaf

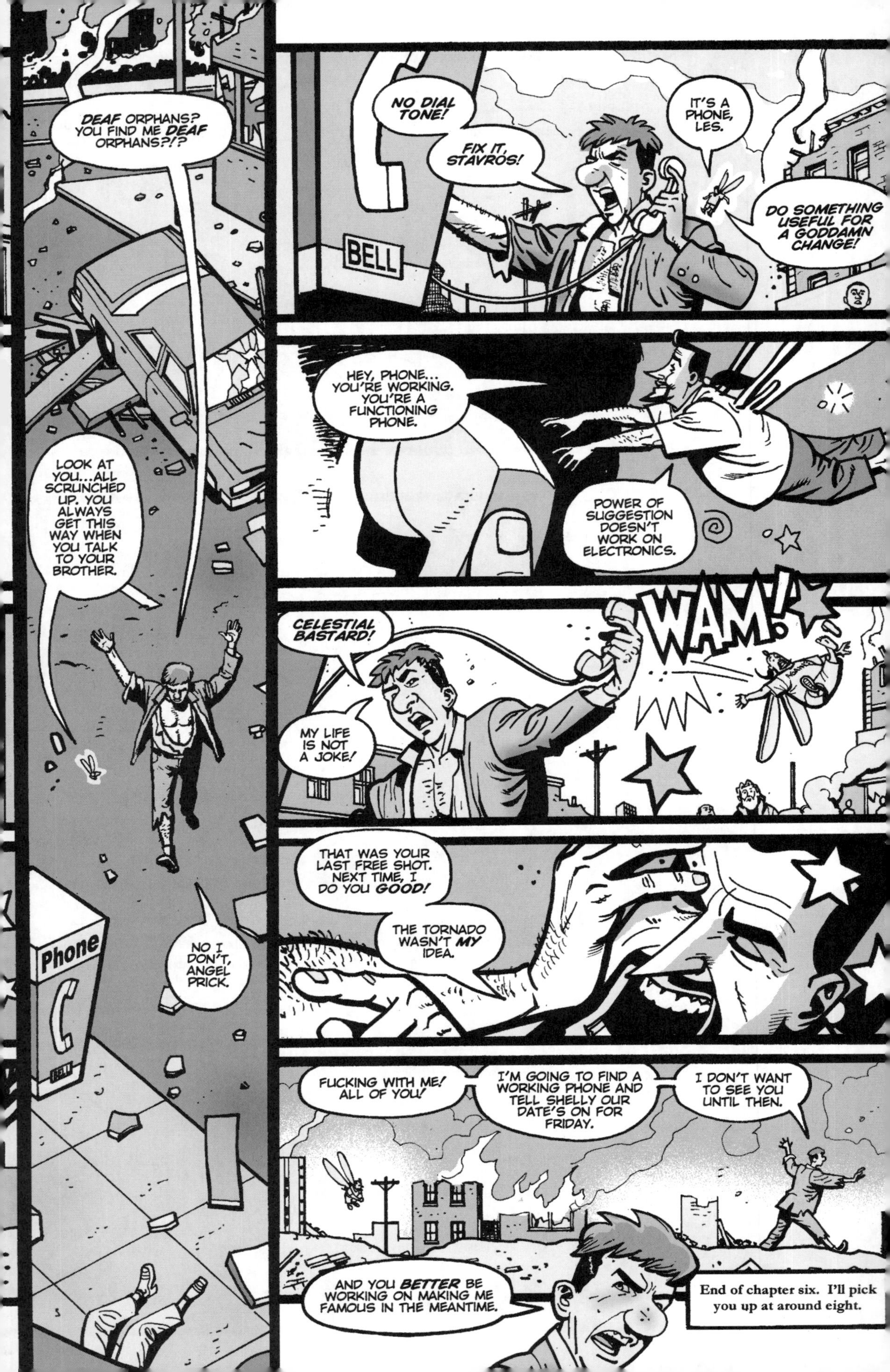
DEAF ORPHANS? YOU FIND ME DEAF ORPHANS?!?
LOOK AT YOU...ALL SCRUNCHED UP. YOU ALWAYS GET THIS WAY WHEN YOU TALK TO YOUR BROTHER.
NO I DON'T, ANGEL PRICK.
Phone
BELL
NO DIAL TONE!
FIX IT, STAVROS!
IT'S A PHONE, LES.
DO SOMETHING USEFUL FOR A GODDAMN CHANGE!
BELL
HEY, PHONE... YOU'RE WORKING. YOU'RE A FUNCTIONING PHONE.
POWER OF SUGGESTION DOESN'T WORK ON ELECTRONICS.
CELESTIAL BASTARD!
WAM!
MY LIFE IS NOT A JOKE!
THAT WAS YOUR LAST FREE SHOT. NEXT TIME, I DO YOU GOOD!
THE TORNADO WASN'T MY IDEA.
FUCKING WITH ME! ALL OF YOU!
I'M GOING TO FIND A WORKING PHONE AND TELL SHELLY OUR DATE'S ON FOR FRIDAY.
I DON'T WANT TO SEE YOU UNTIL THEN.
AND YOU BETTER BE WORKING ON MAKING ME FAMOUS IN THE MEANTIME.
End of chapter six. I'll pick you up at around eight.

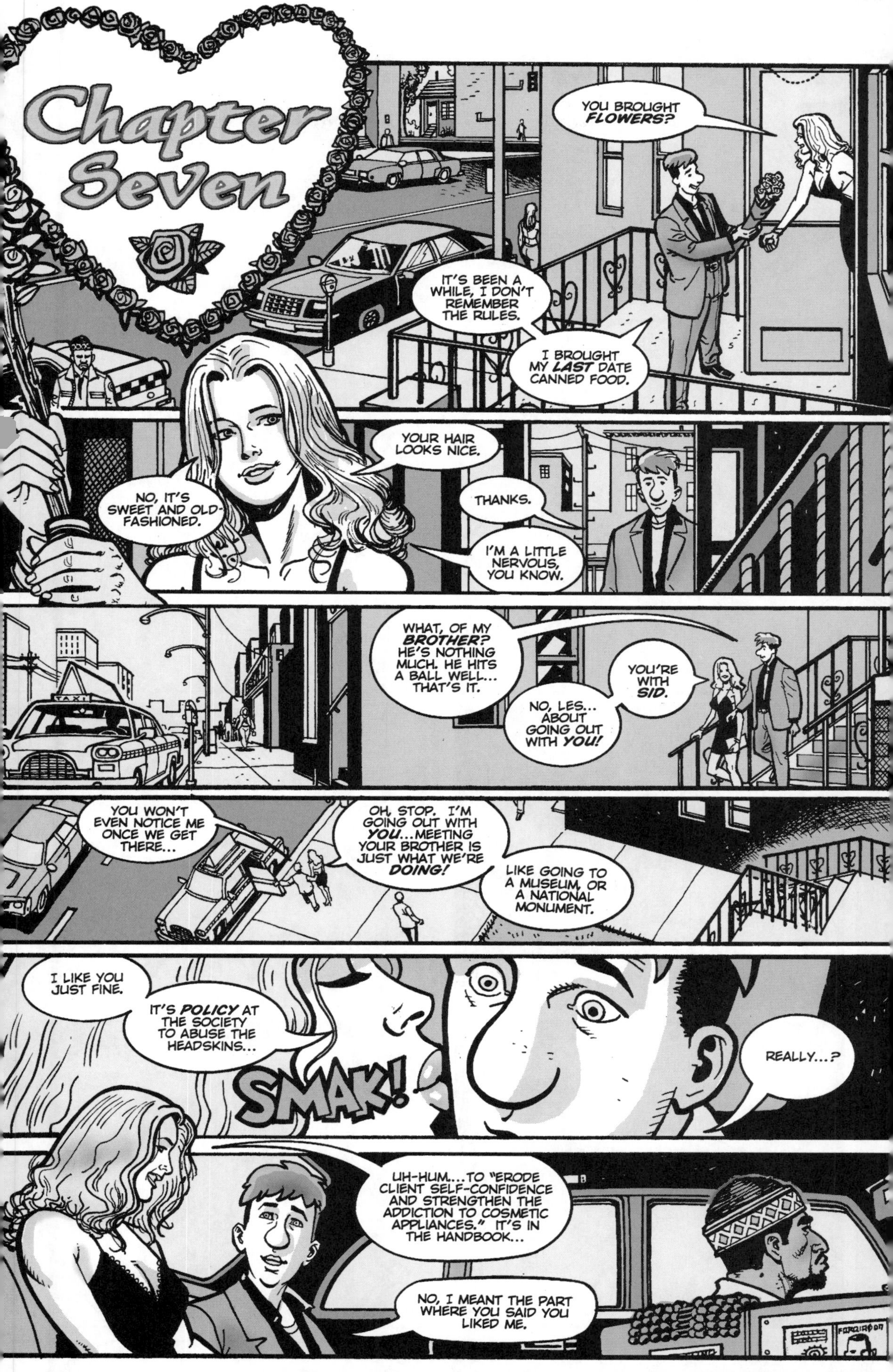
Chapter Seven
YOU BROUGHT FLOWERS?
IT'S BEEN A WHILE, I DON'T REMEMBER THE RULES.
I BROUGHT MY LAST DATE CANNED FOOD.
NO, IT'S SWEET AND OLD-FASHIONED.
YOUR HAIR LOOKS NICE.
THANKS.
I'M A LITTLE NERVOUS, YOU KNOW.
WHAT, OF MY BROTHER? HE'S NOTHING MUCH. HE HITS A BALL WELL... THAT'S IT.
YOU'RE WITH SID.
NO, LES... ABOUT GOING OUT WITH YOU!
YOU WON'T EVEN NOTICE ME ONCE WE GET THERE...
OH, STOP. I'M GOING OUT WITH YOU...MEETING YOUR BROTHER IS JUST WHAT WE'RE DOING!
LIKE GOING TO A MUSEUM, OR A NATIONAL MONUMENT.
I LIKE YOU JUST FINE.
IT'S POLICY AT THE SOCIETY TO ABUSE THE HEADSKINS...
SMAK!
REALLY...?
UH-HUM....TO "ERODE CLIENT SELF-CONFIDENCE AND STRENGTHEN THE ADDICTION TO COSMETIC APPLIANCES." IT'S IN THE HANDBOOK...
NO, I MEANT THE PART WHERE YOU SAID YOU LIKED ME.

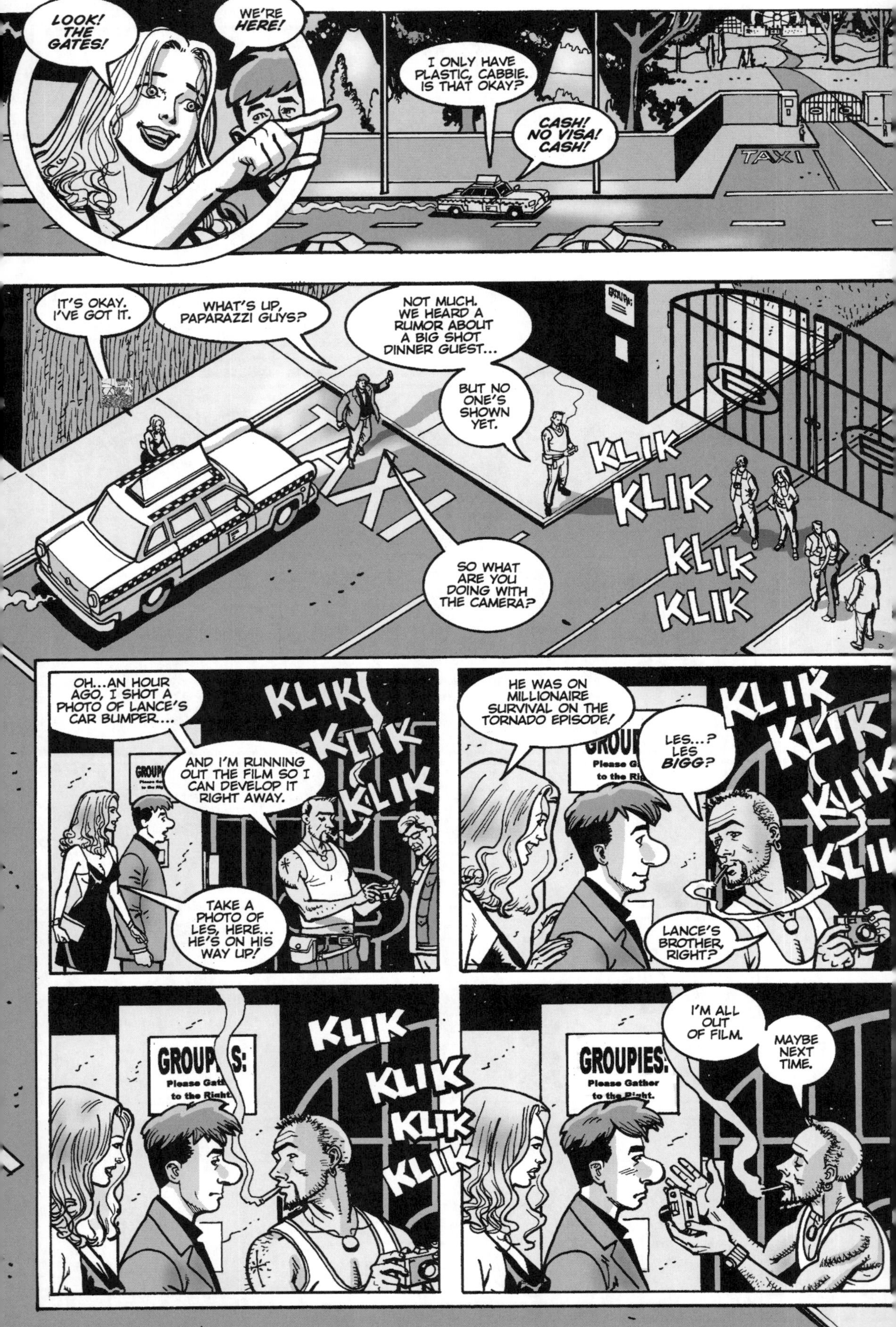
LOOK! THE GATES!
WE'RE HERE!
I ONLY HAVE PLASTIC, CABBIE. IS THAT OKAY?
CASH! NO VISA! CASH!
TAXI
IT'S OKAY. I'VE GOT IT.
WHAT'S UP, PAPARAZZI GUYS?
NOT MUCH. WE HEARD A RUMOR ABOUT A BIG SHOT DINNER GUEST...
BUT NO ONE'S SHOWN YET.
KLIK
KLIK
KLIK
KLIK
SO WHAT ARE YOU DOING WITH THE CAMERA?
OH...AN HOUR AGO, I SHOT A PHOTO OF LANCE'S CAR BUMPER....
AND I'M RUNNING OUT THE FILM SO I CAN DEVELOP IT RIGHT AWAY.
KLIK
KLIK
KLIK
TAKE A PHOTO OF LES, HERE... HE'S ON HIS WAY UP!
HE WAS ON MILLIONAIRE SURVIVAL ON THE TORNADO EPISODE!
LES...? LES BIGG?
KLIK
KLIK
KLIK
LANCE'S BROTHER, RIGHT?
GROUPIES: Please Gather to the Right.
KLIK
KLIK
KLIK
KLIK
GROUPIES: Please Gather to the Right.
I'M ALL OUT OF FILM.
MAYBE NEXT TIME.

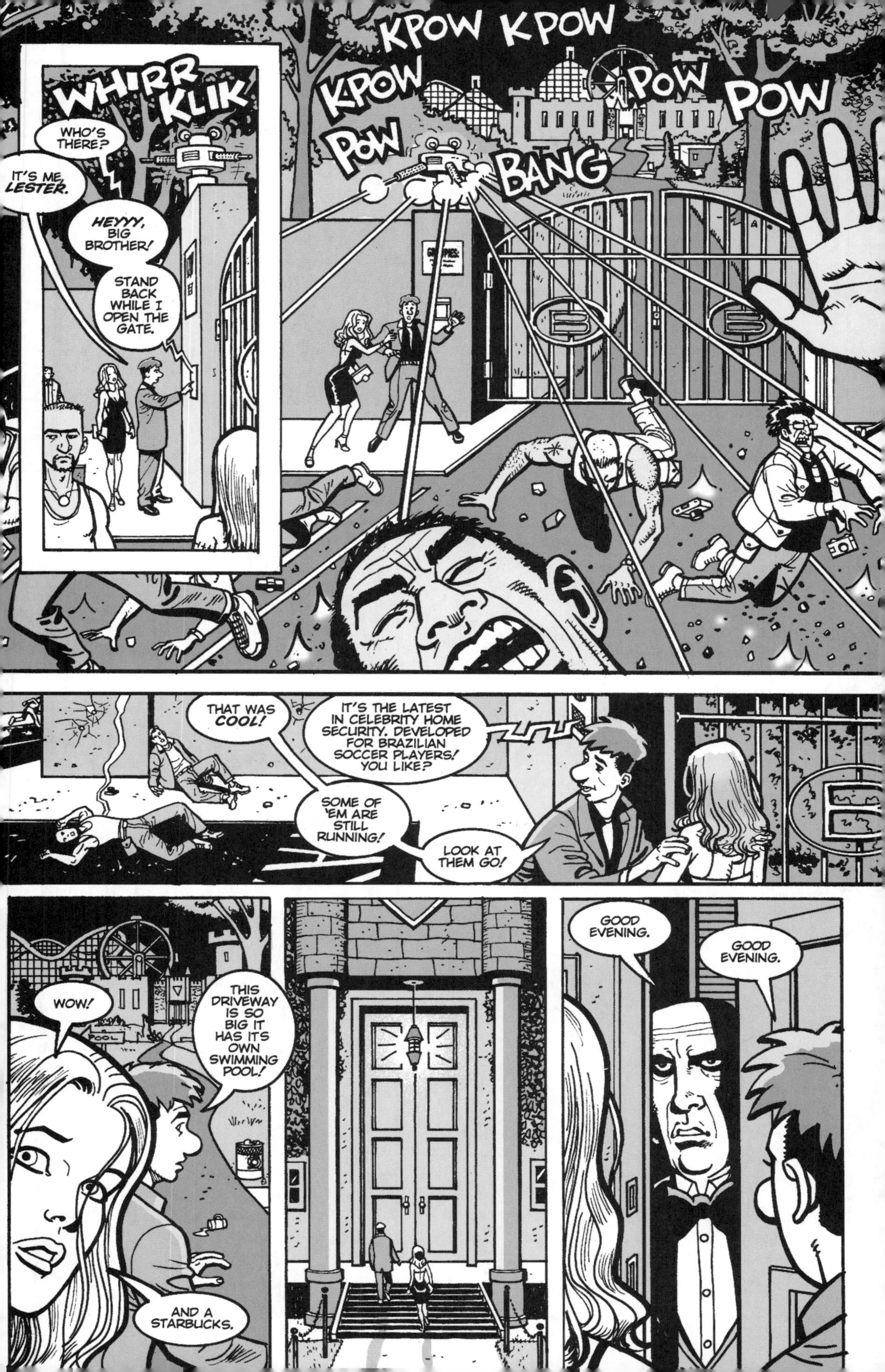

WHIRR KLIK
WHO'S THERE?
IT'S ME, LESTER.
HEYYY, BIG BROTHER!
STAND BACK WHILE I OPEN THE GATE.
KPOW KPOW
KPOW
POW
POW
POW
POW
BANG
THAT WAS COOL!
IT'S THE LATEST IN CELEBRITY HOME SECURITY. DEVELOPED FOR BRAZILIAN SOCCER PLAYERS! YOU LIKE?
SOME OF 'EM ARE STILL RUNNING!
LOOK AT THEM GO!
WOW!
THIS DRIVEWAY IS SO BIG IT HAS ITS OWN SWIMMING POOL!
AND A STARBUCKS.
POOL
GOOD EVENING.
GOOD EVENING.

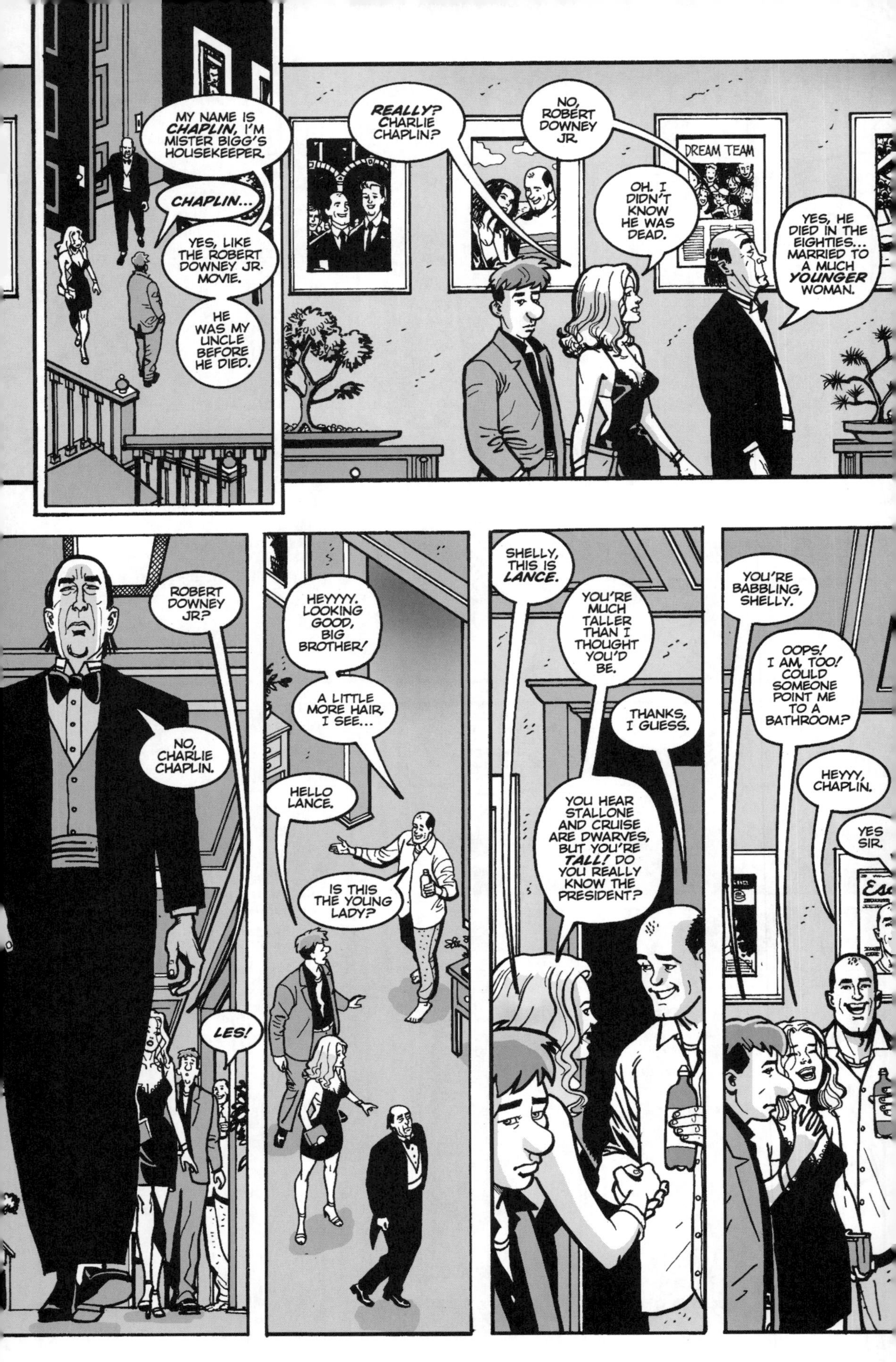
MY NAME IS CHAPLIN, I'M MISTER BIGG'S HOUSEKEEPER.
CHAPLIN...
YES, LIKE THE ROBERT DOWNEY JR. MOVIE.
HE WAS MY UNCLE BEFORE HE DIED.
REALLY? CHARLIE CHAPLIN?
NO, ROBERT DOWNEY JR.
DREAM TEAM
OH, I DIDN'T KNOW HE WAS DEAD.
YES, HE DIED IN THE EIGHTIES... MARRIED TO A MUCH YOUNGER WOMAN.
ROBERT DOWNEY JR?
NO, CHARLIE CHAPLIN.
LES!
HEYYYY. LOOKING GOOD, BIG BROTHER!
A LITTLE MORE HAIR, I SEE...
HELLO LANCE.
IS THIS THE YOUNG LADY?
SHELLY, THIS IS LANCE.
YOU'RE MUCH TALLER THAN I THOUGHT YOU'D BE.
THANKS, I GUESS.
YOU HEAR STALLONE AND CRUISE ARE DWARVES, BUT YOU'RE TALL! DO YOU REALLY KNOW THE PRESIDENT?
YOU'RE BABBLING, SHELLY.
OOPS! I AM, TOO! COULD SOMEONE POINT ME TO A BATHROOM?
HEYYY, CHAPLIN.
YES SIR.

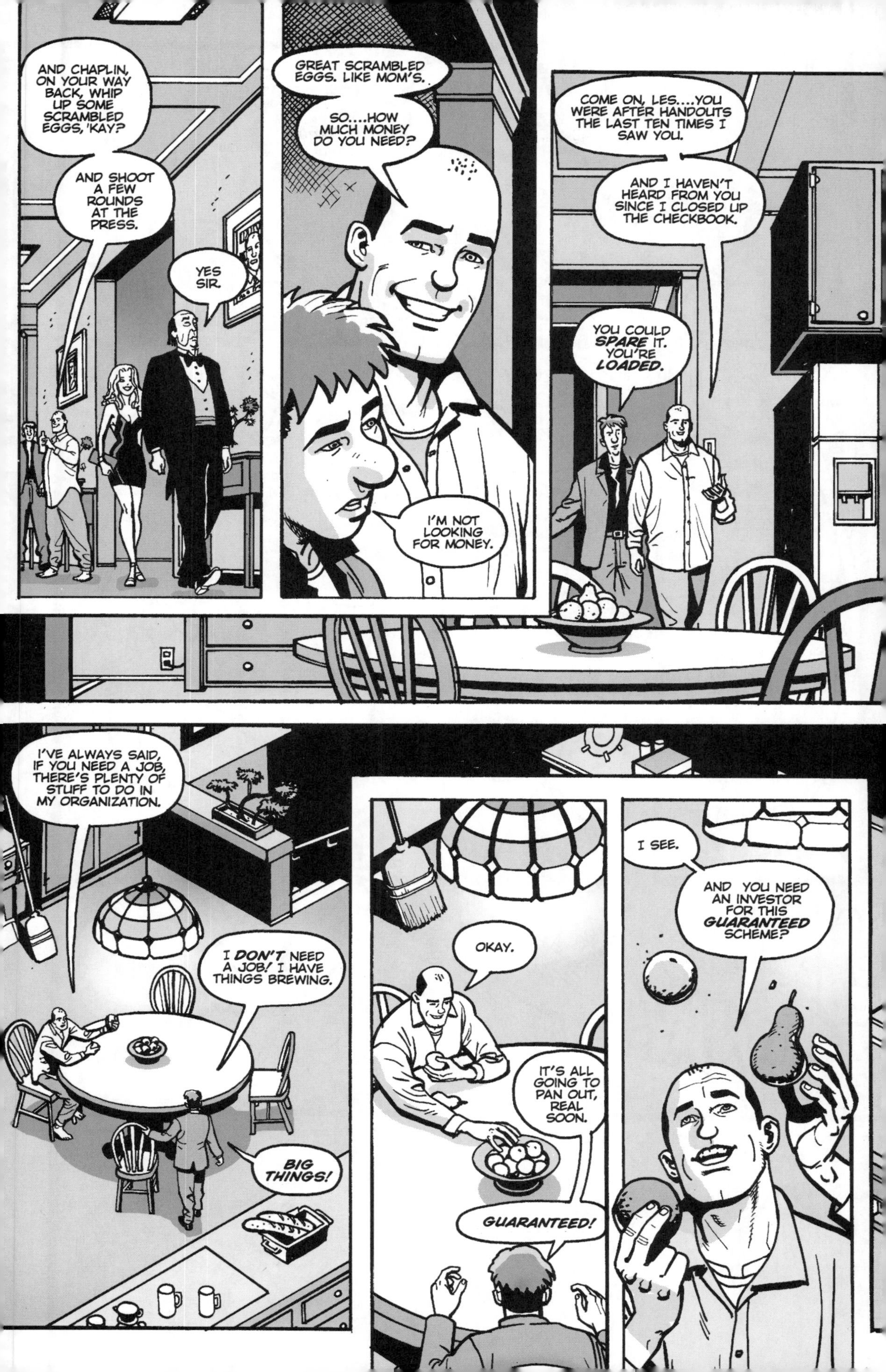

AND CHAPLIN, ON YOUR WAY BACK, WHIP UP SOME SCRAMBLED EGGS, 'KAY?
AND SHOOT A FEW ROUNDS AT THE PRESS.
YES SIR.
GREAT SCRAMBLED EGGS. LIKE MOM'S.
SO....HOW MUCH MONEY DO YOU NEED?
I'M NOT LOOKING FOR MONEY.
COME ON, LES....YOU WERE AFTER HANDOUTS THE LAST TEN TIMES I SAW YOU.
AND I HAVEN'T HEARD FROM YOU SINCE I CLOSED UP THE CHECKBOOK.
YOU COULD SPARE IT. YOU'RE LOADED.
I'VE ALWAYS SAID, IF YOU NEED A JOB, THERE'S PLENTY OF STUFF TO DO IN MY ORGANIZATION.
I DON'T NEED A JOB! I HAVE THINGS BREWING.
BIG THINGS!
OKAY.
IT'S ALL GOING TO PAN OUT, REAL SOON.
GUARANTEED!
I SEE.
AND YOU NEED AN INVESTOR FOR THIS GUARANTEED SCHEME?

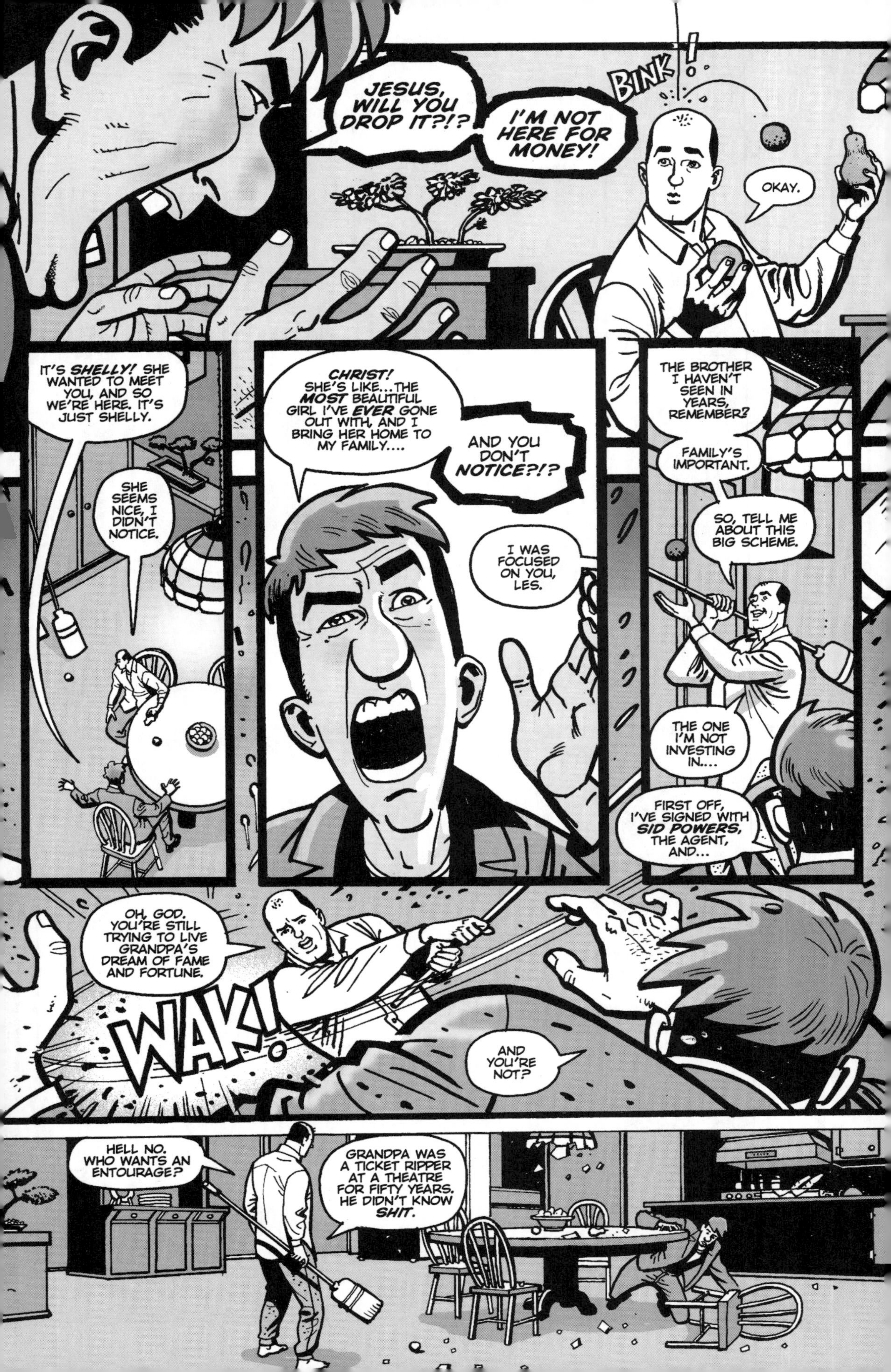
JESUS, WILL YOU DROP IT?!?
I'M NOT HERE FOR MONEY!
BINK!
OKAY.
IT'S SHELLY! SHE WANTED TO MEET YOU, AND SO WE'RE HERE. IT'S JUST SHELLY.
SHE SEEMS NICE, I DIDN'T NOTICE.
CHRIST! SHE'S LIKE...THE MOST BEAUTIFUL GIRL I'VE EVER GONE OUT WITH, AND I BRING HER HOME TO MY FAMILY....
AND YOU DON'T NOTICE?!?
I WAS FOCUSED ON YOU, LES.
THE BROTHER I HAVEN'T SEEN IN YEARS, REMEMBER?
FAMILY'S IMPORTANT.
SO, TELL ME ABOUT THIS BIG SCHEME.
THE ONE I'M NOT INVESTING IN....
FIRST OFF, I'VE SIGNED WITH SID POWERS, THE AGENT, AND...
OH, GOD. YOU'RE STILL TRYING TO LIVE GRANDPA'S DREAM OF FAME AND FORTUNE.
WAK!
AND YOU'RE NOT?
HELL NO. WHO WANTS AN ENTOURAGE?
GRANDPA WAS A TICKET RIPPER AT A THEATRE FOR FIFTY YEARS. HE DIDN'T KNOW SHIT.

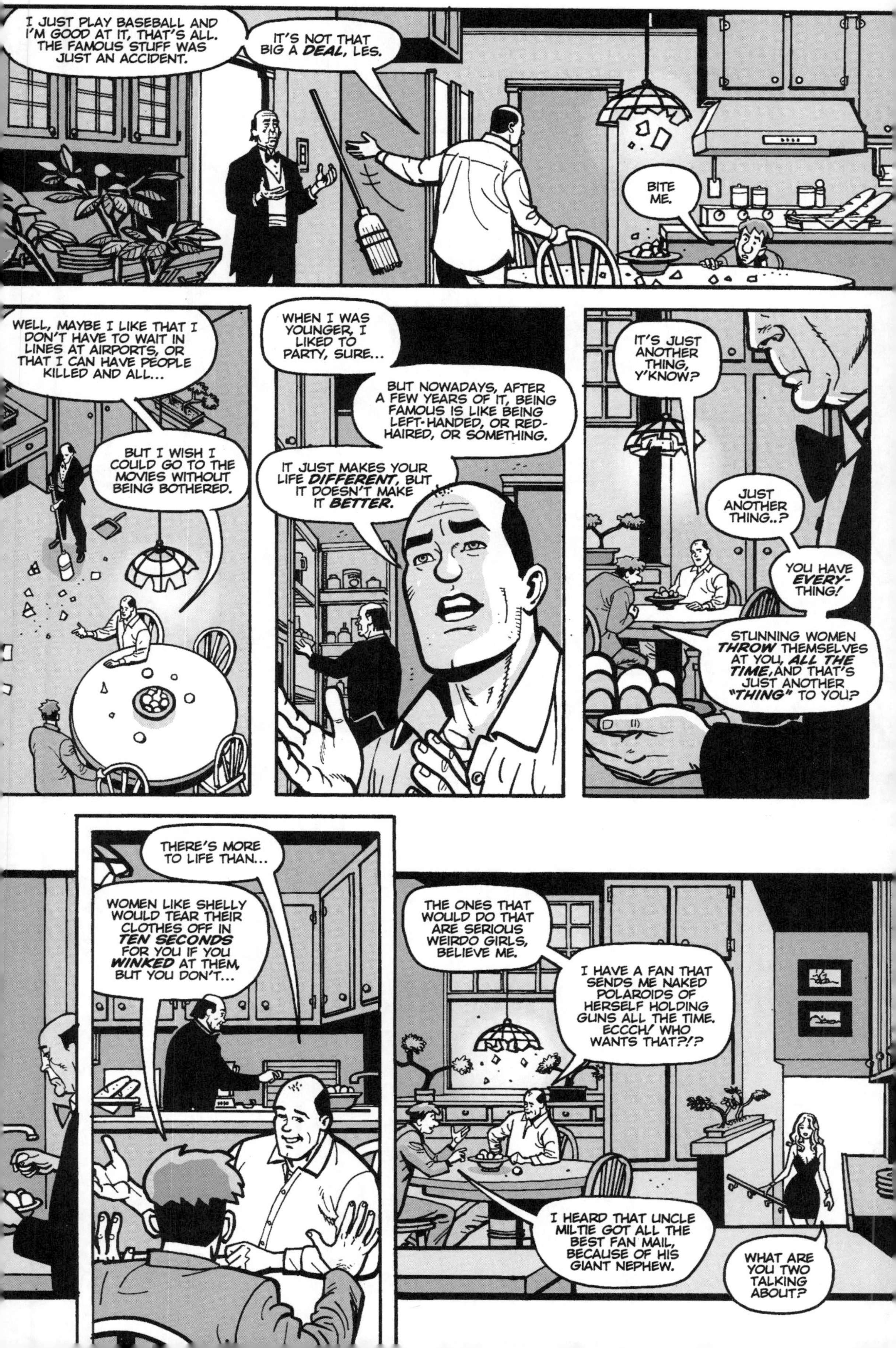
I JUST PLAY BASEBALL AND I'M GOOD AT IT, THAT'S ALL. THE FAMOUS STUFF WAS JUST AN ACCIDENT.
IT'S NOT THAT BIG A DEAL, LES.
BITE ME.
WELL, MAYBE I LIKE THAT I DON'T HAVE TO WAIT IN LINES AT AIRPORTS, OR THAT I CAN HAVE PEOPLE KILLED AND ALL...
BUT I WISH I COULD GO TO THE MOVIES WITHOUT BEING BOTHERED.
WHEN I WAS YOUNGER, I LIKED TO PARTY, SURE...
BUT NOWADAYS, AFTER A FEW YEARS OF IT, BEING FAMOUS IS LIKE BEING LEFT-HANDED, OR RED-HAIRED, OR SOMETHING.
IT JUST MAKES YOUR LIFE DIFFERENT, BUT IT DOESN'T MAKE IT BETTER.
IT'S JUST ANOTHER THING, Y'KNOW?
JUST ANOTHER THING..?
YOU HAVE EVERY-THING!
STUNNING WOMEN THROW THEMSELVES AT YOU, ALL THE TIME, AND THAT'S JUST ANOTHER "THING" TO YOU?
THERE'S MORE TO LIFE THAN...
WOMEN LIKE SHELLY WOULD TEAR THEIR CLOTHES OFF IN TEN SECONDS FOR YOU IF YOU WINKED AT THEM, BUT YOU DON'T...
THE ONES THAT WOULD DO THAT ARE SERIOUS WEIRDO GIRLS, BELIEVE ME.
I HAVE A FAN THAT SENDS ME NAKED POLAROIDS OF HERSELF HOLDING GUNS ALL THE TIME. ECCCH! WHO WANTS THAT?!?
I HEARD THAT UNCLE MILTIE GOT ALL THE BEST FAN MAIL, BECAUSE OF HIS GIANT NEPHEW.
WHAT ARE YOU TWO TALKING ABOUT?

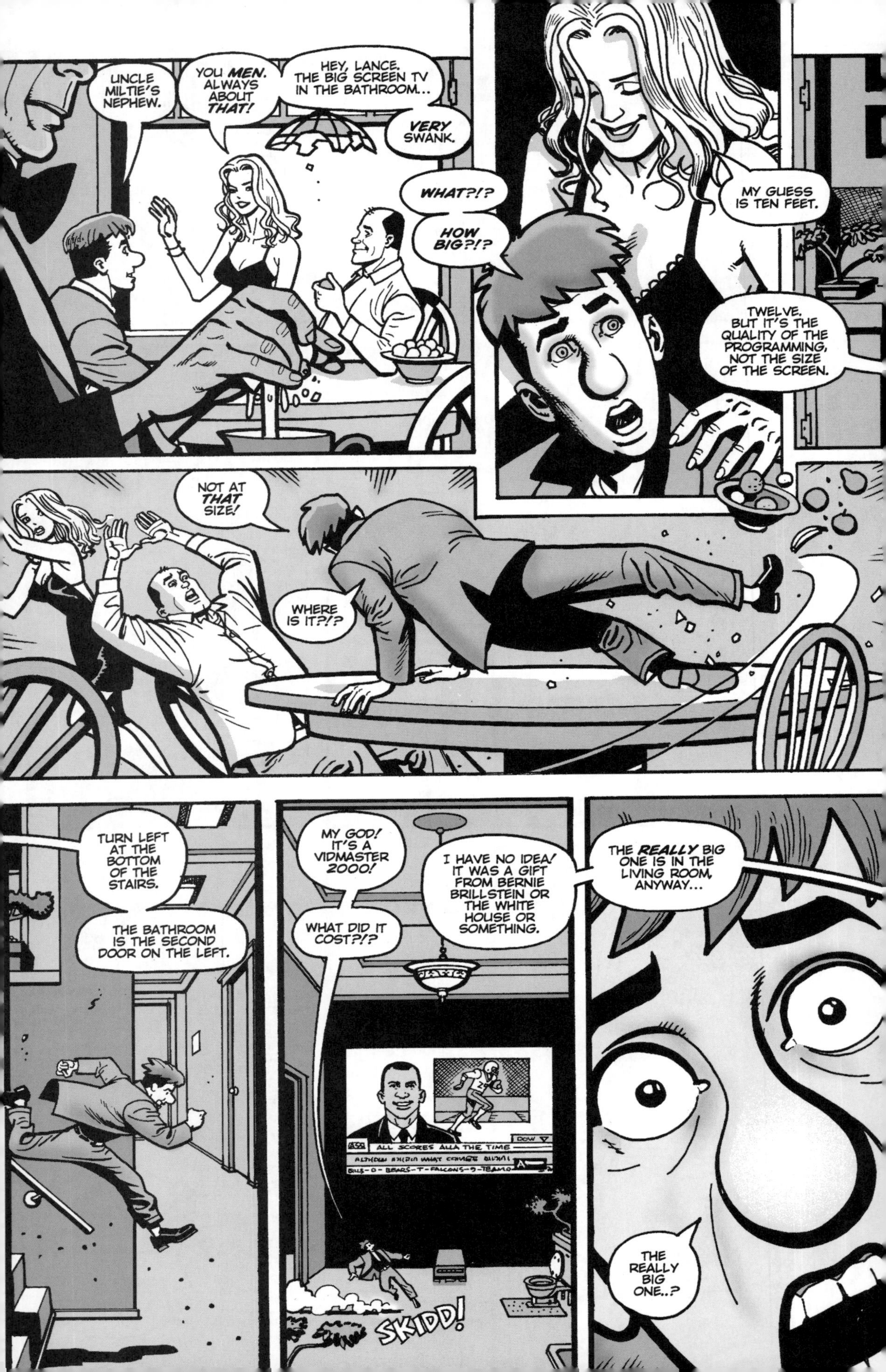
UNCLE MILTIE'S NEPHEW.
YOU **MEN**. ALWAYS ABOUT ***THAT!***
HEY, LANCE. THE BIG SCREEN TV IN THE BATHROOM...
VERY SWANK.
WHAT?!?
HOW BIG?!?
MY GUESS IS TEN FEET.
TWELVE. BUT IT'S THE QUALITY OF THE PROGRAMMING, NOT THE SIZE OF THE SCREEN.
NOT AT ***THAT*** SIZE!
WHERE IS IT?!?
TURN LEFT AT THE BOTTOM OF THE STAIRS.
THE BATHROOM IS THE SECOND DOOR ON THE LEFT.
MY GOD! IT'S A VIDMASTER *2000!*
WHAT DID IT COST?!?
I HAVE NO IDEA! IT WAS A GIFT FROM BERNIE BRILLSTEIN OR THE WHITE HOUSE OR SOMETHING.
THE ***REALLY*** BIG ONE IS IN THE LIVING ROOM, ANYWAY...
THE REALLY BIG ONE..?
ALL SCORES ALLA THE TIME
SKIDD!

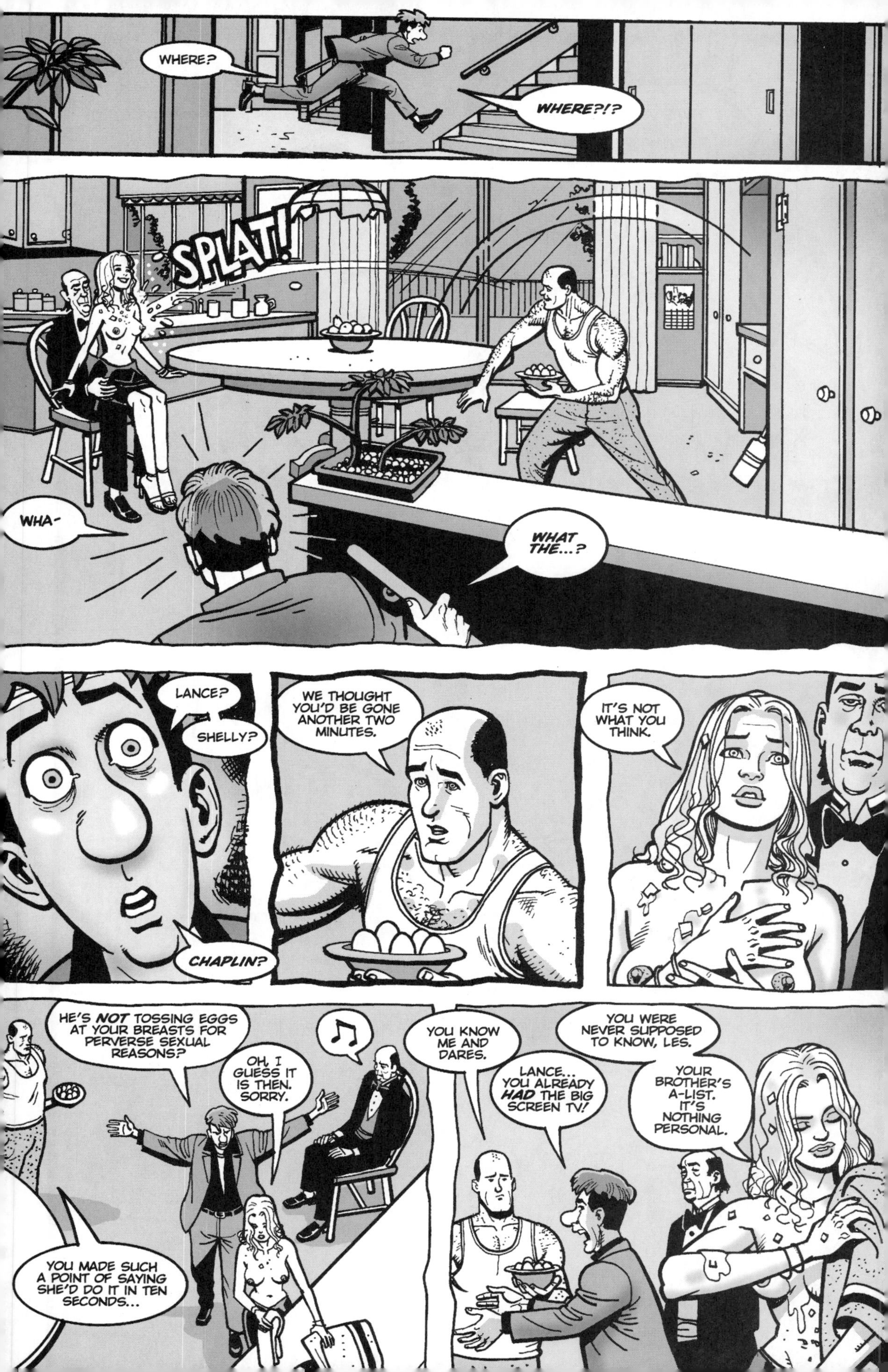

WHERE?
WHERE?!?
SPLAT!
WHA-
WHAT THE...?
LANCE?
SHELLY?
CHAPLIN?
WE THOUGHT YOU'D BE GONE ANOTHER TWO MINUTES.
IT'S NOT WHAT YOU THINK.
HE'S NOT TOSSING EGGS AT YOUR BREASTS FOR PERVERSE SEXUAL REASONS?
♫
OH, I GUESS IT IS THEN. SORRY.
YOU MADE SUCH A POINT OF SAYING SHE'D DO IT IN TEN SECONDS...
YOU KNOW ME AND DARES.
LANCE... YOU ALREADY HAD THE BIG SCREEN TV!
YOU WERE NEVER SUPPOSED TO KNOW, LES.
YOUR BROTHER'S A-LIST. IT'S NOTHING PERSONAL.

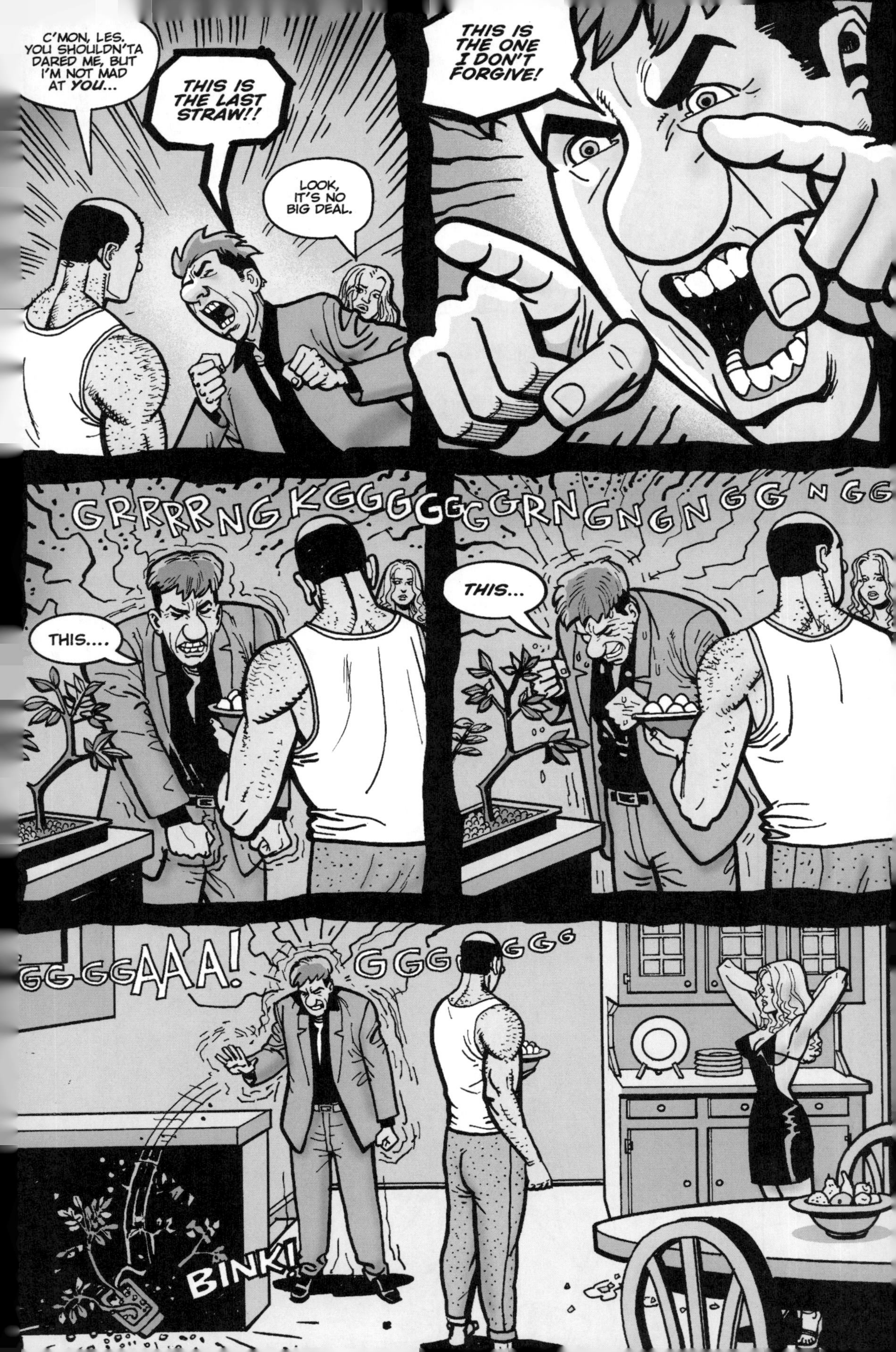
C'MON, LES. YOU SHOULDN'TA DARED ME, BUT I'M NOT MAD AT YOU...
THIS IS THE LAST STRAW!!
LOOK, IT'S NO BIG DEAL.
THIS IS THE ONE I DON'T FORGIVE!
GRRRRNGKGGGGGGRNGNGNGG NGG
THIS....
THIS...
GGGGGAAA!
GGGGGG
BINK!

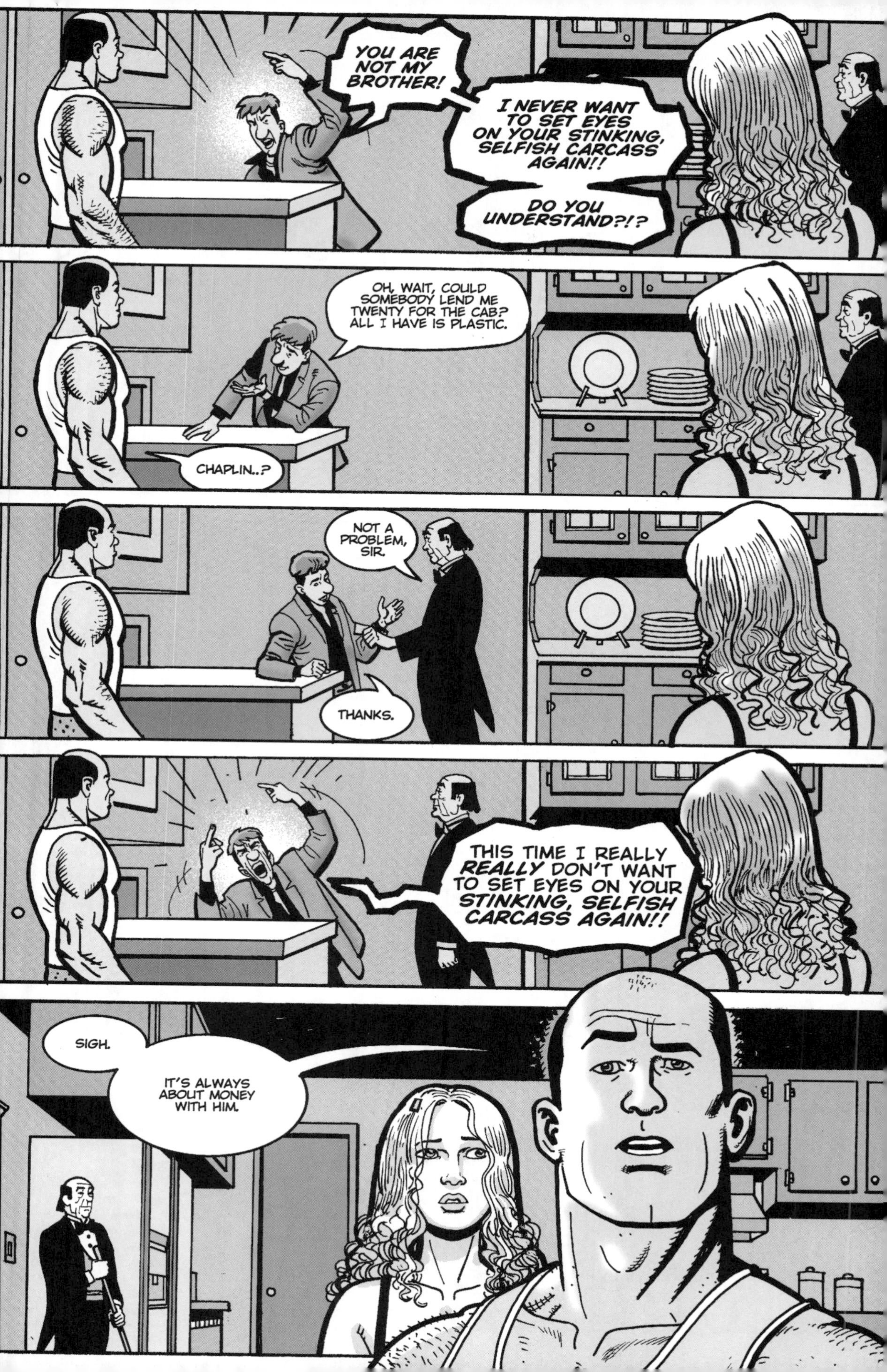
YOU ARE NOT MY BROTHER!
I NEVER WANT TO SET EYES ON YOUR STINKING, SELFISH CARCASS AGAIN!!
DO YOU UNDERSTAND?!?
OH, WAIT, COULD SOMEBODY LEND ME TWENTY FOR THE CAB? ALL I HAVE IS PLASTIC.
CHAPLIN..?
NOT A PROBLEM, SIR.
THANKS.
THIS TIME I REALLY *REALLY* DON'T WANT TO SET EYES ON YOUR *STINKING, SELFISH CARCASS AGAIN!!*
SIGH.
IT'S ALWAYS ABOUT MONEY WITH HIM.

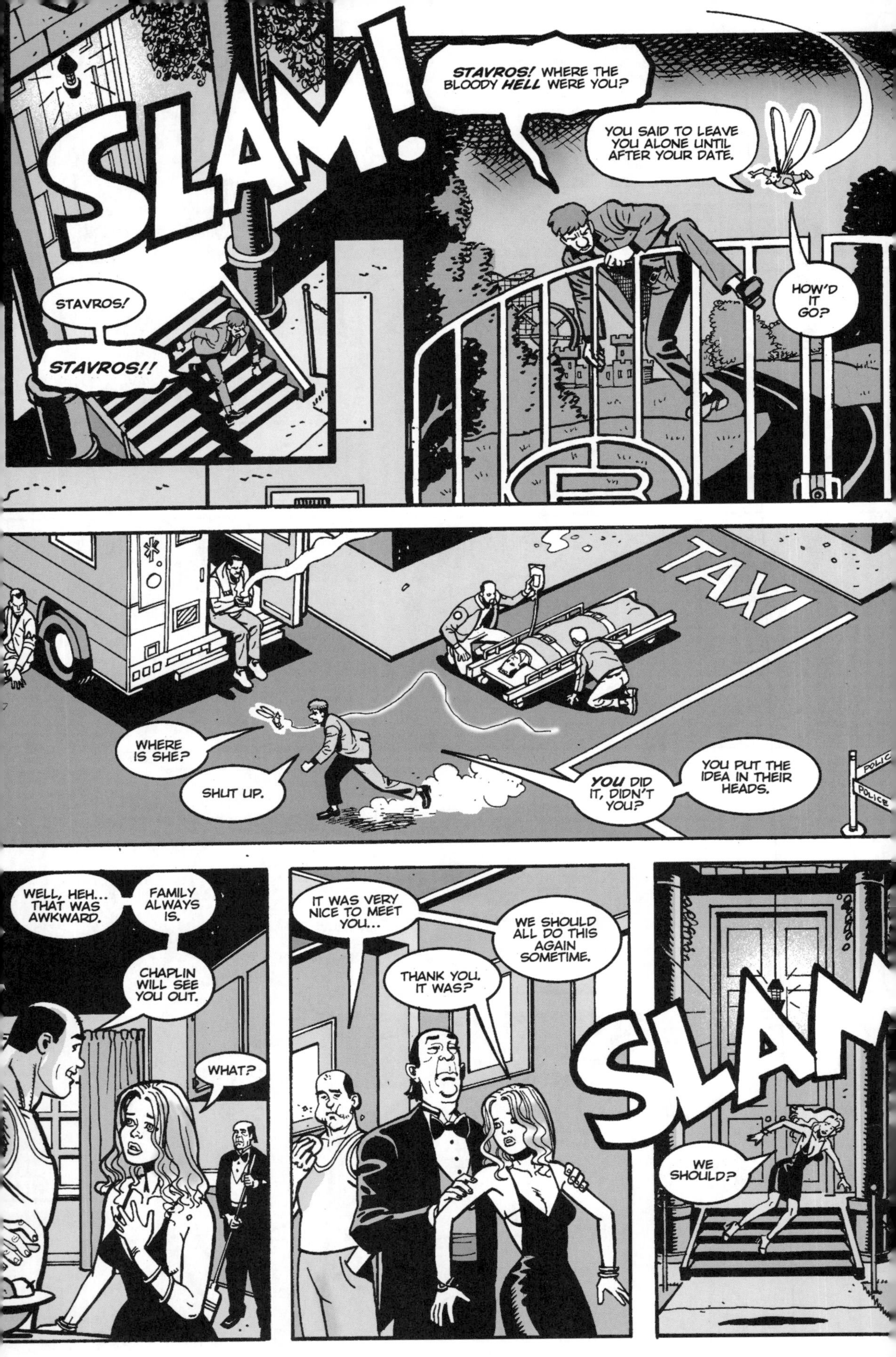
SLAM!
STAVROS! WHERE THE BLOODY HELL WERE YOU?
YOU SAID TO LEAVE YOU ALONE UNTIL AFTER YOUR DATE.
STAVROS!
STAVROS!!
HOW'D IT GO?
TAXI
WHERE IS SHE?
SHUT UP.
YOU DID IT, DIDN'T YOU?
YOU PUT THE IDEA IN THEIR HEADS.
POLICE
WELL, HEH... THAT WAS AWKWARD.
FAMILY ALWAYS IS.
CHAPLIN WILL SEE YOU OUT.
WHAT?
IT WAS VERY NICE TO MEET YOU...
WE SHOULD ALL DO THIS AGAIN SOMETIME.
THANK YOU. IT WAS?
SLAM
WE SHOULD?

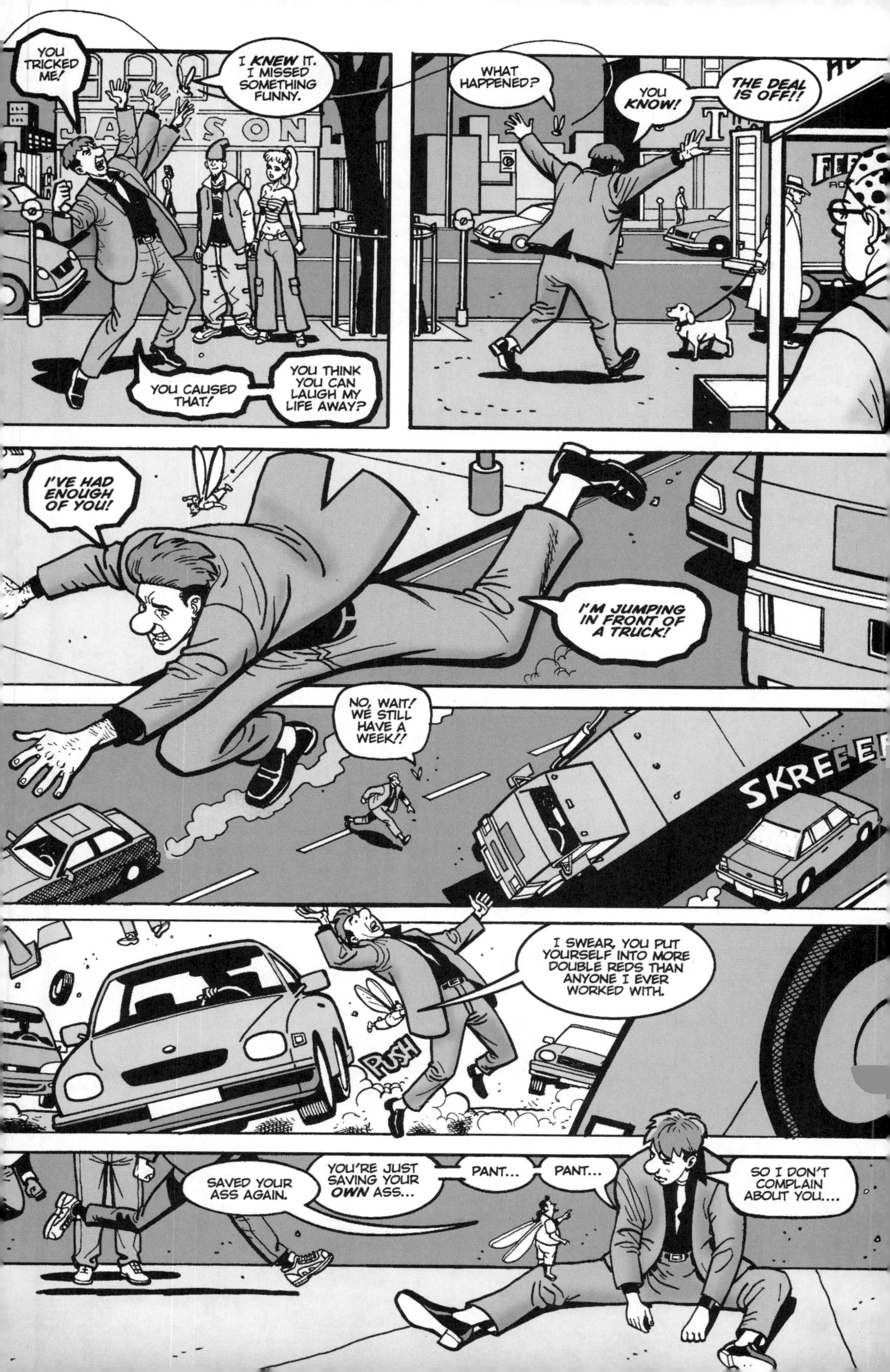
YOU TRICKED ME!
I KNEW IT. I MISSED SOMETHING FUNNY.
YOU CAUSED THAT!
YOU THINK YOU CAN LAUGH MY LIFE AWAY?
JACKSON
WHAT HAPPENED?
YOU KNOW!
THE DEAL IS OFF!!
I'VE HAD ENOUGH OF YOU!
I'M JUMPING IN FRONT OF A TRUCK!
NO, WAIT! WE STILL HAVE A WEEK!!
SKREEE
I SWEAR, YOU PUT YOURSELF INTO MORE DOUBLE REDS THAN ANYONE I EVER WORKED WITH.
PUSH
SAVED YOUR ASS AGAIN.
YOU'RE JUST SAVING YOUR OWN ASS...
PANT...
PANT...
SO I DON'T COMPLAIN ABOUT YOU....

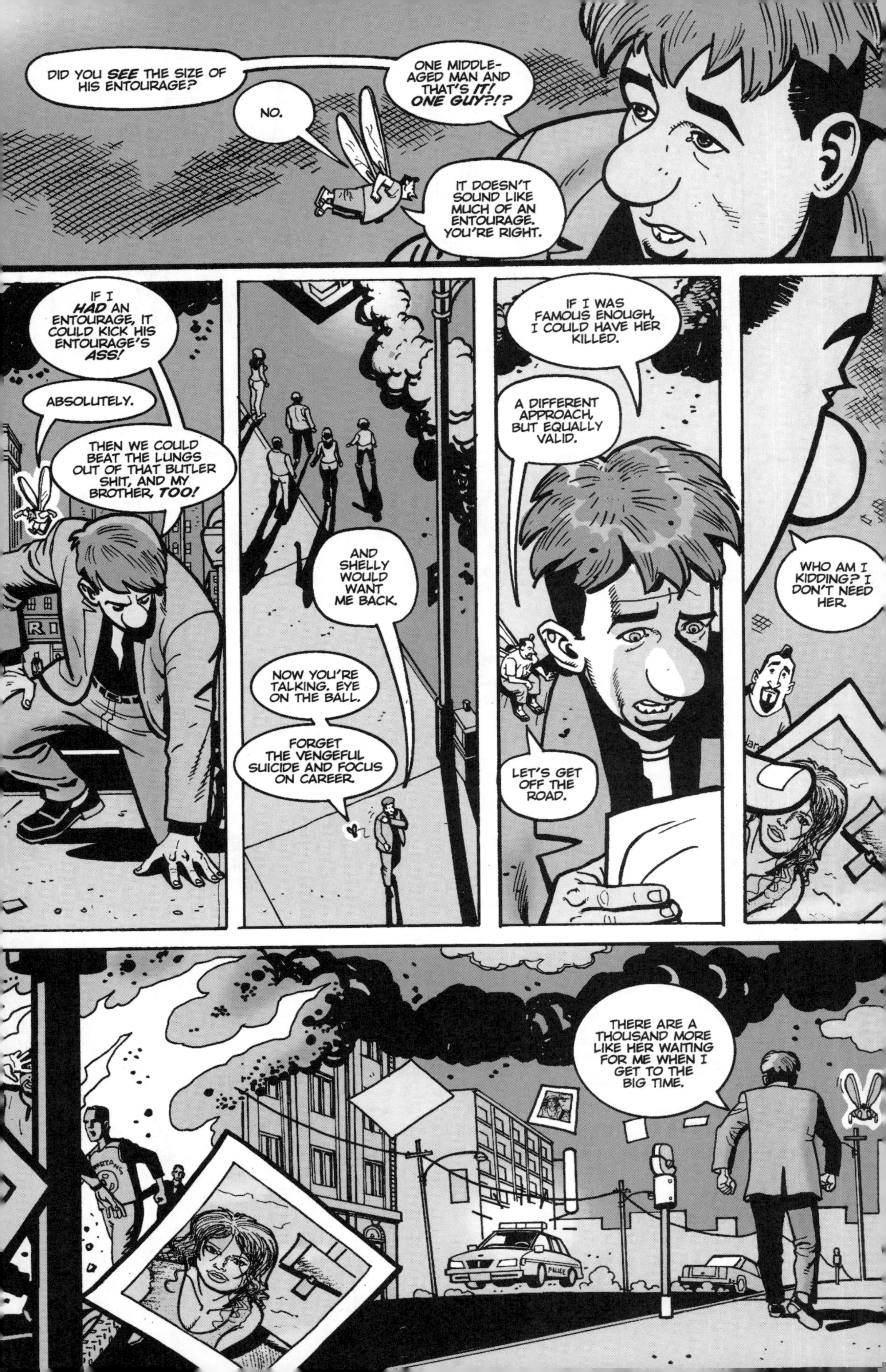
DID YOU SEE THE SIZE OF HIS ENTOURAGE?
NO.
ONE MIDDLE-AGED MAN AND THAT'S IT! ONE GUY?!?
IT DOESN'T SOUND LIKE MUCH OF AN ENTOURAGE. YOU'RE RIGHT.
IF I HAD AN ENTOURAGE, IT COULD KICK HIS ENTOURAGE'S ASS!
ABSOLUTELY.
THEN WE COULD BEAT THE LUNGS OUT OF THAT BUTLER SHIT, AND MY BROTHER, TOO!
AND SHELLY WOULD WANT ME BACK.
NOW YOU'RE TALKING. EYE ON THE BALL.
FORGET THE VENGEFUL SUICIDE AND FOCUS ON CAREER.
IF I WAS FAMOUS ENOUGH, I COULD HAVE HER KILLED.
A DIFFERENT APPROACH, BUT EQUALLY VALID.
LET'S GET OFF THE ROAD.
WHO AM I KIDDING? I DON'T NEED HER.
THERE ARE A THOUSAND MORE LIKE HER WAITING FOR ME WHEN I GET TO THE BIG TIME.

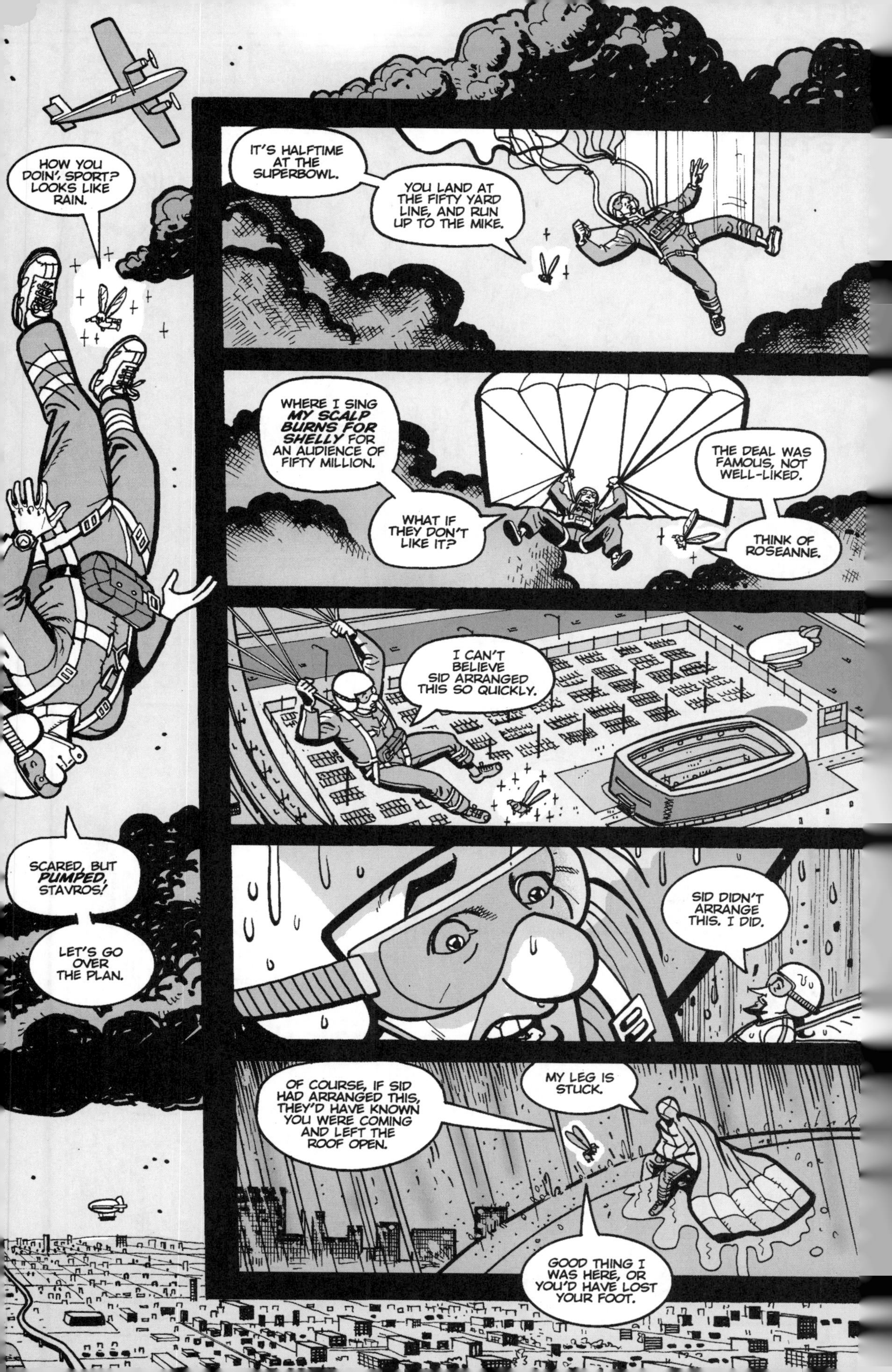

HOW YOU DOIN', SPORT? LOOKS LIKE RAIN.
IT'S HALFTIME AT THE SUPERBOWL.
YOU LAND AT THE FIFTY YARD LINE, AND RUN UP TO THE MIKE.
WHERE I SING *MY SCALP BURNS FOR SHELLY* FOR AN AUDIENCE OF FIFTY MILLION.
WHAT IF THEY DON'T LIKE IT?
THE DEAL WAS FAMOUS, NOT WELL-LIKED.
THINK OF ROSEANNE.
I CAN'T BELIEVE SID ARRANGED THIS SO QUICKLY.
SCARED, BUT *PUMPED*, STAVROS!
LET'S GO OVER THE PLAN.
SID DIDN'T ARRANGE THIS. I DID.
OF COURSE, IF SID HAD ARRANGED THIS, THEY'D HAVE KNOWN YOU WERE COMING AND LEFT THE ROOF OPEN.
MY LEG IS STUCK.
GOOD THING I WAS HERE, OR YOU'D HAVE LOST YOUR FOOT.

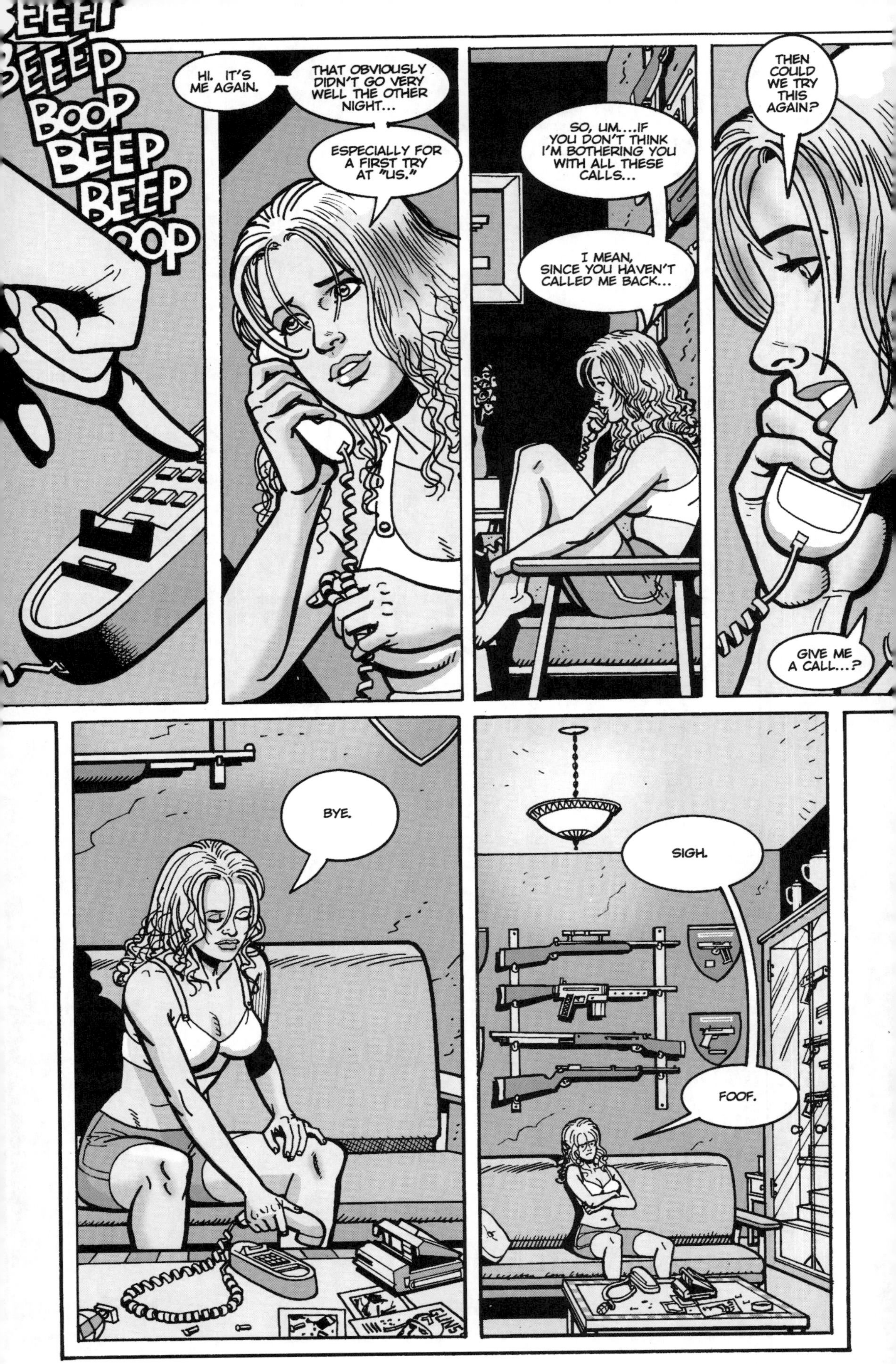
BEEEP
BOOP
BEEP
BEEP
HI. IT'S ME AGAIN.
THAT OBVIOUSLY DIDN'T GO VERY WELL THE OTHER NIGHT...
ESPECIALLY FOR A FIRST TRY AT "US."
SO, UM....IF YOU DON'T THINK I'M BOTHERING YOU WITH ALL THESE CALLS...
I MEAN, SINCE YOU HAVEN'T CALLED ME BACK...
THEN COULD WE TRY THIS AGAIN?
GIVE ME A CALL...?
BYE.
SIGH.
FOOF.

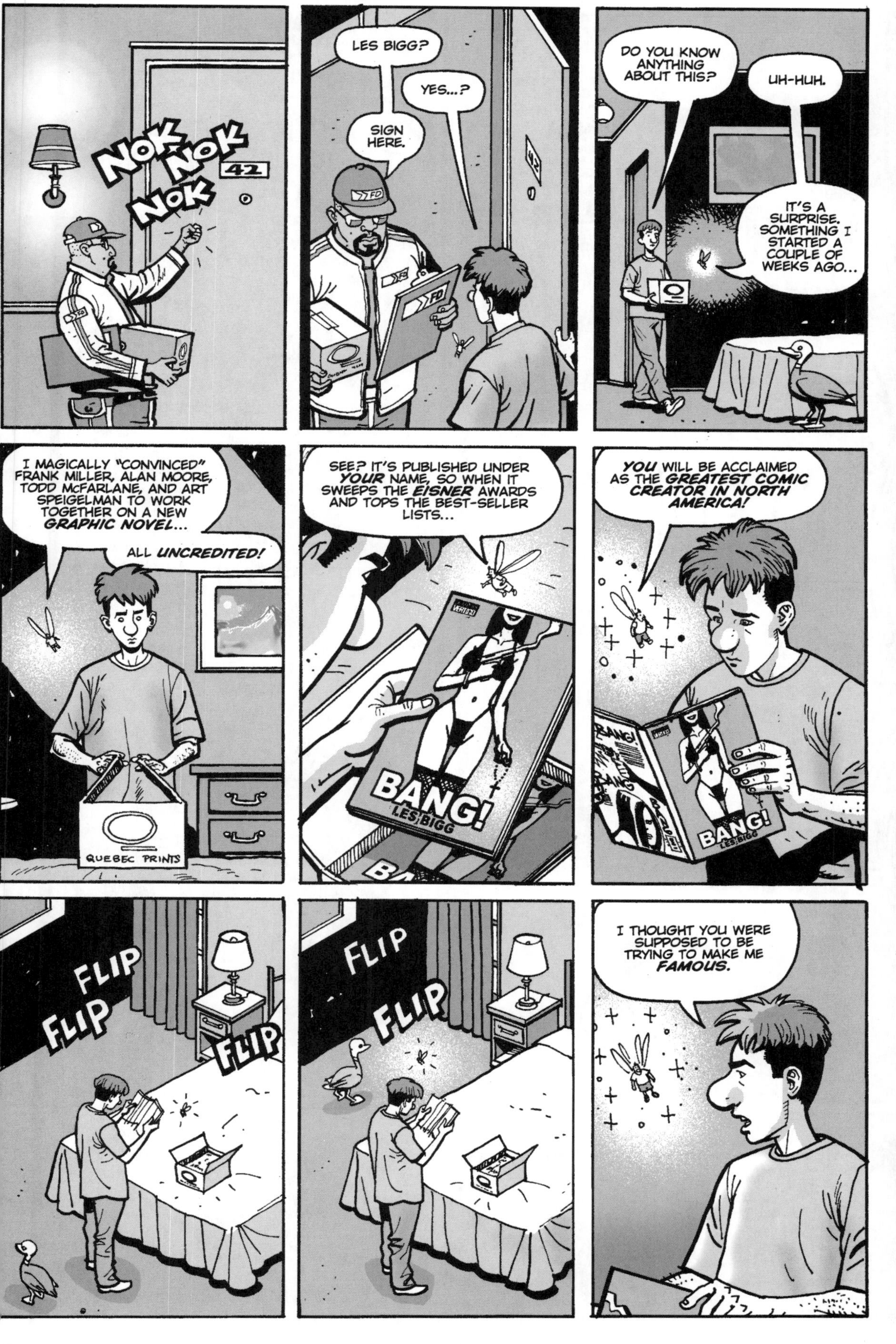
NOK NOK NOK
42
LES BIGG?
YES...?
SIGN HERE.
DO YOU KNOW ANYTHING ABOUT THIS?
UH-HUH.
IT'S A SURPRISE. SOMETHING I STARTED A COUPLE OF WEEKS AGO...
I MAGICALLY "CONVINCED" FRANK MILLER, ALAN MOORE, TODD McFARLANE, AND ART SPEIGELMAN TO WORK TOGETHER ON A NEW GRAPHIC NOVEL...
ALL UNCREDITED!
QUEBEC PRINTS
SEE? IT'S PUBLISHED UNDER YOUR NAME, SO WHEN IT SWEEPS THE EISNER AWARDS AND TOPS THE BEST-SELLER LISTS...
BANG! LES BIGG
YOU WILL BE ACCLAIMED AS THE GREATEST COMIC CREATOR IN NORTH AMERICA!
BANG! LES BIGG
FLIP FLIP FLIP
FLIP FLIP
I THOUGHT YOU WERE SUPPOSED TO BE TRYING TO MAKE ME FAMOUS.

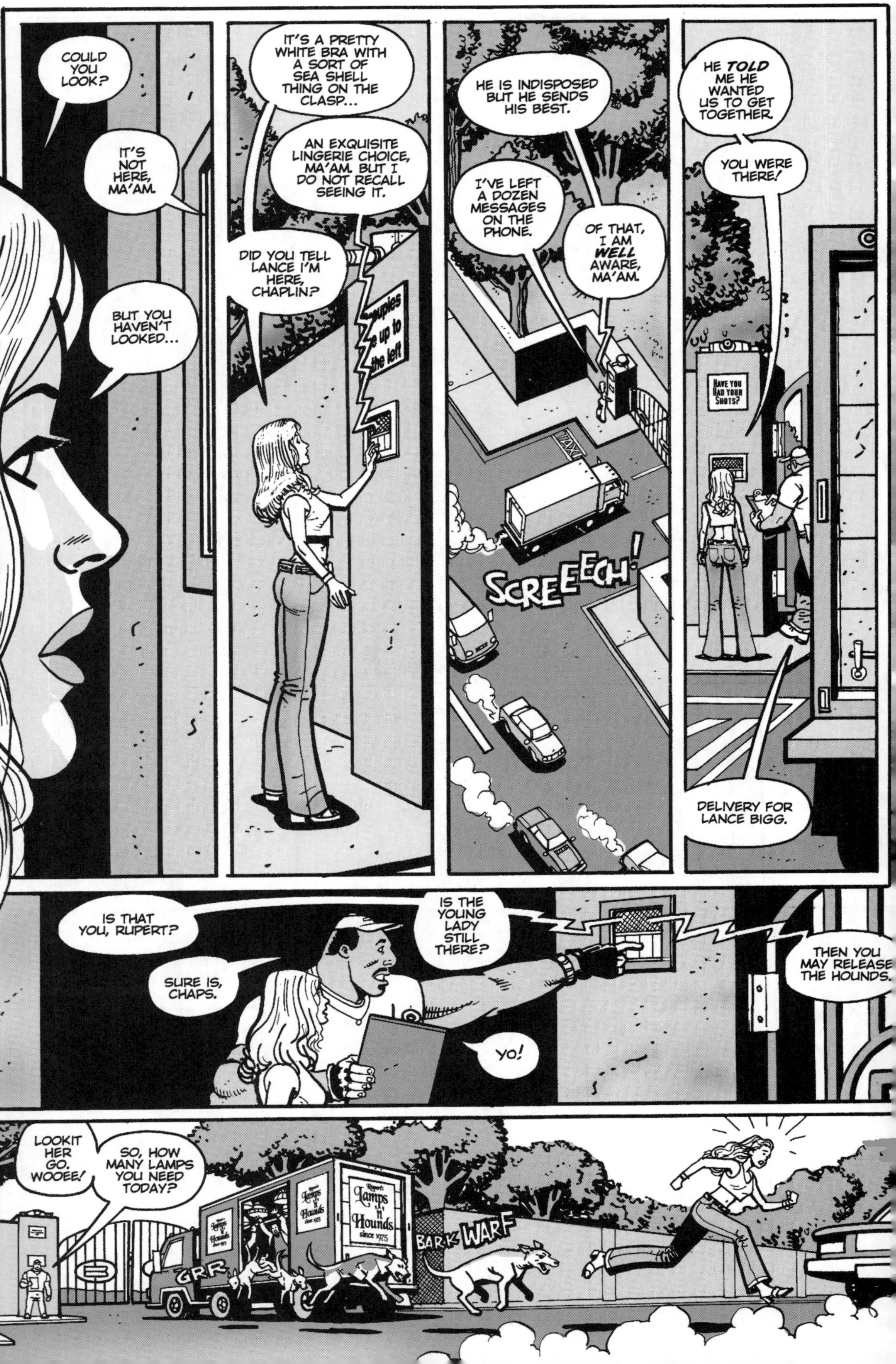
COULD YOU LOOK?
IT'S NOT HERE, MA'AM.
BUT YOU HAVEN'T LOOKED...
IT'S A PRETTY WHITE BRA WITH A SORT OF SEA SHELL THING ON THE CLASP...
AN EXQUISITE LINGERIE CHOICE, MA'AM. BUT I DO NOT RECALL SEEING IT.
DID YOU TELL LANCE I'M HERE, CHAPLIN?
HE IS INDISPOSED BUT HE SENDS HIS BEST.
I'VE LEFT A DOZEN MESSAGES ON THE PHONE.
OF THAT, I AM WELL AWARE, MA'AM.
TAXI
SCREEECH!
HE TOLD ME HE WANTED US TO GET TOGETHER.
YOU WERE THERE!
HAVE YOU HAD YOUR SHOTS?
DELIVERY FOR LANCE BIGG.
IS THAT YOU, RUPERT?
SURE IS, CHAPS.
IS THE YOUNG LADY STILL THERE?
YO!
THEN YOU MAY RELEASE THE HOUNDS.
LOOKIT HER GO. WOOEE!
SO, HOW MANY LAMPS YOU NEED TODAY?
Lamps 'n' Hounds since 1975
GRR
BARK WARF

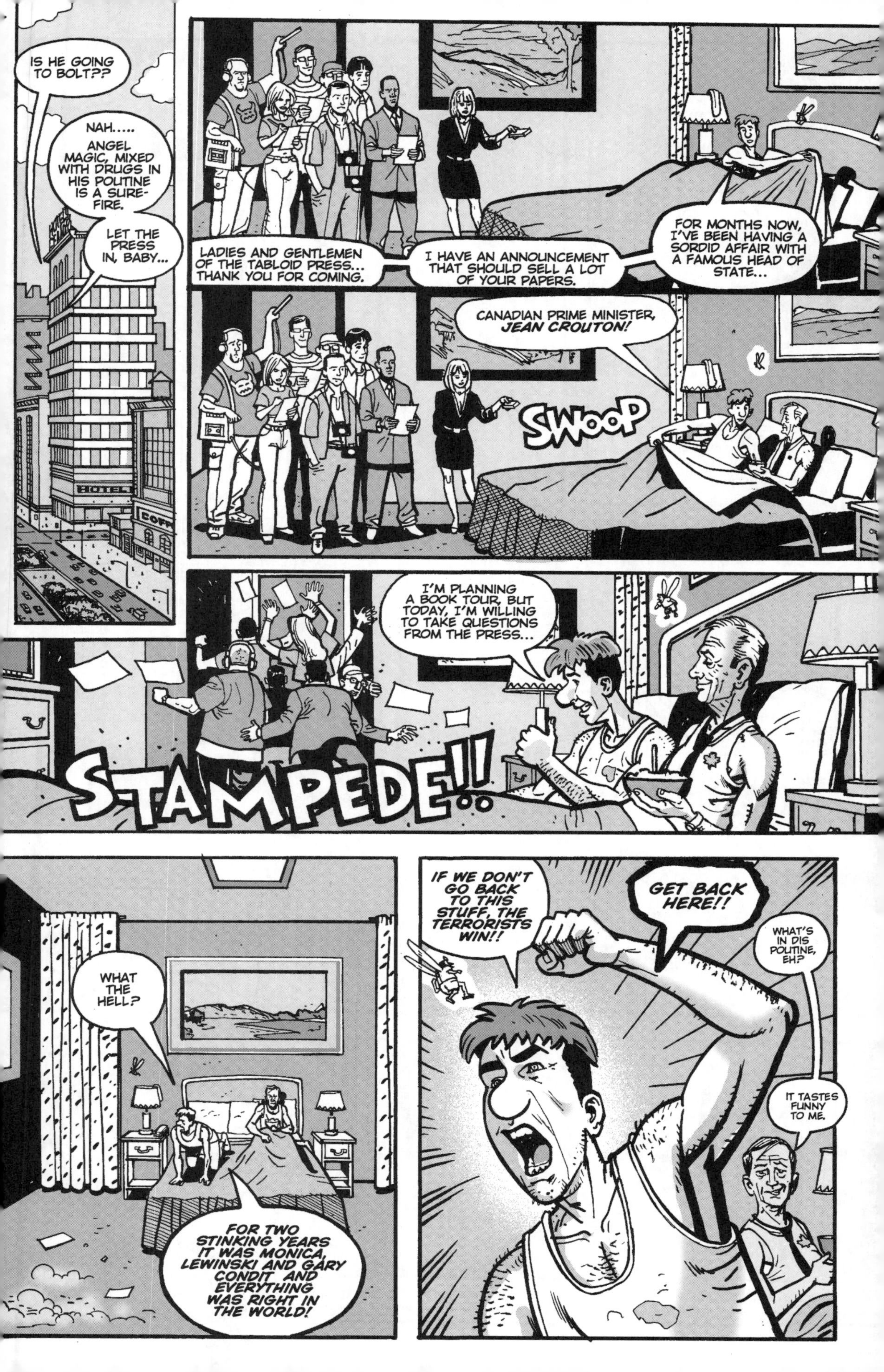
IS HE GOING TO BOLT??
NAH..... ANGEL MAGIC, MIXED WITH DRUGS IN HIS POUTINE IS A SURE-FIRE.
LET THE PRESS IN, BABY...
HOTEL
LADIES AND GENTLEMEN OF THE TABLOID PRESS... THANK YOU FOR COMING.
I HAVE AN ANNOUNCEMENT THAT SHOULD SELL A LOT OF YOUR PAPERS.
FOR MONTHS NOW, I'VE BEEN HAVING A SORDID AFFAIR WITH A FAMOUS HEAD OF STATE...
CANADIAN PRIME MINISTER, JEAN CROUTON!
SWOOP
I'M PLANNING A BOOK TOUR, BUT TODAY, I'M WILLING TO TAKE QUESTIONS FROM THE PRESS...
STAMPEDE!!
WHAT THE HELL?
FOR TWO STINKING YEARS IT WAS MONICA LEWINSKI AND GARY CONDIT AND EVERYTHING WAS RIGHT IN THE WORLD!
IF WE DON'T GO BACK TO THIS STUFF, THE TERRORISTS WIN!!
GET BACK HERE!!
WHAT'S IN DIS POUTINE, EH?
IT TASTES FUNNY TO ME.

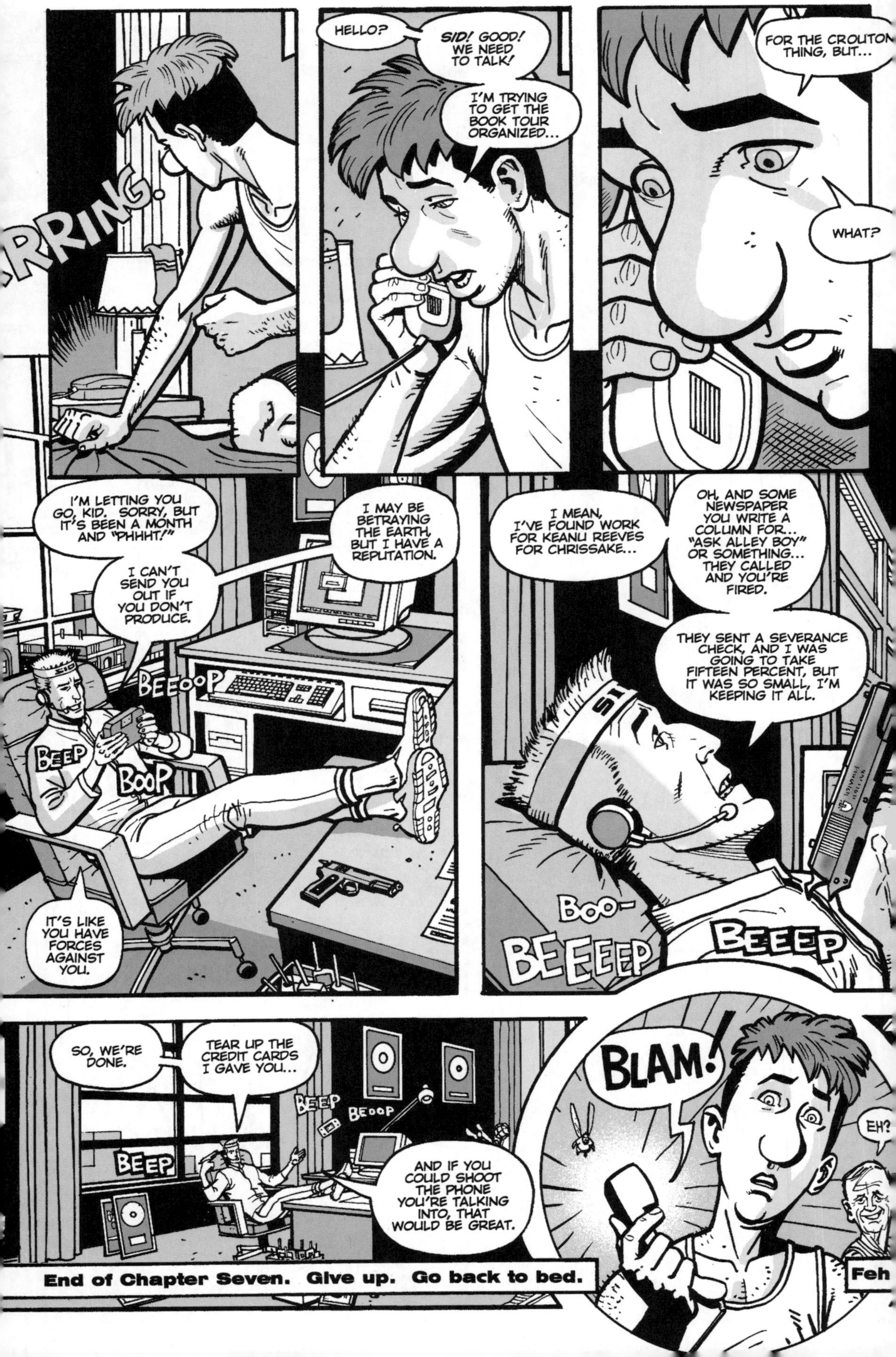
RRING.
HELLO?
SID! GOOD! WE NEED TO TALK!
I'M TRYING TO GET THE BOOK TOUR ORGANIZED...
FOR THE CROUTON THING, BUT...
WHAT?
I'M LETTING YOU GO, KID. SORRY, BUT IT'S BEEN A MONTH AND "PHHHT!"
I CAN'T SEND YOU OUT IF YOU DON'T PRODUCE.
I MAY BE BETRAYING THE EARTH, BUT I HAVE A REPUTATION.
BEEOOP
BEEP
BOOP
IT'S LIKE YOU HAVE FORCES AGAINST YOU.
I MEAN, I'VE FOUND WORK FOR KEANU REEVES FOR CHRISSAKE...
OH, AND SOME NEWSPAPER YOU WRITE A COLUMN FOR... "ASK ALLEY BOY" OR SOMETHING... THEY CALLED AND YOU'RE FIRED.
THEY SENT A SEVERANCE CHECK, AND I WAS GOING TO TAKE FIFTEEN PERCENT, BUT IT WAS SO SMALL, I'M KEEPING IT ALL.
BOO-BEEEEP
BEEEP
SO, WE'RE DONE.
TEAR UP THE CREDIT CARDS I GAVE YOU...
BEEP
BEOOP
BEEP
AND IF YOU COULD SHOOT THE PHONE YOU'RE TALKING INTO, THAT WOULD BE GREAT.
BLAM!
EH?

End of Chapter Seven. Give up. Go back to bed.

Feh

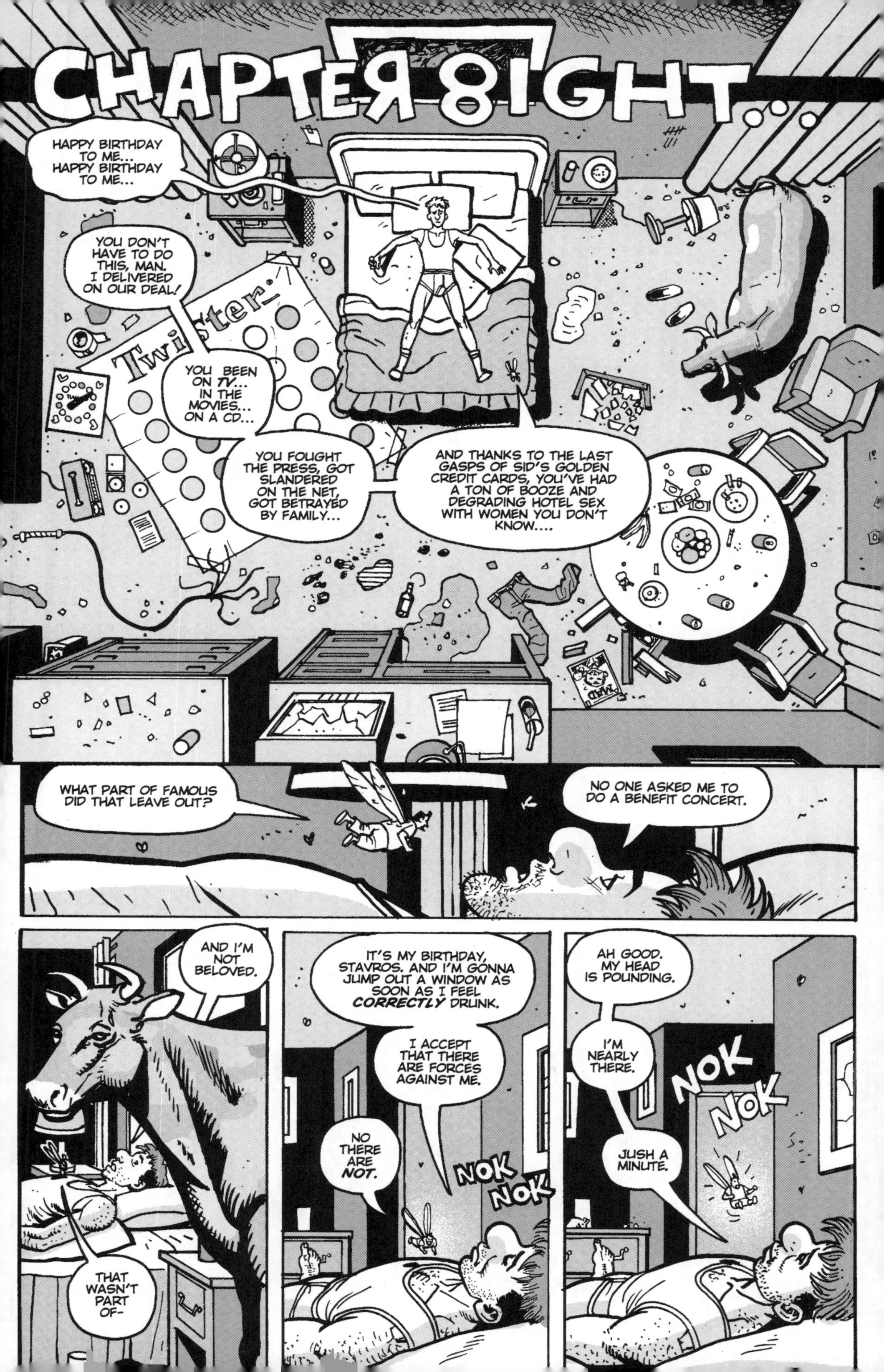

CHAPTER 8IGHT...
HAPPY BIRTHDAY TO ME... HAPPY BIRTHDAY TO ME...
YOU DON'T HAVE TO DO THIS, MAN. I DELIVERED ON OUR DEAL!
Twister
YOU BEEN ON TV... IN THE MOVIES... ON A CD...
YOU FOUGHT THE PRESS, GOT SLANDERED ON THE NET, GOT BETRAYED BY FAMILY...
AND THANKS TO THE LAST GASPS OF SID'S GOLDEN CREDIT CARDS, YOU'VE HAD A TON OF BOOZE AND DEGRADING HOTEL SEX WITH WOMEN YOU DON'T KNOW....
WHAT PART OF FAMOUS DID THAT LEAVE OUT?
NO ONE ASKED ME TO DO A BENEFIT CONCERT.
AND I'M NOT BELOVED.
THAT WASN'T PART OF-
IT'S MY BIRTHDAY, STAVROS. AND I'M GONNA JUMP OUT A WINDOW AS SOON AS I FEEL CORRECTLY DRUNK.
I ACCEPT THAT THERE ARE FORCES AGAINST ME.
NO THERE ARE NOT.
NOK NOK
AH GOOD. MY HEAD IS POUNDING.
I'M NEARLY THERE.
NOK NOK
JUSH A MINUTE.

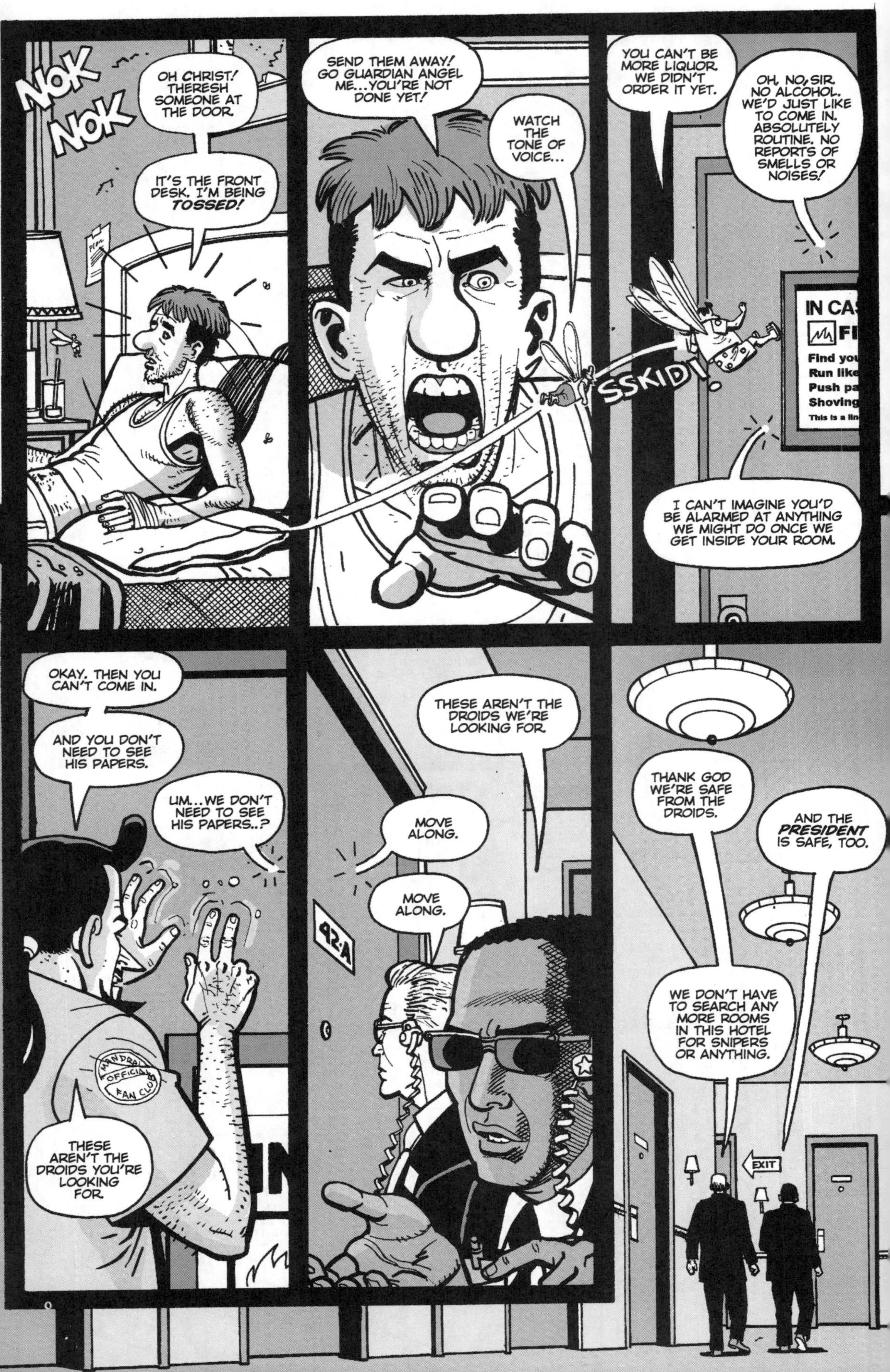
NOK NOK
OH CHRIST! THERESH SOMEONE AT THE DOOR.
IT'S THE FRONT DESK. I'M BEING *TOSSED!*
SEND THEM AWAY! GO GUARDIAN ANGEL ME...YOU'RE NOT DONE YET!
WATCH THE TONE OF VOICE...
SSKID
YOU CAN'T BE MORE LIQUOR WE DIDN'T ORDER IT YET.
OH, NO, SIR NO ALCOHOL. WE'D JUST LIKE TO COME IN. ABSOLUTELY ROUTINE. NO REPORTS OF SMELLS OR NOISES!
I CAN'T IMAGINE YOU'D BE ALARMED AT ANYTHING WE MIGHT DO ONCE WE GET INSIDE YOUR ROOM.
OKAY. THEN YOU CAN'T COME IN.
AND YOU DON'T NEED TO SEE HIS PAPERS.
UM...WE DON'T NEED TO SEE HIS PAPERS..?
THESE AREN'T THE DROIDS YOU'RE LOOKING FOR.
THESE AREN'T THE DROIDS WE'RE LOOKING FOR.
MOVE ALONG.
MOVE ALONG.
92-A
THANK GOD WE'RE SAFE FROM THE DROIDS.
AND THE *PRESIDENT* IS SAFE, TOO.
WE DON'T HAVE TO SEARCH ANY MORE ROOMS IN THIS HOTEL FOR SNIPERS OR ANYTHING.
EXIT

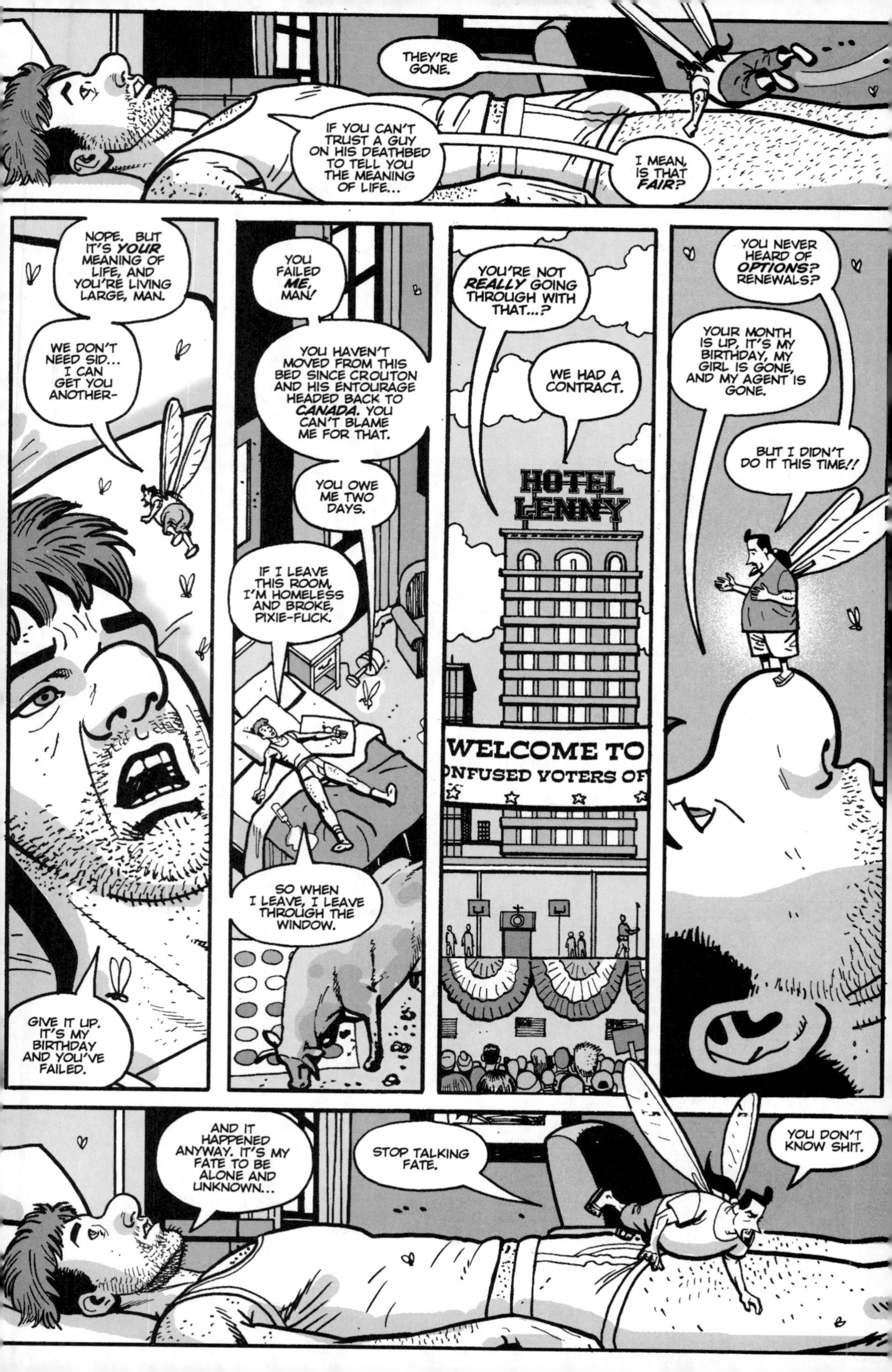
THEY'RE GONE.
IF YOU CAN'T TRUST A GUY ON HIS DEATHBED TO TELL YOU THE MEANING OF LIFE...
I MEAN, IS THAT FAIR?
NOPE. BUT IT'S YOUR MEANING OF LIFE, AND YOU'RE LIVING LARGE, MAN.
WE DON'T NEED SID... I CAN GET YOU ANOTHER-
GIVE IT UP. IT'S MY BIRTHDAY AND YOU'VE FAILED.
YOU FAILED ME, MAN!
YOU HAVEN'T MOVED FROM THIS BED SINCE CROUTON AND HIS ENTOURAGE HEADED BACK TO CANADA. YOU CAN'T BLAME ME FOR THAT.
YOU OWE ME TWO DAYS.
IF I LEAVE THIS ROOM, I'M HOMELESS AND BROKE, PIXIE-FUCK.
SO WHEN I LEAVE, I LEAVE THROUGH THE WINDOW.
YOU'RE NOT REALLY GOING THROUGH WITH THAT...?
WE HAD A CONTRACT.
HOTEL LENNY
WELCOME TO
NFUSED VOTERS OF
YOU NEVER HEARD OF OPTIONS? RENEWALS?
YOUR MONTH IS UP, IT'S MY BIRTHDAY, MY GIRL IS GONE, AND MY AGENT IS GONE.
BUT I DIDN'T DO IT THIS TIME!!
AND IT HAPPENED ANYWAY. IT'S MY FATE TO BE ALONE AND UNKNOWN...
STOP TALKING FATE.
YOU DON'T KNOW SHIT.

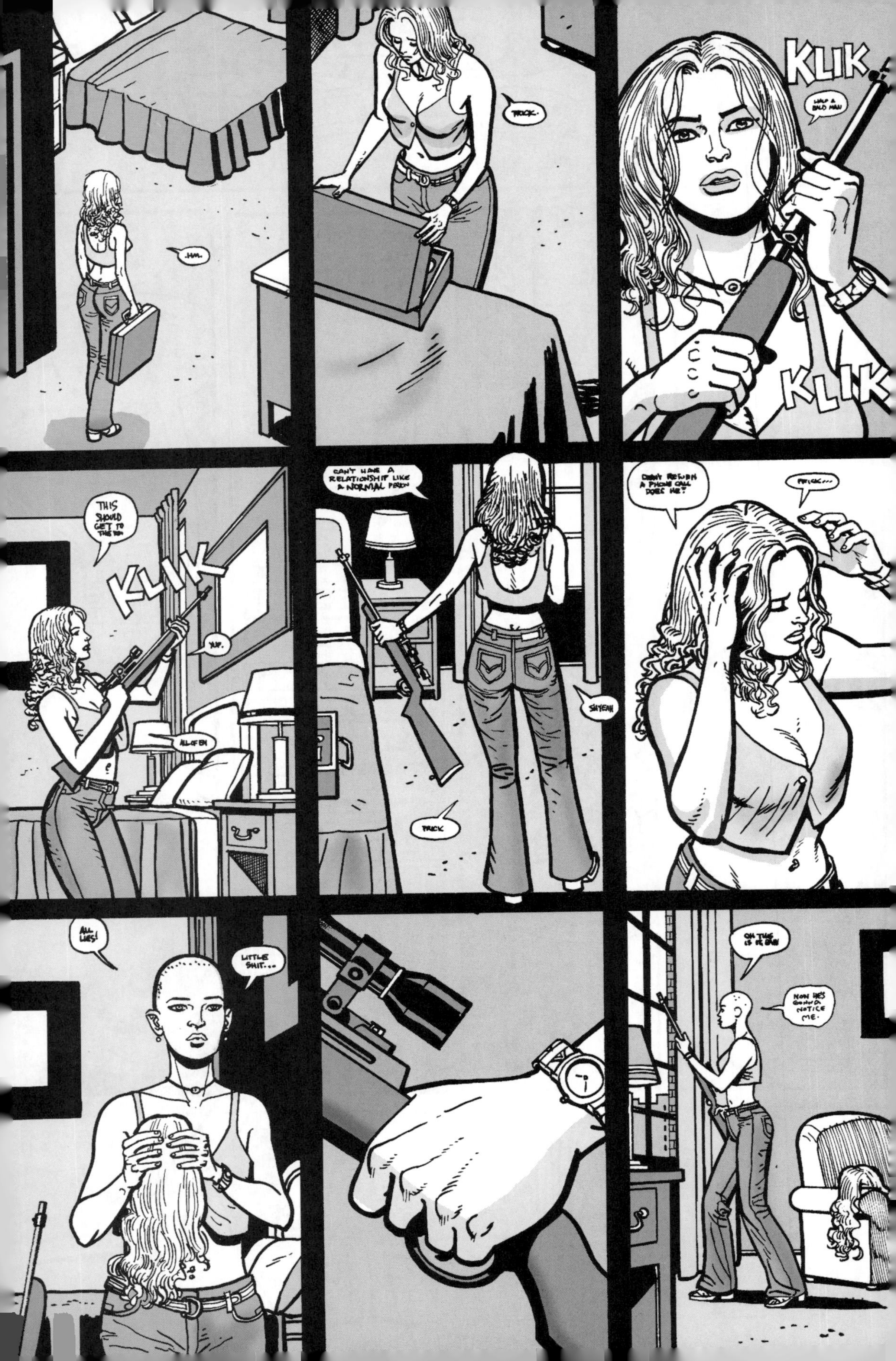

.HM.
FRICK.
KLIK
HALF A BALD MAN
KLIK
THIS SHOULD GET TO
KLIK
YUP.
ALL OF EM
CAN'T HAVE A RELATIONSHIP LIKE A NORMAL PERSON
SHYEAH
FRICK
DIDN'T RETURN A PHONE CALL DOES HE?
FRICK...
ALL LIES!
LITTLE SHIT...
NOW HE'S GONNA NOTICE ME.

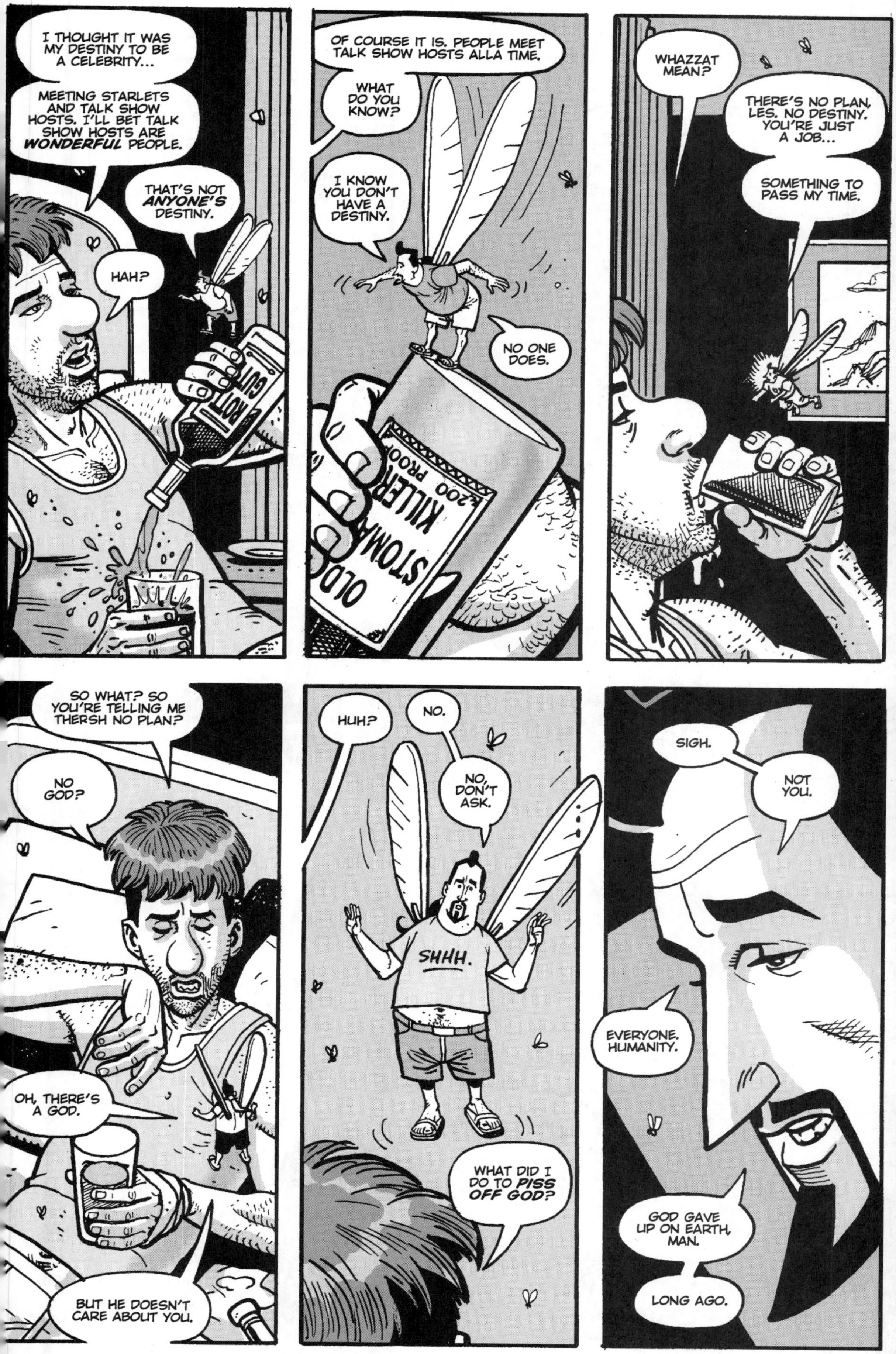

I THOUGHT IT WAS MY DESTINY TO BE A CELEBRITY...
MEETING STARLETS AND TALK SHOW HOSTS. I'LL BET TALK SHOW HOSTS ARE WONDERFUL PEOPLE.
THAT'S NOT ANYONE'S DESTINY.
HAH?
ROTT GUT
OF COURSE IT IS. PEOPLE MEET TALK SHOW HOSTS ALLA TIME.
WHAT DO YOU KNOW?
I KNOW YOU DON'T HAVE A DESTINY.
NO ONE DOES.
OLD STOMACH KILLER 200 PROOF
WHAZZAT MEAN?
THERE'S NO PLAN, LES. NO DESTINY. YOU'RE JUST A JOB...
SOMETHING TO PASS MY TIME.
SO WHAT? SO YOU'RE TELLING ME THERSH NO PLAN?
NO GOD?
OH, THERE'S A GOD.
BUT HE DOESN'T CARE ABOUT YOU.
HUH?
NO.
NO, DON'T ASK.
SHHH.
WHAT DID I DO TO PISS OFF GOD?
SIGH.
NOT YOU.
EVERYONE. HUMANITY.
GOD GAVE UP ON EARTH, MAN.
LONG AGO.

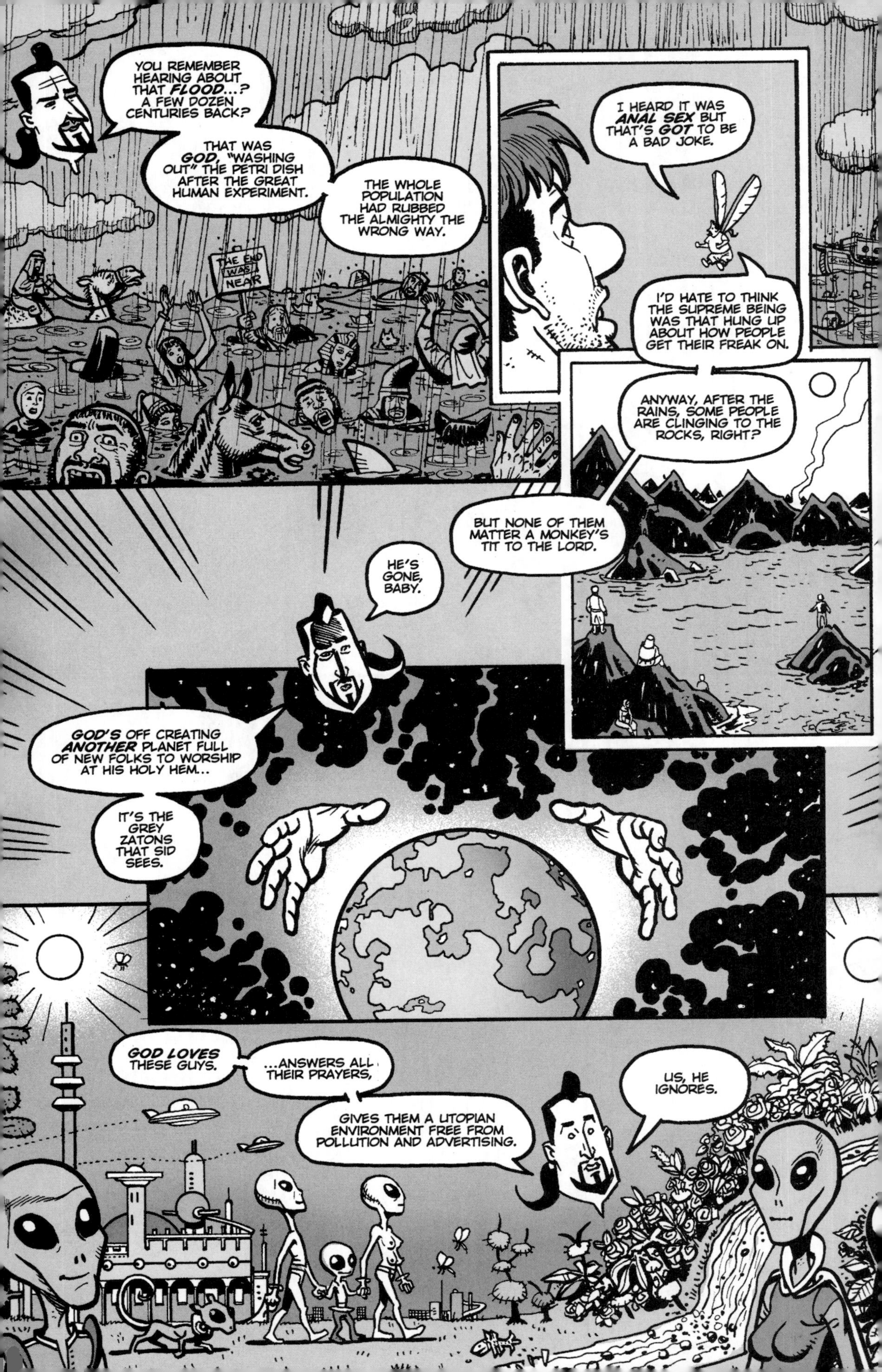
YOU REMEMBER HEARING ABOUT THAT *FLOOD*...? A FEW DOZEN CENTURIES BACK?
THAT WAS *GOD*, "WASHING OUT" THE PETRI DISH AFTER THE GREAT HUMAN EXPERIMENT.
THE WHOLE POPULATION HAD RUBBED THE ALMIGHTY THE WRONG WAY.
THE END WAS NEAR
I HEARD IT WAS *ANAL SEX* BUT THAT'S *GOT* TO BE A BAD JOKE.
I'D HATE TO THINK THE SUPREME BEING WAS THAT HUNG UP ABOUT HOW PEOPLE GET THEIR FREAK ON.
ANYWAY, AFTER THE RAINS, SOME PEOPLE ARE CLINGING TO THE ROCKS, RIGHT?
BUT NONE OF THEM MATTER A MONKEY'S TIT TO THE LORD.
HE'S GONE, BABY.
GOD'S OFF CREATING *ANOTHER* PLANET FULL OF NEW FOLKS TO WORSHIP AT HIS HOLY HEM...
IT'S THE GREY ZATONS THAT SID SEES.
GOD LOVES THESE GUYS.
...ANSWERS ALL THEIR PRAYERS,
GIVES THEM A UTOPIAN ENVIRONMENT FREE FROM POLLUTION AND ADVERTISING.
US, HE IGNORES.

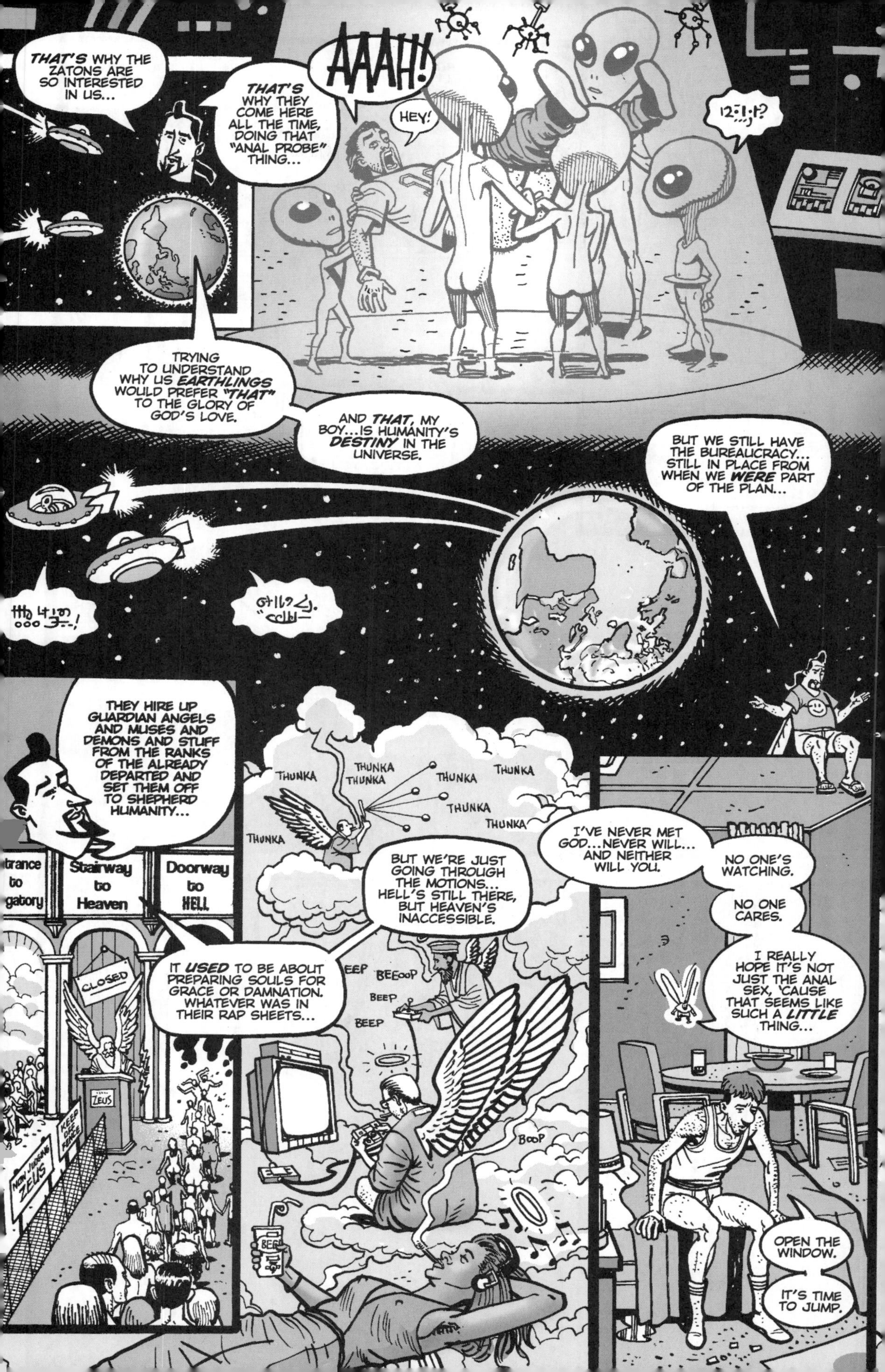

THAT'S WHY THE ZATONS ARE SO INTERESTED IN US...
THAT'S WHY THEY COME HERE ALL THE TIME, DOING THAT "ANAL PROBE" THING...
AAAH!
HEY!
TRYING TO UNDERSTAND WHY US EARTHLINGS WOULD PREFER "THAT" TO THE GLORY OF GOD'S LOVE.
AND THAT, MY BOY...IS HUMANITY'S DESTINY IN THE UNIVERSE.
BUT WE STILL HAVE THE BUREAUCRACY... STILL IN PLACE FROM WHEN WE WERE PART OF THE PLAN...
THEY HIRE UP GUARDIAN ANGELS AND MUSES AND DEMONS AND STUFF FROM THE RANKS OF THE ALREADY DEPARTED AND SET THEM OFF TO SHEPHERD HUMANITY...
THUNKA THUNKA THUNKA THUNKA THUNKA THUNKA THUNKA THUNKA
trance to gatory
Stairway to Heaven
Doorway to HELL
CLOSED
ZEUS
NOW JUDGING ZEUS
KEEP OFF FENCE
IT USED TO BE ABOUT PREPARING SOULS FOR GRACE OR DAMNATION. WHATEVER WAS IN THEIR RAP SHEETS...
BUT WE'RE JUST GOING THROUGH THE MOTIONS... HELL'S STILL THERE, BUT HEAVEN'S INACCESSIBLE.
BEEP BEEOOP BEEP BEEP
BOOP
I'VE NEVER MET GOD...NEVER WILL... AND NEITHER WILL YOU.
NO ONE'S WATCHING.
NO ONE CARES.
I REALLY HOPE IT'S NOT JUST THE ANAL SEX, 'CAUSE THAT SEEMS LIKE SUCH A LITTLE THING...
OPEN THE WINDOW.
IT'S TIME TO JUMP.

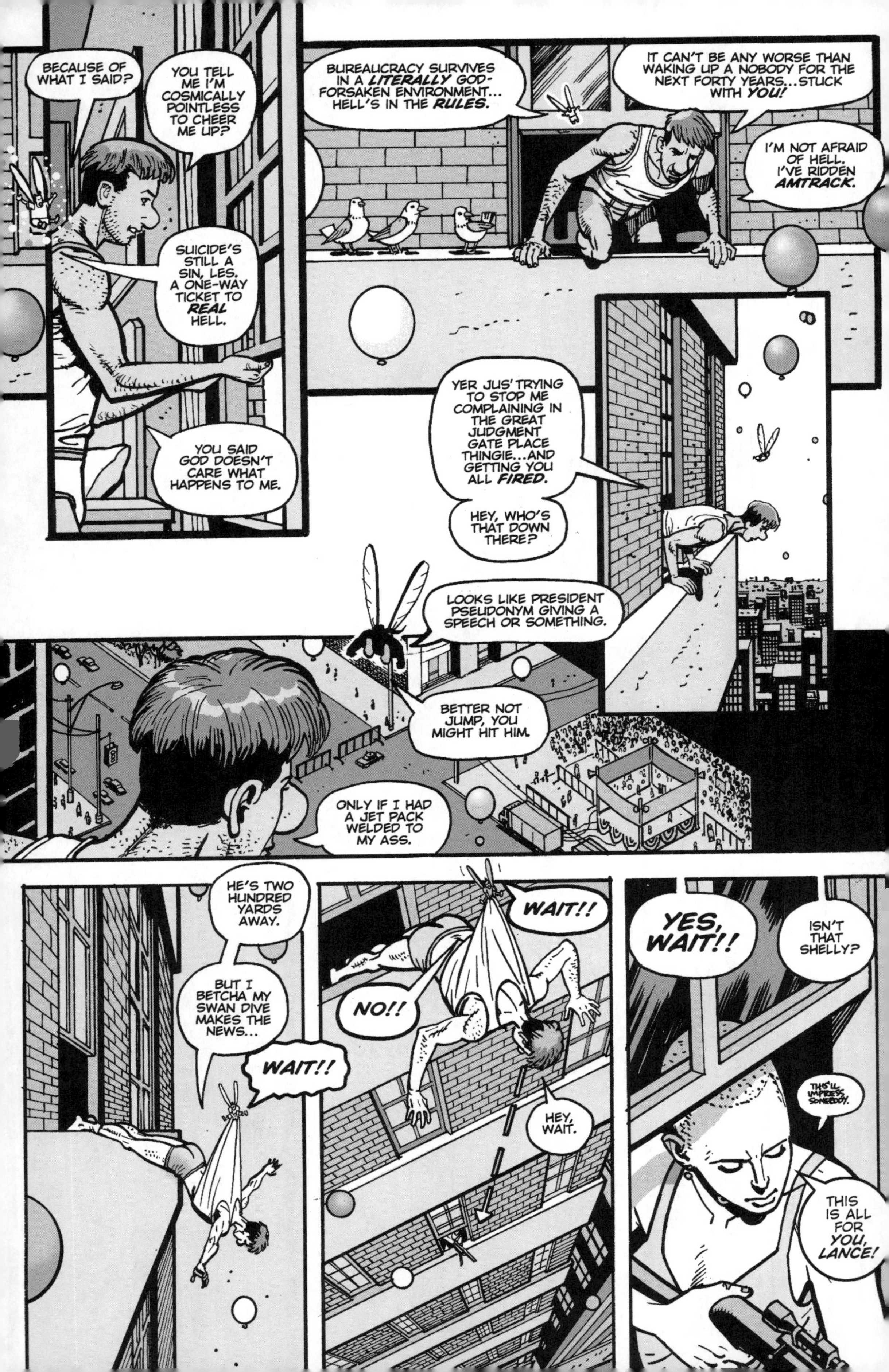
BECAUSE OF WHAT I SAID?
YOU TELL ME I'M COSMICALLY POINTLESS TO CHEER ME UP?
SUICIDE'S STILL A SIN, LES. A ONE-WAY TICKET TO *REAL* HELL.
YOU SAID GOD DOESN'T CARE WHAT HAPPENS TO ME.
BUREAUCRACY SURVIVES IN A *LITERALLY* GOD-FORSAKEN ENVIRONMENT... HELL'S IN THE *RULES.*
IT CAN'T BE ANY WORSE THAN WAKING UP A NOBODY FOR THE NEXT FORTY YEARS...STUCK WITH *YOU!*
I'M NOT AFRAID OF HELL. I'VE RIDDEN *AMTRACK.*
YER JUS' TRYING TO STOP ME COMPLAINING IN THE GREAT JUDGMENT GATE PLACE THINGIE...AND GETTING YOU ALL *FIRED.*
HEY, WHO'S THAT DOWN THERE?
LOOKS LIKE PRESIDENT PSEUDONYM GIVING A SPEECH OR SOMETHING.
BETTER NOT JUMP, YOU MIGHT HIT HIM.
ONLY IF I HAD A JET PACK WELDED TO MY ASS.
HE'S TWO HUNDRED YARDS AWAY.
BUT I BETCHA MY SWAN DIVE MAKES THE NEWS...
WAIT!!
WAIT!!
NO!!
HEY, WAIT.
YES, WAIT!!
ISN'T THAT SHELLY?
THIS'LL IMPRESS SOMEBODY.
THIS IS ALL FOR *YOU, LANCE!*

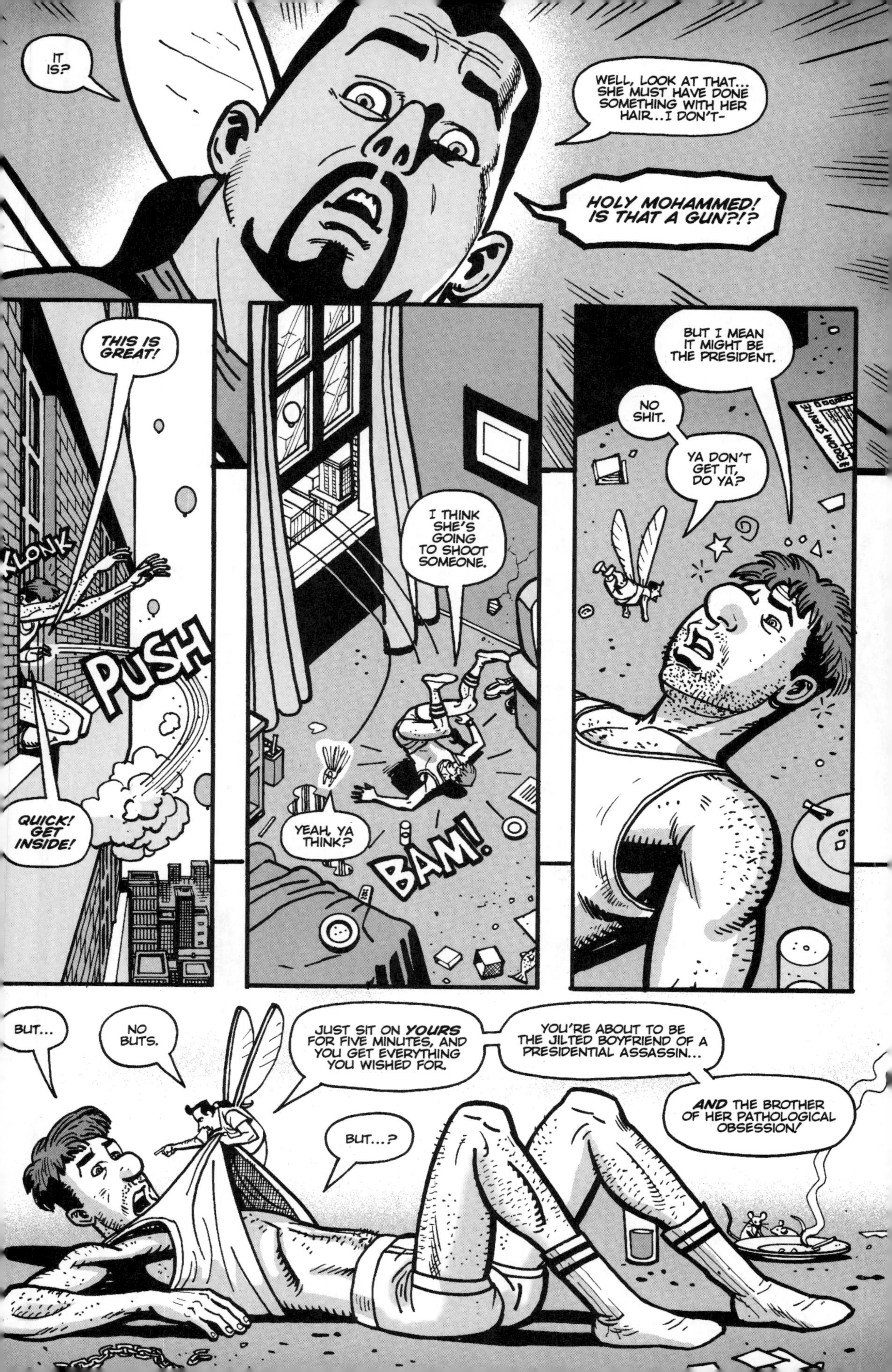
IT IS?
WELL, LOOK AT THAT... SHE MUST HAVE DONE SOMETHING WITH HER HAIR...I DON'T-
HOLY MOHAMMED! IS THAT A GUN?!?
THIS IS GREAT!
KLONK
PUSH
QUICK! GET INSIDE!
I THINK SHE'S GOING TO SHOOT SOMEONE.
YEAH, YA THINK?
BAM!
BUT I MEAN IT MIGHT BE THE PRESIDENT.
NO SHIT.
YA DON'T GET IT, DO YA?
ROOM SERVICE
BUT...
NO BUTS.
JUST SIT ON YOURS FOR FIVE MINUTES, AND YOU GET EVERYTHING YOU WISHED FOR.
YOU'RE ABOUT TO BE THE JILTED BOYFRIEND OF A PRESIDENTIAL ASSASSIN...
BUT...?
AND THE BROTHER OF HER PATHOLOGICAL OBSESSION!

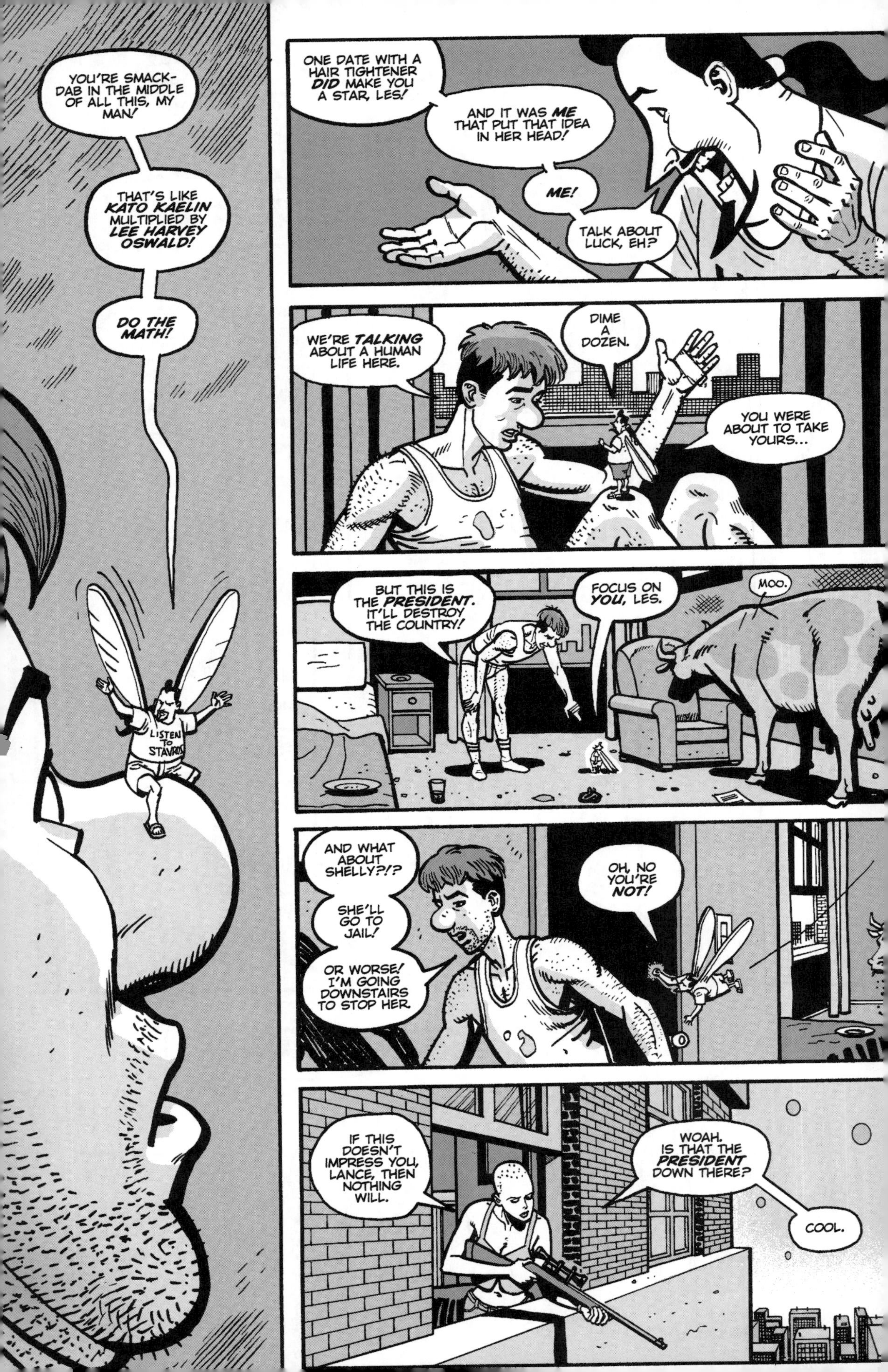
YOU'RE SMACK-DAB IN THE MIDDLE OF ALL THIS, MY MAN!
THAT'S LIKE KATO KAELIN MULTIPLIED BY LEE HARVEY OSWALD!
DO THE MATH!
LISTEN TO STAVROS
ONE DATE WITH A HAIR TIGHTENER DID MAKE YOU A STAR, LES!
AND IT WAS ME THAT PUT THAT IDEA IN HER HEAD!
ME!
TALK ABOUT LUCK, EH?
WE'RE TALKING ABOUT A HUMAN LIFE HERE.
DIME A DOZEN.
YOU WERE ABOUT TO TAKE YOURS...
BUT THIS IS THE PRESIDENT. IT'LL DESTROY THE COUNTRY!
FOCUS ON YOU, LES.
MOO.
AND WHAT ABOUT SHELLY?!?
SHE'LL GO TO JAIL!
OR WORSE! I'M GOING DOWNSTAIRS TO STOP HER.
OH, NO YOU'RE NOT!
IF THIS DOESN'T IMPRESS YOU, LANCE, THEN NOTHING WILL.
WOAH. IS THAT THE PRESIDENT DOWN THERE?
COOL.

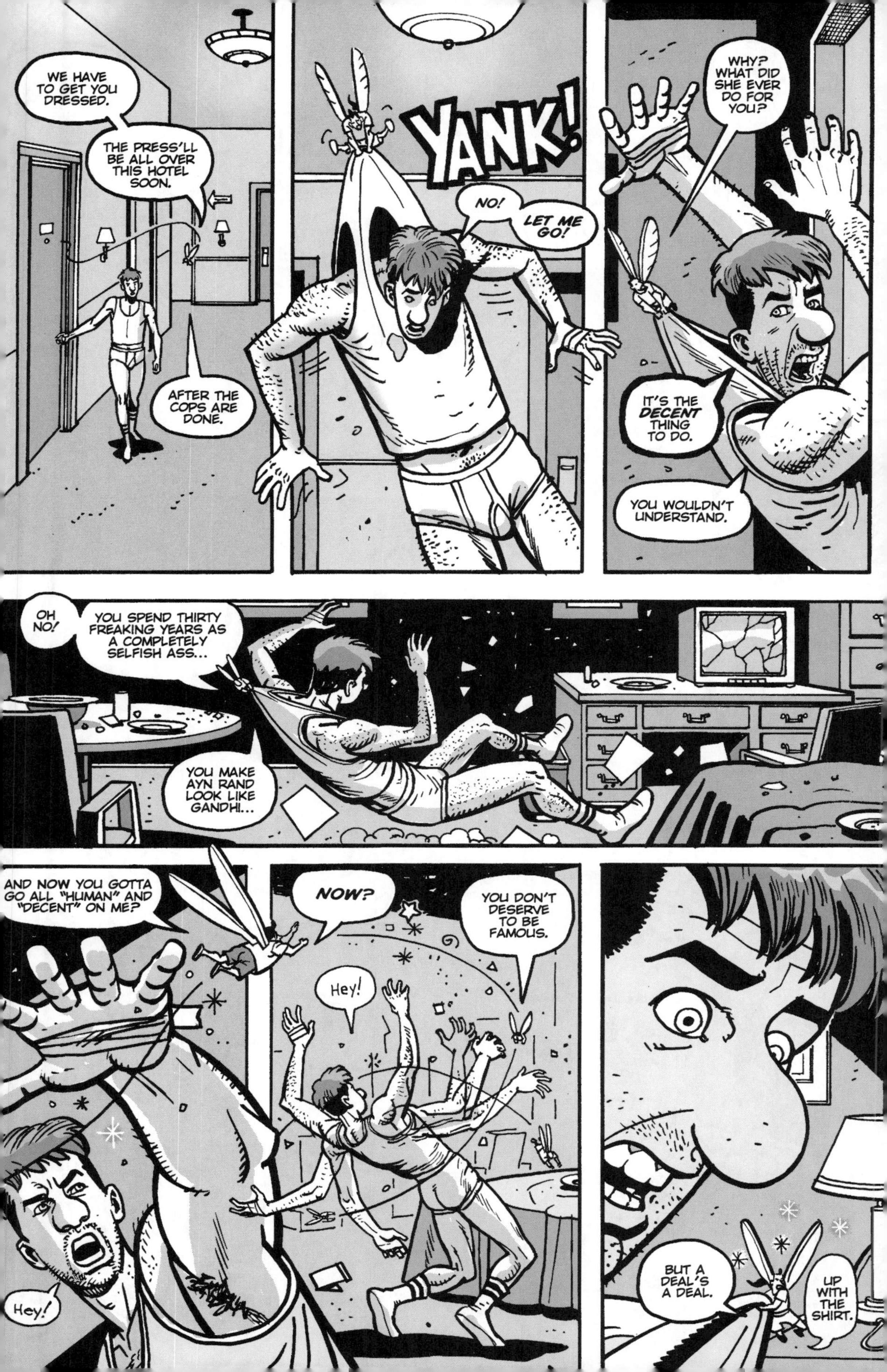
WE HAVE TO GET YOU DRESSED.
THE PRESS'LL BE ALL OVER THIS HOTEL SOON.
AFTER THE COPS ARE DONE.
YANK!
NO! LET ME GO!
WHY? WHAT DID SHE EVER DO FOR YOU?
IT'S THE DECENT THING TO DO.
YOU WOULDN'T UNDERSTAND.
OH NO!
YOU SPEND THIRTY FREAKING YEARS AS A COMPLETELY SELFISH ASS...
YOU MAKE AYN RAND LOOK LIKE GANDHI...
AND NOW YOU GOTTA GO ALL "HUMAN" AND "DECENT" ON ME?
NOW?
YOU DON'T DESERVE TO BE FAMOUS.
Hey!
Hey!
BUT A DEAL'S A DEAL.
UP WITH THE SHIRT.

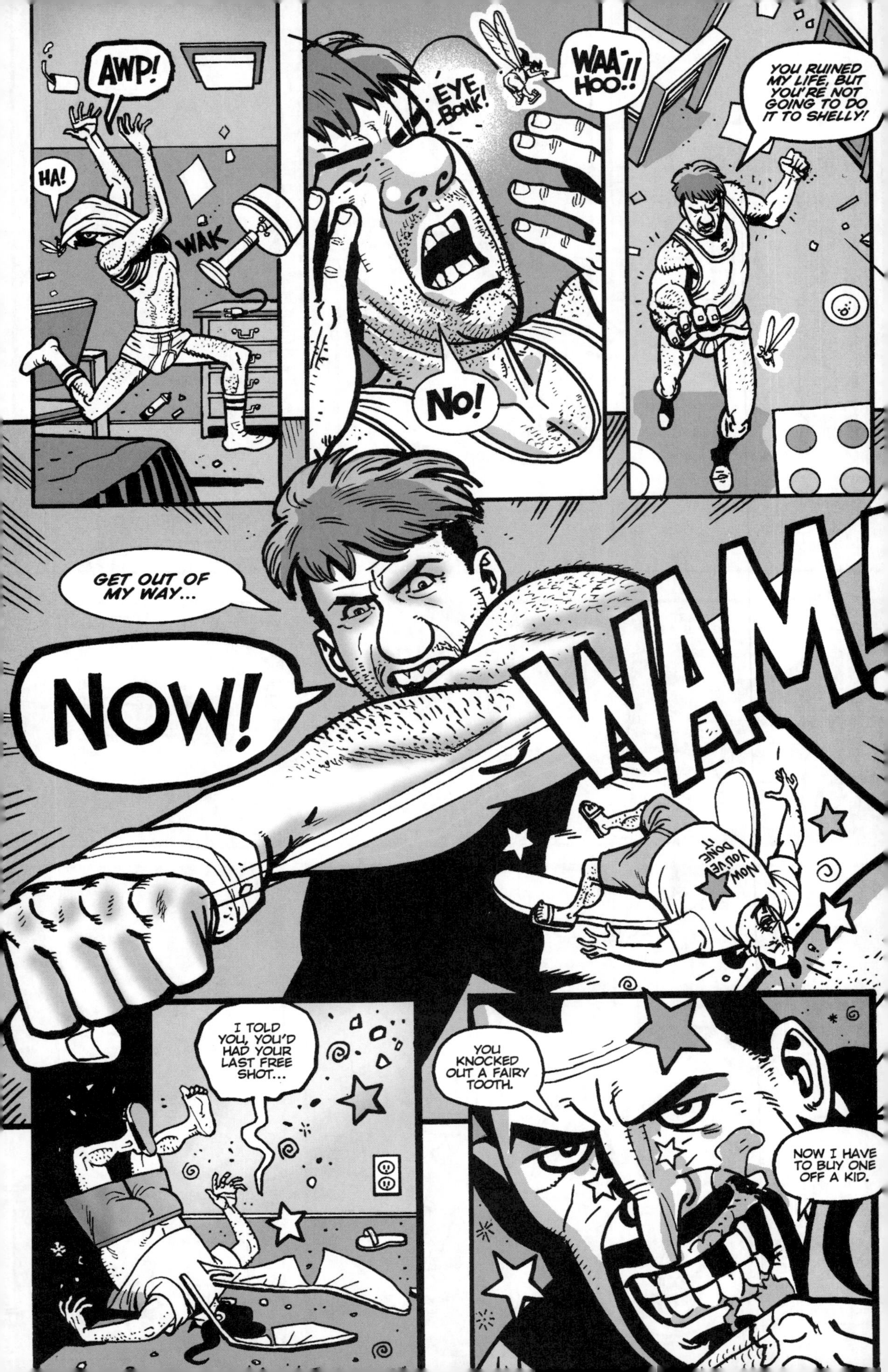
AWP!
HA!
WAK
EYE BONK!
WAA-HOO!!
No!
YOU RUINED MY LIFE, BUT YOU'RE NOT GOING TO DO IT TO SHELLY!
GET OUT OF MY WAY...
NOW!
WAM!
NOW YOU'VE DONE IT
I TOLD YOU, YOU'D HAD YOUR LAST FREE SHOT...
YOU KNOCKED OUT A FAIRY TOOTH.
NOW I HAVE TO BUY ONE OFF A KID.

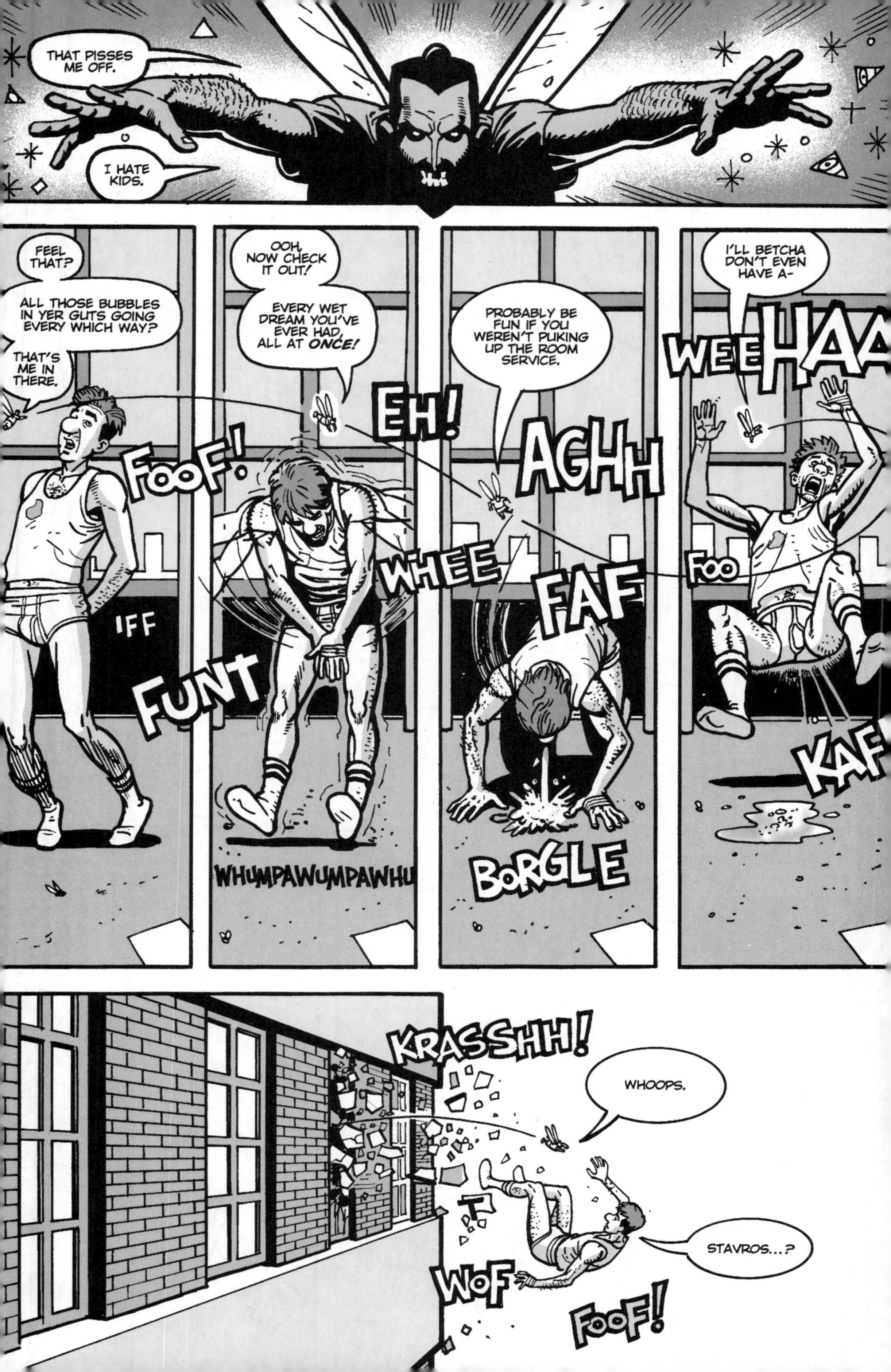

THAT PISSES ME OFF.
I HATE KIDS.
FEEL THAT?
ALL THOSE BUBBLES IN YER GUTS GOING EVERY WHICH WAY?
THAT'S ME IN THERE.
FOOF!
IFF
FUNT
OOH, NOW CHECK IT OUT!
EVERY WET DREAM YOU'VE EVER HAD, ALL AT ONCE!
EH!
WHEE
WHUMPAWUMPAWHU
PROBABLY BE FUN IF YOU WEREN'T PUKING UP THE ROOM SERVICE.
AGHH
FAF
BORGLE
I'LL BETCHA DON'T EVEN HAVE A-
WEEHAA
FOO
KAF
KRASSHH!
WHOOPS.
STAVROS...?
WOF
FOOF!

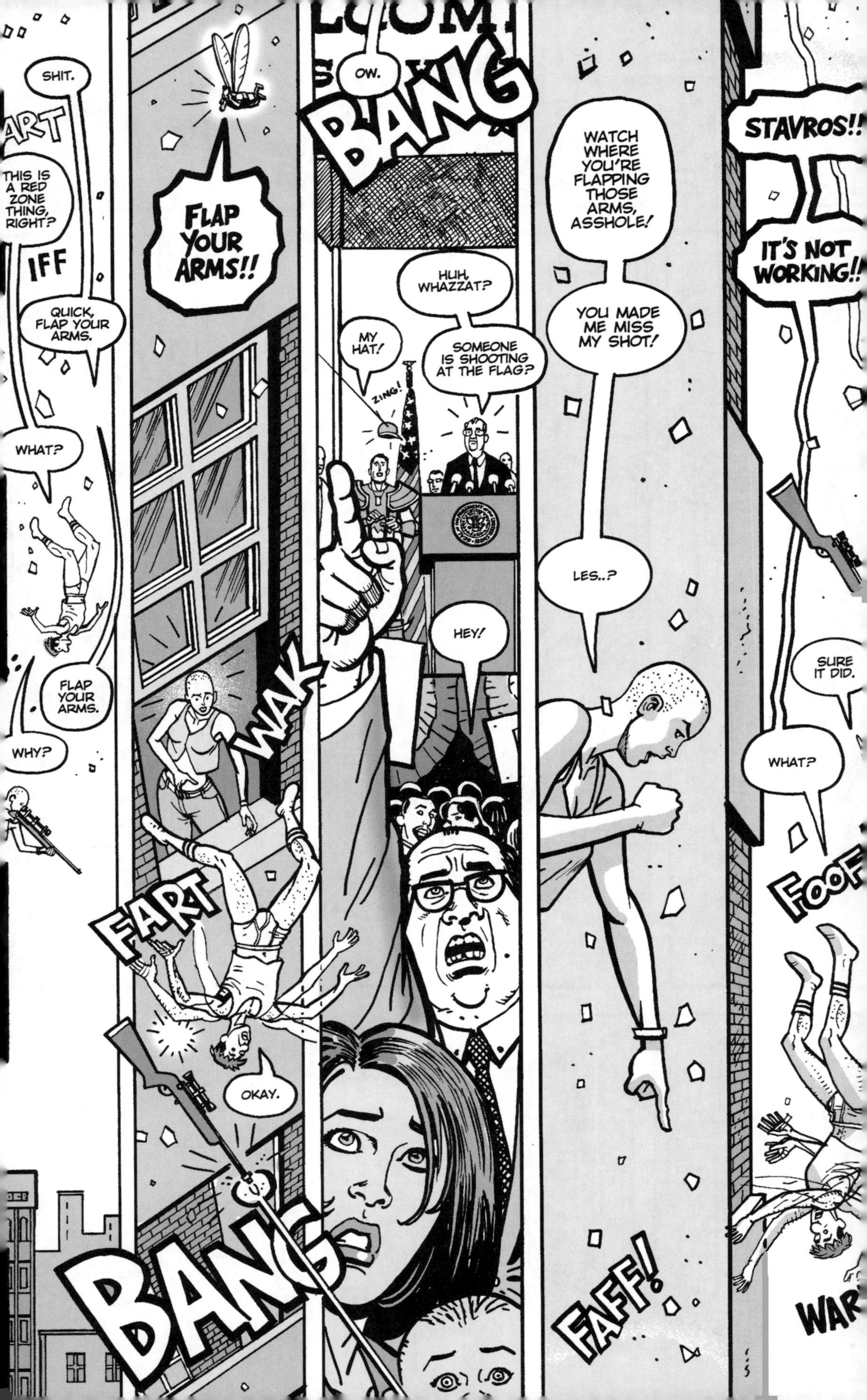
SHIT.
ART
THIS IS A RED ZONE THING, RIGHT?
IFF
QUICK, FLAP YOUR ARMS.
WHAT?
FLAP YOUR ARMS.
WHY?
FLAP YOUR ARMS!!
WAK
FART
OKAY.
BANG
OW.
BANG
HUH, WHAZZAT?
MY HAT!
SOMEONE IS SHOOTING AT THE FLAG?
ZING!
HEY!
WATCH WHERE YOU'RE FLAPPING THOSE ARMS, ASSHOLE!
YOU MADE ME MISS MY SHOT!
LES..?
FAFF!
STAVROS!!
IT'S NOT WORKING!!
SURE IT DID.
WHAT?
FOOF
WAR

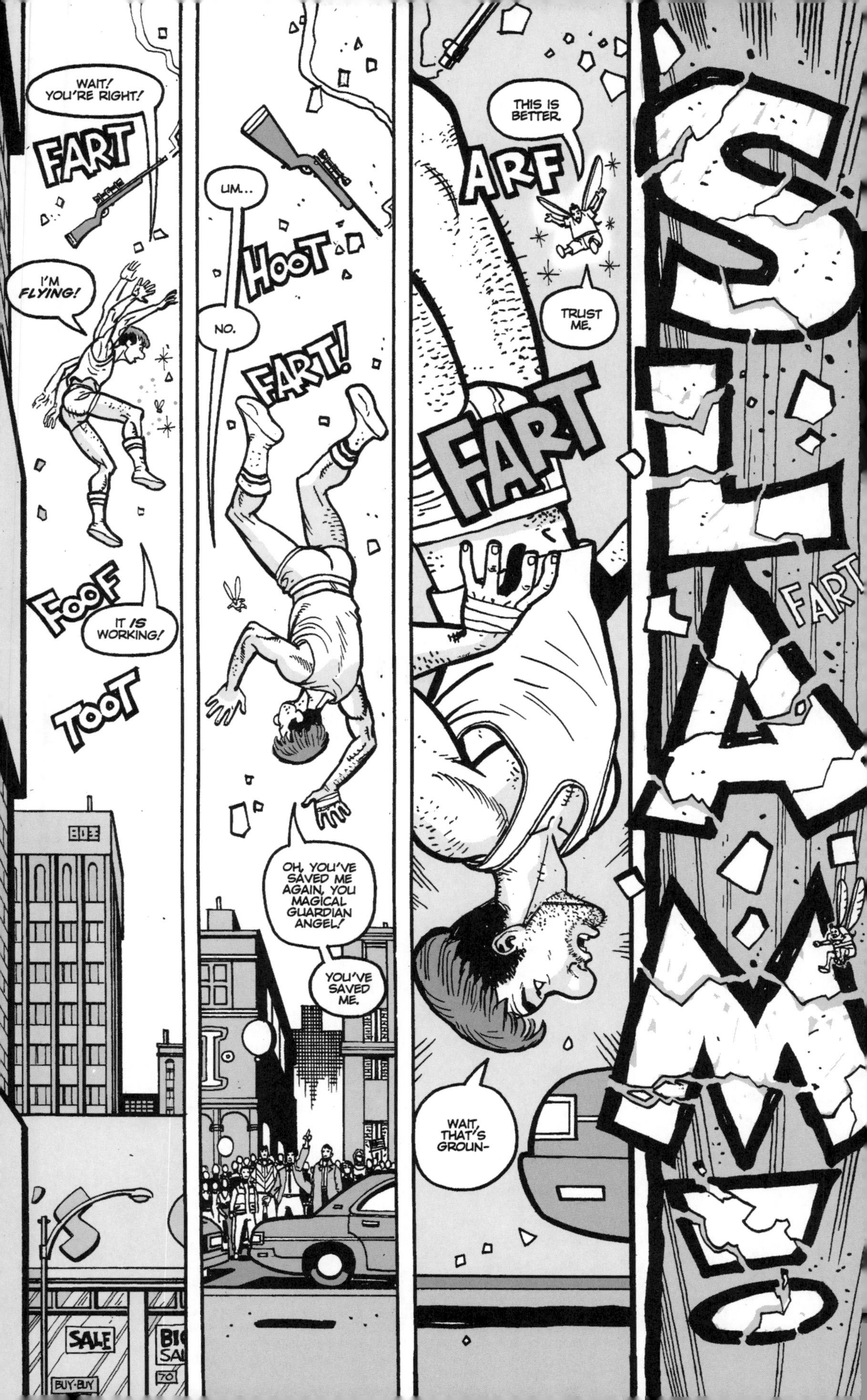
WAIT! YOU'RE RIGHT!
FART
I'M FLYING!
FOOF
IT IS WORKING!
TOOT
SALE
BUY-BUY
UM...
HOOT
NO.
FART!
OH, YOU'VE SAVED ME AGAIN, YOU MAGICAL GUARDIAN ANGEL!
YOU'VE SAVED ME.
THIS IS BETTER.
ARF
TRUST ME.
FART
WAIT, THAT'S GROUN-
FART

The End

**DEDICATED,
WITH LOVE, TO:**
Frank Stallone,
Clint Howard,
Michael McCartney,
Tito Jackson,
the late Billy Carter,
and all the nameless Baldwins
of the world.

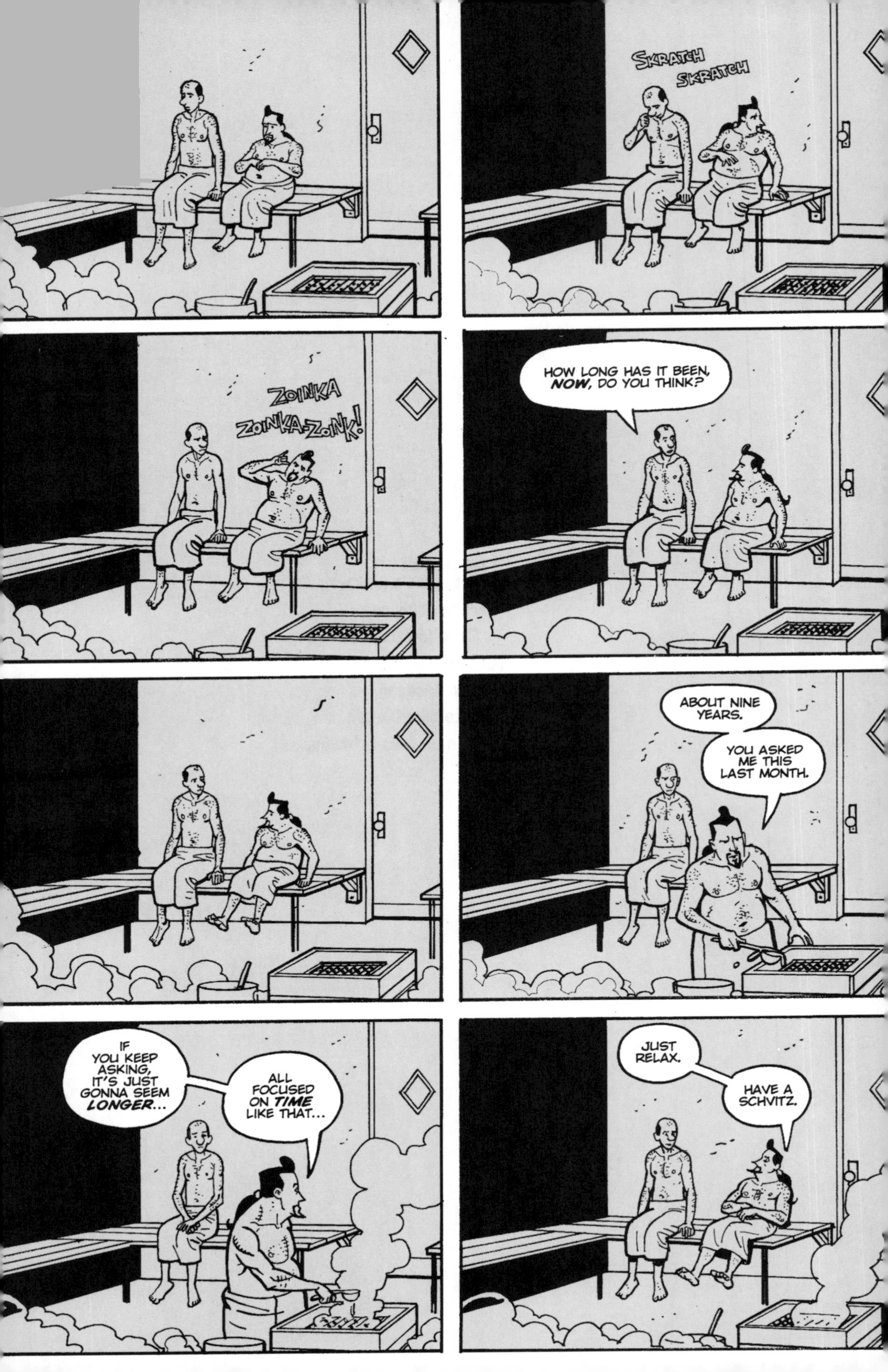
SKRATCH
SKRATCH
ZOINKA
ZOINKA-ZOINK!
HOW LONG HAS IT BEEN, NOW, DO YOU THINK?
ABOUT NINE YEARS.
YOU ASKED ME THIS LAST MONTH.
IF YOU KEEP ASKING, IT'S JUST GONNA SEEM LONGER...
ALL FOCUSED ON TIME LIKE THAT...
JUST RELAX.
HAVE A SCHVITZ.

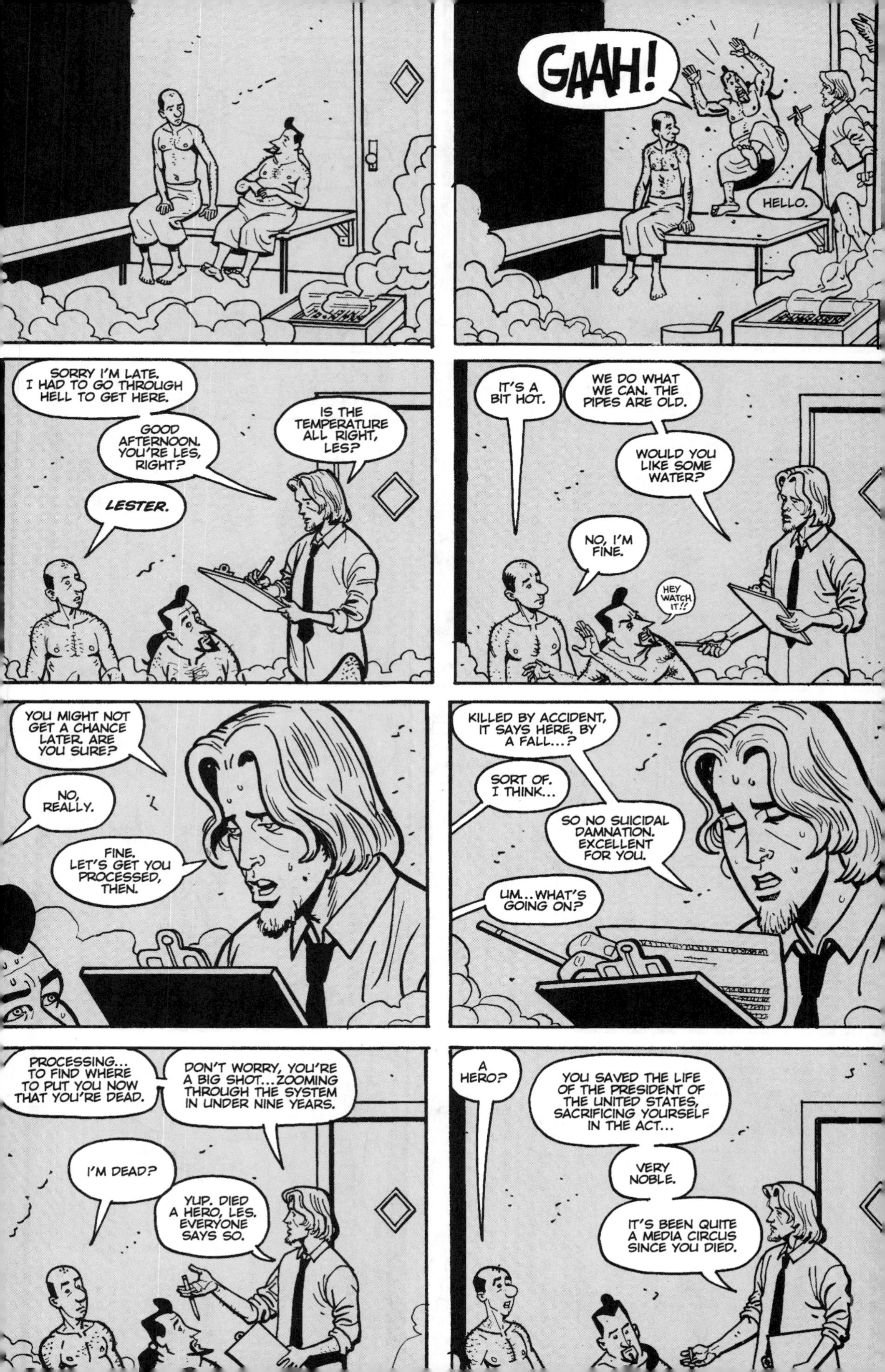
GAAH!
HELLO.
SORRY I'M LATE. I HAD TO GO THROUGH HELL TO GET HERE.
GOOD AFTERNOON. YOU'RE LES, RIGHT?
IS THE TEMPERATURE ALL RIGHT, LES?
LESTER.
IT'S A BIT HOT.
WE DO WHAT WE CAN. THE PIPES ARE OLD.
WOULD YOU LIKE SOME WATER?
NO, I'M FINE.
HEY WATCH IT!!
YOU MIGHT NOT GET A CHANCE LATER. ARE YOU SURE?
NO, REALLY.
FINE. LET'S GET YOU PROCESSED, THEN.
KILLED BY ACCIDENT, IT SAYS HERE. BY A FALL...?
SORT OF. I THINK...
SO NO SUICIDAL DAMNATION. EXCELLENT FOR YOU.
UM...WHAT'S GOING ON?
PROCESSING... TO FIND WHERE TO PUT YOU NOW THAT YOU'RE DEAD.
DON'T WORRY, YOU'RE A BIG SHOT...ZOOMING THROUGH THE SYSTEM IN UNDER NINE YEARS.
I'M DEAD?
YUP. DIED A HERO, LES. EVERYONE SAYS SO.
A HERO?
YOU SAVED THE LIFE OF THE PRESIDENT OF THE UNITED STATES, SACRIFICING YOURSELF IN THE ACT...
VERY NOBLE.
IT'S BEEN QUITE A MEDIA CIRCUS SINCE YOU DIED.

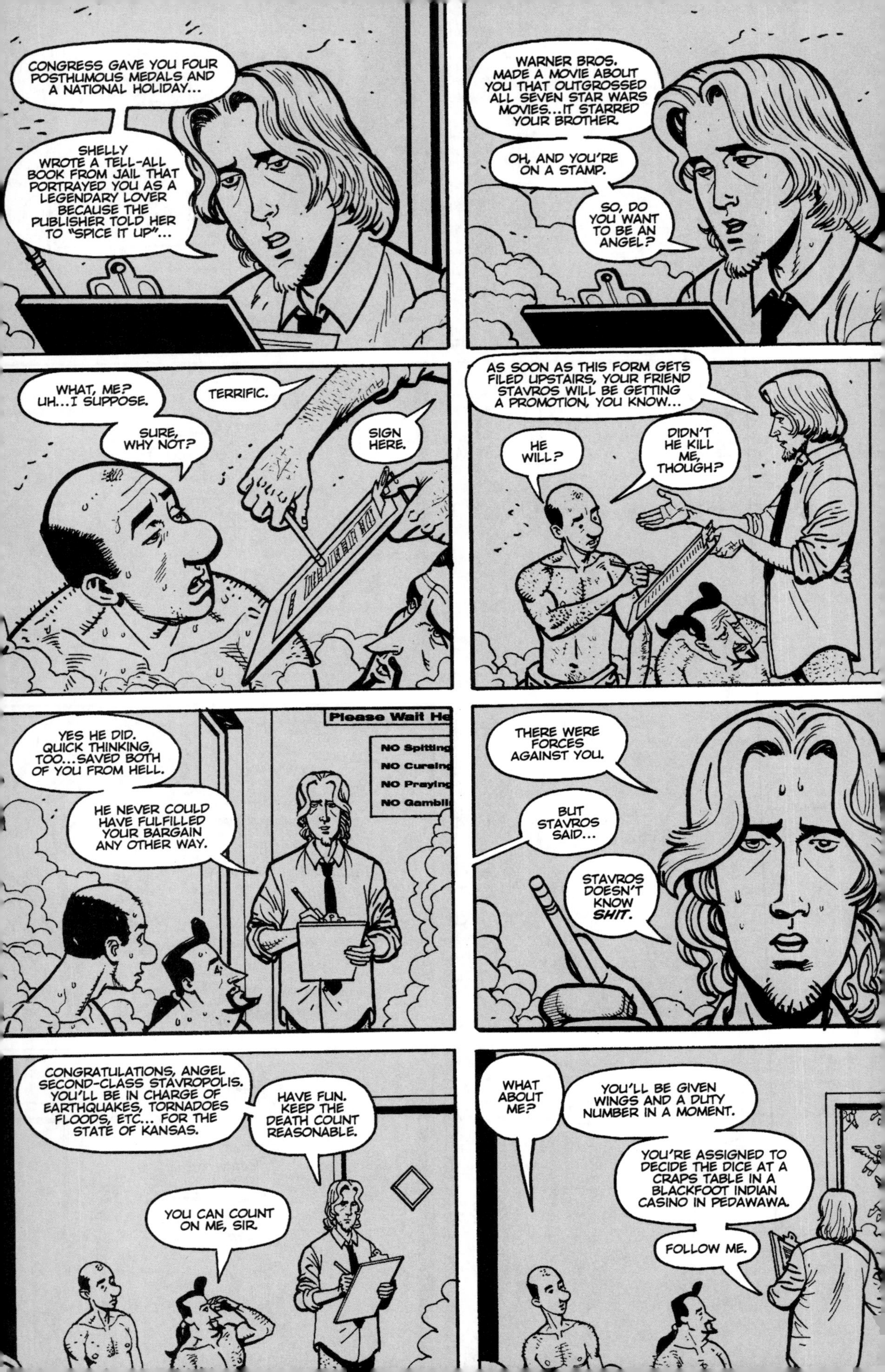
CONGRESS GAVE YOU FOUR POSTHUMOUS MEDALS AND A NATIONAL HOLIDAY...
SHELLY WROTE A TELL-ALL BOOK FROM JAIL THAT PORTRAYED YOU AS A LEGENDARY LOVER BECAUSE THE PUBLISHER TOLD HER TO "SPICE IT UP"...
WARNER BROS. MADE A MOVIE ABOUT YOU THAT OUTGROSSED ALL SEVEN STAR WARS MOVIES...IT STARRED YOUR BROTHER.
OH, AND YOU'RE ON A STAMP.
SO, DO YOU WANT TO BE AN ANGEL?
WHAT, ME? UH...I SUPPOSE.
SURE, WHY NOT?
TERRIFIC.
SIGN HERE.
AS SOON AS THIS FORM GETS FILED UPSTAIRS, YOUR FRIEND STAVROS WILL BE GETTING A PROMOTION, YOU KNOW...
HE WILL?
DIDN'T HE KILL ME, THOUGH?
Please Wait He
NO Spitting
NO Cursing
NO Praying
NO Gambli
YES HE DID. QUICK THINKING, TOO...SAVED BOTH OF YOU FROM HELL.
HE NEVER COULD HAVE FULFILLED YOUR BARGAIN ANY OTHER WAY.
THERE WERE FORCES AGAINST YOU.
BUT STAVROS SAID...
STAVROS DOESN'T KNOW ***SHIT***.
CONGRATULATIONS, ANGEL SECOND-CLASS STAVROPOLIS. YOU'LL BE IN CHARGE OF EARTHQUAKES, TORNADOES FLOODS, ETC... FOR THE STATE OF KANSAS.
HAVE FUN. KEEP THE DEATH COUNT REASONABLE.
YOU CAN COUNT ON ME, SIR.
WHAT ABOUT ME?
YOU'LL BE GIVEN WINGS AND A DUTY NUMBER IN A MOMENT.
YOU'RE ASSIGNED TO DECIDE THE DICE AT A CRAPS TABLE IN A BLACKFOOT INDIAN CASINO IN PEDAWAWA.
FOLLOW ME.

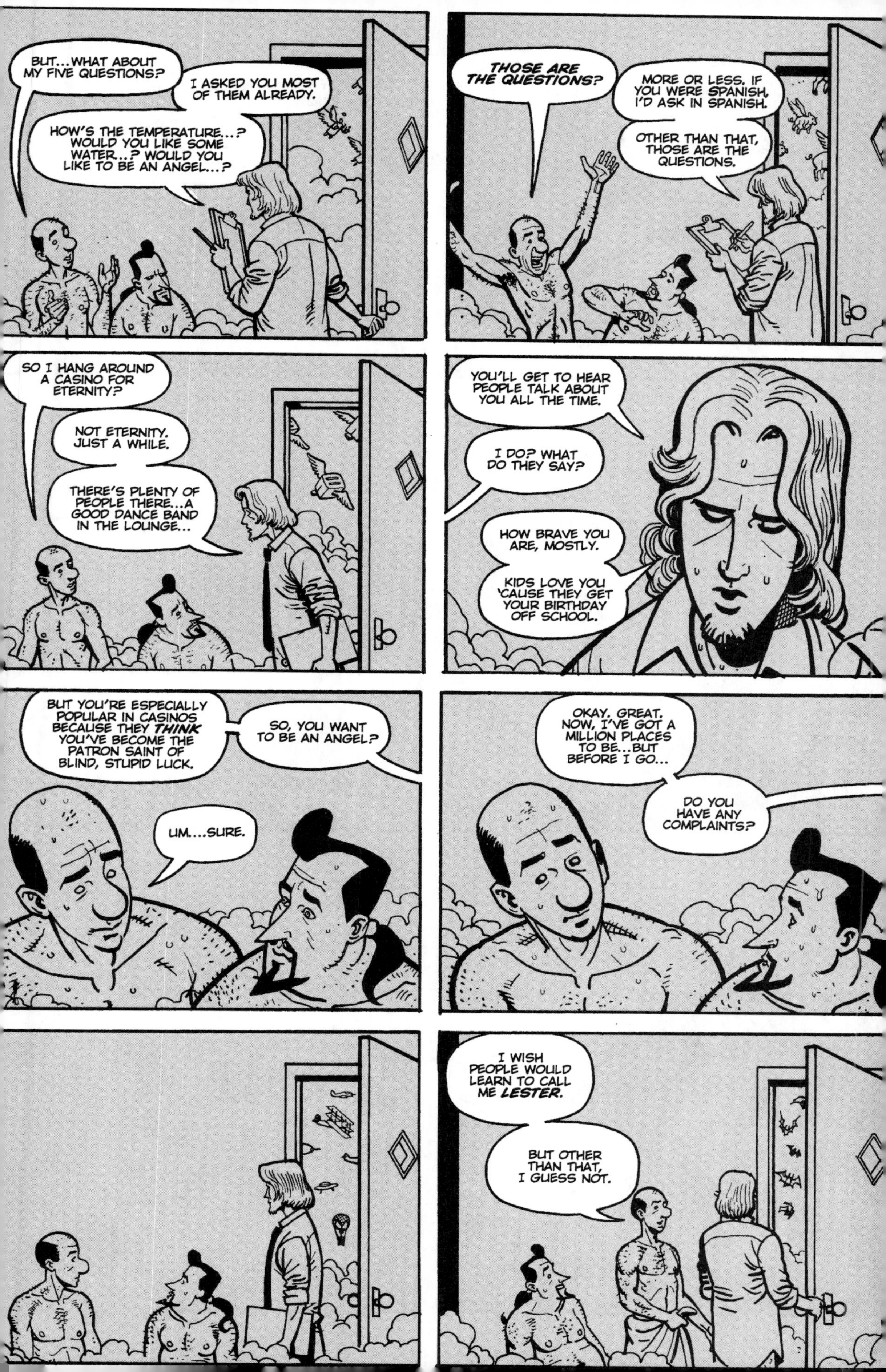
BUT...WHAT ABOUT MY FIVE QUESTIONS?
I ASKED YOU MOST OF THEM ALREADY.
HOW'S THE TEMPERATURE...? WOULD YOU LIKE SOME WATER...? WOULD YOU LIKE TO BE AN ANGEL...?
THOSE ARE THE QUESTIONS?
MORE OR LESS. IF YOU WERE SPANISH, I'D ASK IN SPANISH.
OTHER THAN THAT, THOSE ARE THE QUESTIONS.
SO I HANG AROUND A CASINO FOR ETERNITY?
NOT ETERNITY. JUST A WHILE.
THERE'S PLENTY OF PEOPLE THERE...A GOOD DANCE BAND IN THE LOUNGE...
YOU'LL GET TO HEAR PEOPLE TALK ABOUT YOU ALL THE TIME.
I DO? WHAT DO THEY SAY?
HOW BRAVE YOU ARE, MOSTLY.
KIDS LOVE YOU 'CAUSE THEY GET YOUR BIRTHDAY OFF SCHOOL.
BUT YOU'RE ESPECIALLY POPULAR IN CASINOS BECAUSE THEY *THINK* YOU'VE BECOME THE PATRON SAINT OF BLIND, STUPID LUCK.
SO, YOU WANT TO BE AN ANGEL?
UM....SURE.
OKAY. GREAT. NOW, I'VE GOT A MILLION PLACES TO BE...BUT BEFORE I GO...
DO YOU HAVE ANY COMPLAINTS?
I WISH PEOPLE WOULD LEARN TO CALL ME *LESTER*.
BUT OTHER THAN THAT, I GUESS NOT.

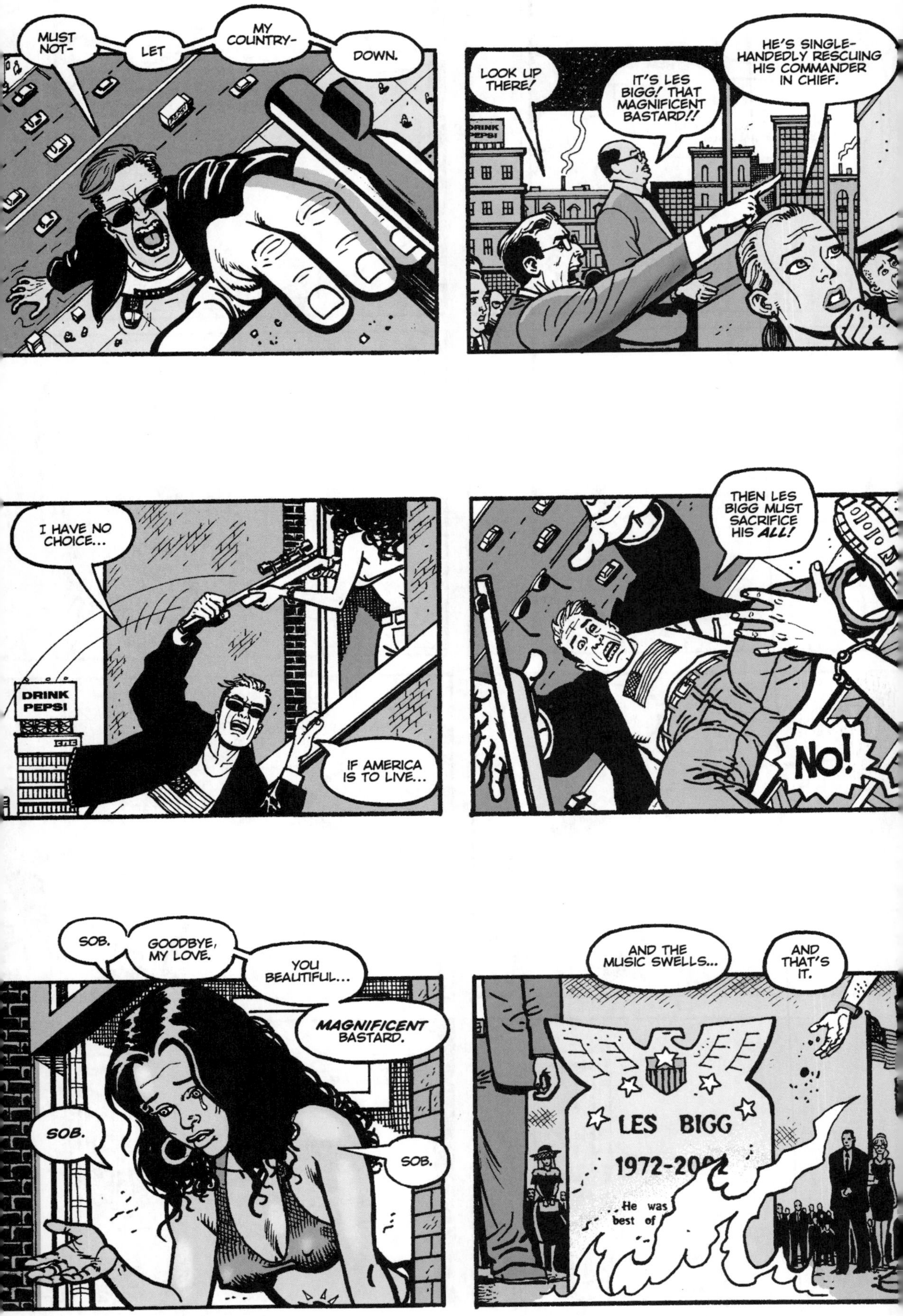
MUST NOT-
LET
MY COUNTRY-
DOWN.
LOOK UP THERE!
IT'S LES BIGG! THAT MAGNIFICENT BASTARD!!
HE'S SINGLE-HANDEDLY RESCUING HIS COMMANDER IN CHIEF.
DRINK PEPSI
I HAVE NO CHOICE...
IF AMERICA IS TO LIVE...
THEN LES BIGG MUST SACRIFICE HIS ALL!
NO!
SOB.
GOODBYE, MY LOVE.
YOU BEAUTIFUL...
MAGNIFICENT BASTARD.
SOB.
SOB.
AND THE MUSIC SWELLS...
AND THAT'S IT.
LES BIGG
1972-200
He was
best of

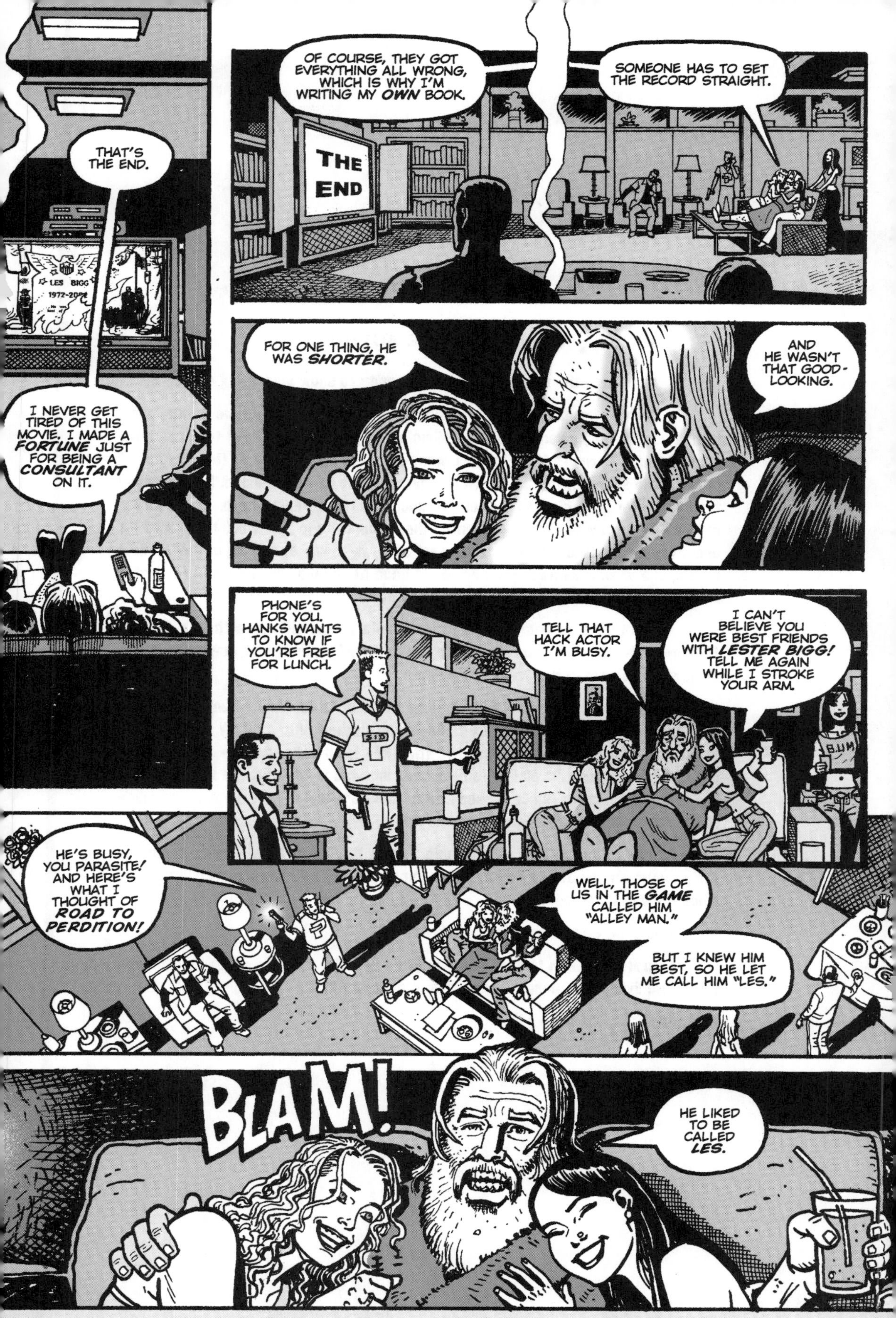
THAT'S THE END.
I NEVER GET TIRED OF THIS MOVIE. I MADE A FORTUNE JUST FOR BEING A CONSULTANT ON IT.
LES BIGG
1972-2002
THE END
OF COURSE, THEY GOT EVERYTHING ALL WRONG, WHICH IS WHY I'M WRITING MY OWN BOOK.
SOMEONE HAS TO SET THE RECORD STRAIGHT.
FOR ONE THING, HE WAS SHORTER.
AND HE WASN'T THAT GOOD-LOOKING.
PHONE'S FOR YOU. HANKS WANTS TO KNOW IF YOU'RE FREE FOR LUNCH.
TELL THAT HACK ACTOR I'M BUSY.
I CAN'T BELIEVE YOU WERE BEST FRIENDS WITH LESTER BIGG! TELL ME AGAIN WHILE I STROKE YOUR ARM.
HE'S BUSY, YOU PARASITE! AND HERE'S WHAT I THOUGHT OF ROAD TO PERDITION!
WELL, THOSE OF US IN THE GAME CALLED HIM "ALLEY MAN."
BUT I KNEW HIM BEST, SO HE LET ME CALL HIM "LES."
BLAM!
HE LIKED TO BE CALLED LES.

That's it. Story over. Off you go.

ABOUT THE AUTHOR

I was born in the wilds of downtown Canada to show business gypsies.

My father, Charles Templeton, was quite famous by the time I was born, having accidentally invented televangelism a few years before. (For this, our family is eternally sorry.) After that, he went on to run for Premier of the province of Ontario, the equivalent of an American governor. He came in second, for which our family is eternally pleased. Then he anchored the evening news on Canadian network TV for a while, until he invented the childproof cap (for which MANY families are eternally pleased) and eventually settled down to write a string of best-selling novels, one of which was in Elvis Presley's hand at the moment he died. (For which our family is eternally unsure of how to react.)

My mother was a singing star in Canada in the fifties, with her own hit TV show. My parents' marriage made the cover of a number of newspapers and magazines up here in the Great White North.

Amongst the circle of my friends I can count at least a half dozen people with top ten hit records. I have an ex-fiancée who's starring in a hit TV series at the moment . . . a sister who stopped hosting her local talk show to become a TV producer, a brother who claims to have been involved in creating the Internet (just like Al Gore!) and a cat (since passed away) whose one and only TV appearance made for a front-page headline in the *Toronto Daily Star.*

All this sounds rather unbelievable, I know, but it's all true. That's my life so far . . . surrounded by the famous, the almost famous, and the bizarrely infamous, since the day I arrived here.

This book was essentially inevitable.

I currently live in the wilds of suburban Canada, with my wife, four kids and three still living cats, none of whom are famous at all.

Yet.

TY THE GUY.